MW00626015

Me: A Rewrite!

From Vanity Insanity to Self-Acceptance (sort of)

ANNA JORGENSEN

Brave Little Bird Publishing

Copyright © 2016 Anna Jorgensen

All rights reserved. This book or any portion thereof may not be reproduced or used in any manner whatsoever without the express written permission of the publisher except for the use of brief quotations in a book review.

ISBN: 978-0-9937979-0-3

Anna Jorgensen
anna@annajorgensen.com
www.annajorgensen.com

DEDICATION

Dedicated to all the women who have ever, for a second, wanted to run away!

And

My Little Mom, for her unfaltering belief in me.

Always in my heart. . .

Maria Jorgensen: October 1932-October 2016

CONTENTS

ANNA JORGENSEN

ACKNOWLEDGMENTS

Thank you to the brave, real women who have faced their fears and overcome them, and stepped outside their comfort zones to reach out for something more, whatever that more is for you. You inspire me! In other words, it's your fault I'm here.

Thank you to The Film School, in Seattle, Washington, and its instructors. The program changed my life! (Special thanks to Tom Skerritt and John Jacobsen.)

Thank you to the men who have touched my life and added another step to my journey, while giving me great writing material in the process. For privacy sake, I'll refrain from naming names, except for Steve Santagati. Thank you for writing *The Manual* and *Code of Honor*, and for being my pen pal and friend, and for answering my dumbass relationship advice questions.

Thank you to Melissa and Richard for your loyalty and dedication.

Thank you to my Editor, Emma K. Lyders of Emma Edits, for putting up with me, getting it, and helping me get it together!

Thank you to StudioEi8ty8 for designing the cover and exercising an abyss of patience with OCD-perfectionist-mind-changing me.

Thank you, Karen Salmansohn, my favorite "better-me" author, for your positive words, encouragement, and inspiration. xo

Thank you to the women in this book for sharing their stories and offering their shoulders to cry on.

Thank you to my closest girlfriends for supporting, encouraging, understanding, and accepting me during my "rewrite," and for complying with my endless requests for feedback on titles, covers, and the works. You're the best cheerleading squad ever, especially Jessie, Philippa, Tracy, Melissa, Dawn, and Larissa.

Thank you to Maëris Boudreau, my long time loyal friend for always being there.

Thank you to my family for putting up with me and loving me in spite of my "quirks"!

Thank you, especially, to My Little Mom (MLM), for your strength, wisdom, confidence, pride in me, and endless prayers! Words cannot express how much I miss you.

And thank you to God for making me me.

PROLOGUE

Really, I just want to warn you that there are 72 uses of the word *fuck*, or Anna-derivatives of the word, in this memoir—73 now—but my editor assures me they are moderately and appropriately placed and totally don't take away from the readers' viewing pleasure.

Also, I've evolved a lot since these fucking shenanigans and am now a classy fucking lady. Seventy-five.[1]

xo

Anna J

[1]As you'll find out, I am a wee bit obsessive compulsive, hence the seventy-five *f-bombs*. OCD people will understand.

FOREWORD: A FORTY-SOMETHING MID-LIFE CRISIS

I'm in a late-thirties crisis. I'm not calling it a mid-life crisis because that might greatly reduce my life expectancy and I'm hoping to have more sane years left, unless this book is a hit—then I'll make a full time career of it, the crises that is, because, truth be told, the insanity bit might be ingrained. In fact, since I have been a drama addict up to this point, a crisis could be a fun gig.

Anyway, this thirties crisis started when my marriage fell apart almost ten years ago. My husband was, and still is, a really good man—we're talking really, super great—but not a really *right* man for me. Well, he was right for almost thirteen years, but apparently not for forever. I unconsciously craved a new life because I was discontent with my career and life in general, but I didn't know any better, so...I admit it, I blamed my marriage. Totally selfish, I know, but that's how it was. Or how I was. Damn it. Despite the great sadness between us, as any growing apart can evoke, we divorced amicably, and as of this writing, I'm still his realtor. (Either he really *is* a good man, or I'm just that good at sales, as in selling him on the idea of keeping me as his land pimp! I will reference him as Good Man in these pages.)

Like so many single women entering the Freeway of Forty, I find myself on a journey of self-discovery, self-understanding, self-enlightenment, and self-acceptance (sort of). *Case in point*: The books on my coffee table

1

include the likes of *Feel The Fear and Do It Anyway*® (by Dr. Susan Jeffers); *You Can Heal Your Life* (by Louise Hay)*; In The Meantime: Finding the Love You Want* (by Iyanla Vanzant); and *Eat, Love, Pray* (by Elizabeth Gilbert). You get the idea. If the titles don't tell it all, the folded corners and side notes and key-coded highlighting might: *this chick needs professional help.* You'll also find the requisite stack of SeattleMet magazines. I love Seattle. (I live in Comox, B.C., Canada, a municipality of sixty thousand. Not quite the same.) Victoria's Secret catalogues go promptly into the recycling bin after the depressing motivating, stop-stuffing-my-face factor—usually while fanning through the pages—has worn off.

My journey follows a route of randomness (though, if asked, I'll totally deny that and say I planned it all out—with bullet point lists and highlighter pens). While on this journey, nothing seems to make sense, even though the library of books I've read about how to make sense of life appear *so* logical as to be downright annoying, damn it. I get it, *intellectually*, but implementation's a bitch. Yeah, yeah, *love thyself.* Yeah, yeah, *if you stop looking, love will find you.* Yeah, yeah, *be authentic, follow your dreams.* Yeah, yeah, *quit your job, travel the world, have a life.* Yeah, yeah, yeah. Easier said than done, damn it! (Plus, didn't Gilbert get a fat *advance* to go travelling the world? *Exactly.*)

When you're about to hit forty, and you're single, and you have no kids and no pets and no (living) plants—guess what? You are alone. *Alone.* Aloneness can be sad, *sure*, but it can also make a girl restless. *Restless.* And even if you have great friends and family (or kids, or pets, or a fig tree, or a fern), when you're still that shy, under-socialized, misfit child inside, you can't avoid the disconnected, lonely feeling. *Lonely.*

And when you've been at your same job for twenty years, let's say as Anna J the Realtor, and doing pretty well at it, and you live in a small town, and you're known all over as the consummate professional, and your sign with your smiling face on it is plastered all over said town because you've done a bang-up job of marketing yourself (and your listings, too, of course), and really the only thing you want to say to the next person who asks you, "How's the market?," is "Today's my day off," which you're not allowed to have, and *that's the censored version...*well, it's time to do something else.

And say you really want to write. And by "you," I mean me.

So what's a girl to do?

She's to run away from her small town of Comox, on Vancouver Island (an island, no less!) à la *Eat, Pray, Love,* to the Big City—in this case, Seattle—seven-road (and ferry-boat) travel hours away, to live an adventurous, anonymous, alias, secret life as an aspiring writer! And by writing, I mean blogging about said secret life. (Though I have also started writing a screenplay!) The "new" life has to be kept secret, because otherwise my clients might not be too happy about it. There's an unspoken expectation that realtors eat, love, and produce in real estate—and engaging in any other pursuits is deemed unacceptable. After all, it's just taking away from "selling my house" or "finding me a house to buy," which means any personal time is questioned, and certainly *personal time being lived in another country* is grounds for tanking a hard-earned career— even though *I am doing the exact same marketing job from afar, people!* But I can do this! My clients in Canada would never have to know that I'm hanging out in Seattle, err *working from* Seattle! Plus, what if I want to turn this writing "hobby" into a new career? And I don't do too well right off the bat. You know, the whole "what if I fail" thing. So an alias it is. Genius, right?

My alias: Elaine. Elaine Elizabeth Kaufman, otherwise known as EEK. This book is my coming out party. You get to know the real deal. Elaine is Anna, Anna is Elaine. The jig is up.

What you're about to read started as a blog, by EEK, entitled "Random Rantings of a Spicy Mexican (Viking) Redhead," though alternately I could have just titled it "Sexless Single in Seattle." It tells the story of my secret life as EEK. EEK's a bit of a mess.

Disclaimer: No clients were harmed in the making of my new life. My real estate team and I fulfilled our fiduciary duties. (I checked with my lawyer, so ha!) Also, I should warn you now that this book contains swears, politically-incorrect musings, crass humor, sarcasm, satire, God references (with a sacrilegious bent), egotistical self-proclamations, and, as my editor tells me, enough offensive material to hit every demographic from here to Fernie. Excellent. If you're not offended at least once while reading this, let me know and I'll try harder next time. And we should also meet up for coffee.

What this book does not contain: Co-ed sex scenes. (Disappointed? Trust me, not as much as I was.)

Part One is perhaps a bit serious, but again my editor tells me, "Anna, there's a lot of getting chased by boys [and girls] and either making a lot of money or not having to work. You come across as kind of narcissistic, and the readers need something to sympathize with. They don't know you like I've come to know you or how people who know you know you. Does that make sense?" But but but! I *am* shallow and narcissistic and write things one shouldn't even think. But I am also kind and generous and tender, plus

3

I got to be this way through what some might consider a "sympathy-worthy" childhood. That's when I sent her a point-by-point list of my childhood memories. (My little mom [MLM] gave me the okay to relate these events, just in case you were wondering.) My editor can only say, "You poor thing. Put as much of that in as you can." So, what follows is a brief history of my life, and it is heavy if stark. I'll save the rest for another memoir if anyone gives a care.

I'd like to note that I write to the best of my memory and the memories of my immediate family members. If any of the following is inaccurate, *it's the reality that's been stuck in my head for almost forty years, people.* I'm not sure if the protagonist (that would be me) learns anything or goes through some major "character arc," but really, I'm just here to entertain.

If there are any heterosexual men reading this, stop. *Now.* You will never be able to sexually objectify women (at least me) again. You really don't want to know this stuff. However, you may learn something about the way women think, which could get you laid more often. It's a toss-up. Your call.[1]

Finally, I spew wordy diarrhea and go through moods and possess a lot of different personalities and get off track and jump around at times and eat too much cheese. My affinity for dairy isn't a good thing because then I don't "go," and since MLM has Crohn's Disease, I *should* really be careful, but I'm not a big fan of the word *should*, as I think it's a guilt-inducing word and we *shouldn't* guilt ourselves or others, which means we *shouldn't should* on ourselves or others and, *fuckstick, where was I?* Oh, right, I also tend to ramble.

Bear with me.

∗∗∗

---

[1] Certain exceptions and exclusions apply, namely The Gerry. The Gerry is not permitted to read this. If you are The Gerry: close this book, but first know that I don't poop, fart, sweat, or burp, like ever. Because I'm a classy fucking lady, after all!

PART ONE: FAMILY & HISTORY AKA THE SERIOUS STUFF

(Otherwise Known As: If We Don't Laugh at Life, We'll go Stark-Raving Mad)

SNIPPETS OF A LIFE

I've always been a perfectionist, which sucks because perfection doesn't exist. I got this way in part because of My Little Mom (MLM)—she stands proud at 4'10"—who *has* forever used the phrase, "Perfect." And for which I complete in my mind with, "but never good enough." Indeed, MLM only ever says the single word, "Perfect." I can't remember the specifics from childhood because I've blocked a lot out—some of it sucked balls at the time (note I'm refraining from throwing in a distasteful sexual innuendo). Now I'm all, "Oh yeah, super glad *that* happened, because it made me who I am today [*read*: nuts]."

For example, here's a totally fabricated story that might have been true, but I'm not swearing it is, and in fact it probably isn't so forgive me for the fib. When I was four years old, MLM taught me how to tie my shoelaces. If I made perfectly even bows, she would praise me with "Perfect!" and a hug for good measure. If I didn't tie them perfectly, she would have retied them for me "perfectly," showing me how I *should* have done it in the first place. Granted, it's not as if she would beat me or throw harsh Mexican words at me. Maybe she was a Zen Mama practicing the art of discipline in the miniscule. I've thought about going to hypnotherapy to recall these details, but it's taken me nearly forty years to keep them safely suppressed, thank you. But, truthfully, *that never happened*. MLM adored me and sang me bedtime songs while tickling my back, but *how's that going to build sympathy?* Exactly. Her singing sounded like an angel's.

But her favorite word *is* "perfect." That much is absolutely true.

7

Though I didn't cater to MLM's idea of perfection, I did cobble together my own high standards, for which I can only blame myself. I was too withdrawn and under-socialized (more on that later) to join clubs or sports in school, plus I'd been adored and adorned in pretty dresses from birth—my mother says, "You were like a little doll, Dolly." So, you guessed it: I relied on my appearance. I was born with some "Western Society Standards" good fortune in that area, even though I did go through an ugly awkward stage, *only for me it lasted from grade three through grade eight*, probably part of why I used attire to garner more self-esteem (and later cosmetic enhancements).

As a teenager, name-brand clothing filled in what I considered the gap to betterment and acceptance, though I didn't know why I was doing it then. Although we couldn't afford designer clothes (especially after my dad died), I sewed Esprit and Benetton labels coffered from thrift store finds onto my own K-Mart sweaters and shirts. In case you don't know, because I sure as shit didn't at the time, folks who can afford designer duds *know what's on this season's rack.* (I finally figured this out years later when I bought the legit shit myself.) Unknowingly, I labeled myself a fraud and a misfit early on. Sure, now it's all the rage—the misfit bit, not the fraud part—but when you're young, it's a whole other ball game. (And, by the way, there's no way I'd play ball. *Hell, no.*) My one friend knew but never said. Thank you, Miss Janet, for not outing me in the first inning.

Also, I have, for as long as I can remember, possessed the drive to be the best at whatever I tried, and if I didn't believe (*know*) I could be the best, well, then, I wouldn't try. What a brat, right? I agree (now). As an example, I tried out for track and field in grade six. Where I got the courage to do this, I don't know, because I was clinically shy—before you get ahead of yourself, that's a self-diagnosis.

On the day of the track meet, I stood on the field in my blue velour shorts with white piping and looked at the crowds of people in the stands, aka a dozen dozy parents. It felt like a stadium to me. I stood rigid with fear of failure and shame since anything less than First Place would have qualified as such in my mind.

I pled with the coach, a hand on my head and the other on my gut, "I don't feel well. I'm sick." At the time, I wasn't fibbing. I would have either vomited on the red dirt track or passed out on his sneakers if he hadn't caved. My guts had turned inside out. I could see from the look on his face that he knew what was up—that it was anxiety, not indigestion—but he must have also feared I really would have blown chunks if he made me compete. He let me go home. I felt better as soon as I was far enough away that he couldn't call me back to the track.

Speaking of my mom, MLM is, and always will be, Mexican—despite her resistance of that fact. She was born in Mexico City of rape, and resembled her biological father. (Get it? She looked like the man that had raped her mom.) That didn't sit well with her mother, *who was fourteen at the time.* Every time my grandmother (my mom's mom) looked at her, she must have been reminded of the conception, a very horrible memory, indeed. At least, that's how MLM first interpreted her mother's unaffectionate and strict child-rearing.

"I would get my ear pinched if I was bad, but I deserve it."

MLM tells me *bad* might be fidgeting from sitting too long on the hard, wooden chair while doing homework. Her mother and my grandmother, Carmen—MLM calls her Carmelita—was a stunning, green-eyed, natural auburn redhead. Yep, we're both the same shade of red. (I always kind of felt ripped off that I didn't also inherit her exotic, green eyes. Then again, I wouldn't be able to use the phrase, "I'm so full of shit my eyes are brown.")

MLM remembers walking down the street with her mom. "'Muy bonita Camelita,' they all called her, Anna Maria. And everyone looks at her like she is a movie star . . . pretty soon all the ladies in the area have the same color hair . . . like a movie star . . ."

From the time I was six, I started getting teased at school for my fire-red hair, but not by MLM. I didn't exactly buy into the compliment, but I loved the way her eyes glaze over as she imagines the aureole of Carmelita. (In case you didn't know, *aureole* is a hallowed halo not a nipple halo, which is an *areola*. And don't even try to tell me you didn't get distracted!)

MLM lived with Carmelita's older sister, because even in Mexico in the 1930s, getting pregnant out of wedlock at the age of thirteen wasn't cool. But MLM's aunt treated her like the daughter she wasn't. When Carmelita was seventeen, she married a man twenty-eight years her senior and MLM went back home to live with her mom and new stepfather, who was a gentleman that treated them both well. Even though Carmelita wasn't yet thirty, she remained loyal to him even after his death. She was never with a man again.

MLM lived her life until she fell in love with a musician, and at the age of seventeen, bore him a son, Fernando. She didn't find out until later that she wasn't the only one giving birth on behalf of the Latin rock star. Suffice it to say, he broke her heart. She went to work in a nightclub selling cigarettes, while Carmelita took care of Fernando, and there, within a year, met her first husband, a stoic military Englishman.

When MLM came to Canada in 1953, having married that military gentleman and, by default, his conservative "traditional" parents, she

9

longed to leave Mexico behind in its entirety.

Except, there was little two-year-old Fernando to think about. She couldn't bring both him and Carmelita to Canada and the two wouldn't be separated, so she made a difficult choice: a new life. *Hug for my little mom.*

Once in Canada, MLM adopted Englishness to the best of her ability, but still couldn't leave behind the evidence of her heritage in her accent or appearance, her black hair and Spanish-descent features forever her nemesis. When the world changed and cosmetic surgery became available, it created a window of opportunity for MLM to rewrite her history, to become someone new. (Interjection: *Holy crap! I just realized I'm reliving my mother's life of escape.* Okay, carry on.) In a perverted, loving way, my mother wanted to give me permission to be happy in the same way, i.e., by changing my appearance for the better, whatever that "better" meant to me.

"I want to give my children everything I didn't have," MLM has declared many times. This "what I didn't have" included emotional support, but for me translated into her encouragement of my plastic surgery endeavors. (More on that later.)

After her divorce from the Englishman—when my sister was fifteen and my brother was eight (out of respect for them, I'll refrain from revealing anything more than that)—MLM met my dad, a broken bear of a man who was drinking his way through grief. He'd just lost his wife and three children (two boys and a girl) in a train accident. (I know, right? Talk about the fated intersection of two tragic lives.)

He eventually met MLM, newly divorced, in the café she owned in Comox, B.C. Two souls sorting through lost loves, they made a perfect pair.

My dad was a poor farmer's son from the lonely Saskatchewan prairies. He was the largest of five children, though not the eldest. According to what I've been told, his parents didn't have the means to feed him, and sent him off with five dollars at the age of twelve. What more does a twelve-year-old need, after all?

Dad persuaded a friend to join him. The twosome survived by stealing food out of cellars and sleeping in barns, until they somehow made their way to the wet West Coast of Canada and began a new life. He eventually found work in the logging industry (*read*: forest rape) as a log truck driver.

Dad got married and had three children (as aforementioned) that he cherished—my father was a big kid and, like MLM, wanted to give his kids the loving attention he never received. Having lost his children once, he didn't want children again, but either by accident or not (MLM's eyes betray her), when MLM was thirty-nine, I was born. And adored.

As I said, my dad was a big man, weighing in at over 250lbs and standing at 6'1" with a big voice and a bigger heart. When I was little, he would run through the raked-up maple leaves, chasing me as I squealed and giggled. He would bring home logging truck inner tubes and bounce my friends and me on them, or slide down 6th Street on a toboggan when too much snow called for it to be closed. I was never spanked. MLM tells me how, even from the age of three, I was the boss of him.

"You would make a little fist and point you little finger and say, 'Don't you dare, Daddy, don't you dare.'"

He never dared. He loved me with smothering affection and grizzly bear protection. *Hug for my dad.*

Dad's parents died before I was born. Had his mother been alive when I was young, I might have had that fat-gushy-granny-baking-cookies experience. Or perhaps ordered to collect chicken eggs from the hen house. Either way, I didn't have a "grandparents" experience.

My formative years were spent in remote, logging camps—Toba Inlet, Burman River, Tzowen River. If it had the word "river" in its name or running through it, there's a good chance I was there. Some were accessible only by boat or harbor (water landing) plane, i.e., not road. Toba Inlet was the first. *Population:* 300 seasonal, 24 permanent, including maybe three children my own age. (My best friend was a girl a few months older than me who had Down Syndrome. I never noticed there was anything "different" about her. Such is the innocence of children.) *For urban-dwelling readers:* A logging camp is a place where modern lumberjacks (aka loggers) live. Loggers cut down forests to transport raw logs to the needy or, more accurately put, lumber mills that process the wood and ship it out of country, only to be bought back by Canadian consumers as bookcases from China. (*Yeah, not too bright, are we?*)

A lot of the crew abides in what is called a bunkhouse, a barged-in (no roads, remember), hostel-type, metal structure with rows of compact bedrooms for filthy, dirty-minded workmen to tape a lot of photos ripped from the pages of Hustler and Playboy to the walls. How do I know this? *What the hell else was there for a four-year-old to do?* Anyway, after that, it was off to another remote logging camp with more naked-lady wallpaper. We lived in a fifteen-foot travel trailer. Yes, the kind you tow behind a dually. (A *dually* is redneck slang for a one or two-ton truck with two double wheels on the back axle, in case you didn't grow up in Redneck Ville.)

Mine was a simple, innocent existence. Another childless couple, who knew my dad from the days of his first family, lived in one of these camps, too, for a while. The Wife was so happy that my dad had a second chance at family (and life) that I was equally spoiled by her affection. For one birthday party, she spent the entire morning blowing up oblong balloons to affix to birthday hats. Okay, it only took ten minutes because there were only three kids, but still. (Actually, this was later at a larger camp with more kids.) She did bake a cake. One time she even chased a grizzly bear with a broom because it was giving me the *are-you-my-breakfast* eye through the white picket fence. As you can see, I was well protected.

When I was five, my mom ended up in the hospital for an extended period of time (I don't know why) and my dad had to work, so they sent me to stay with a family I didn't know—father, mother, daughter (a year older than I), and son (a year younger)—in a nearby, slightly-less-tiny community. I'd never been away from my parents. Maybe from trauma of being sent to live with strangers or the terrifying drive to their mobile home (*read:* larger trailer)—along a narrow, single-lane road bordered by cliffs that evaporated into a water-filled gorge—or perhaps for some entirely different reason, I became a bed-wetter. As you can imagine, this development made me super popular with the laundry-doer lady of the house, if *popular* meant getting a lot of spankings. Now, I was not only with a family I didn't know, but being beaten silly for soiling their sheets. *Awesome.* Fortunately, I got to go home on weekends. I never told my parents about the corporal punishment.

Maybe a month later, neither MLM nor I remember exactly, MLM came home from the hospital and my dad left to get me. The next day, when that ill-humored family took their regular Friday drive to the grocery store, they accidentally drove off the embankment and drowned. Typically, they would have dropped me off at my parents' place en route. Maybe, sometimes, God's not so funny.

Since the camp didn't have a schoolhouse, at kindergarten age I was shipped off to the childless family's home—remember, The Wife saved me from the grizzly—in the Comox Valley, comprised of the Municipality of Courtenay, Town of Comox, and Village of Cumberland. It was awesome for about two minutes because The Wife would take me to Leung's Grocery Store in downtown Courtenay, where I'd get to wear my pretty dresses and she'd get me a milkshake in those old-fashioned aluminum containers. Then it got less awesome. Her Husband did naughty NC17 adult-only things-that-should-not-be-done-to-children to my little-girl self for the whole time I was there, which wasn't quite a whole year, though it sure felt like it. Whatever, it was long enough for me to know that Tuesday was liver and onions night and Thursday was meatloaf night. The Wife, the very one who put her life on the line for me, punished *me* by putting me in the closet. (*How fucked up is that?*) (*Answer:* Very fucked up.) Hurt people hurt people? In all fairness, she didn't actually *put me* in the closet, she only *yelled at me until I backed my six-year-old self away from her six-foot tall frame into it.* I would resort to hiding there amongst my frilly dresses after each incident, until she would find me and yell at me some more. She cut my waist-length hair into a not-very-cute, one-inch boy cut not long after. I guess she thought Her Husband wouldn't be interested in a little boy in frilly frocks. Yeah, um, wishful thinking. Of course, there were no more milkshakes dates. (Very fucked up.) I never told my parents.[1]

After my release from pedophile prison, my parents left the logging camp and moved us to Campbell River, B.C., a small, industry-based community with mining, fishing, logging, and a saw mill as its base, aka Redneck *City*. By this time, I'd aged a lot, and my unabashed joyousness was replaced with jumpy skepticism. It didn't help that we moved to a new house in a different school district what felt like every four days, which meant I was the "new kid in class" at four elementary schools.

Three weeks before my twelfth birthday, on April 30, 1983, my dad died of a heart attack, his third. He'd smoked a joint on the sundeck and then collapsed, along with my world, halfway in my parents' bedroom closet. (The joint had nothing to do with the premature death. But, it was my first association with marijuana and, to this day, wacky tobacky is a total dealbreaker, end of story, not up for negotiation. Plus, if I can love life after all the shit I've been through without artificial highs–aside from the cosmetic surgery, *but that hardly counts, people*–then I want a man who can handle it all au natural, too. Did I mention one of my endearing qualities is hypocrisy?)

I remember looking at my dad, lying there in his white briefs, belly protruding, while my mother hand-pumped his chest and tried to breathe life back into him. "Give me one more breath, Henry, just one more."

At some point, I ran out of the bedroom to call 911, but was too shaky to press the digits, so my niece called her mom, my sister, and she called the ambulance. The septum in his heart had burst. He was dead and not coming back. I sat on the bed, staring at him and his pale freckled skin, and at my mom in her long nightgown. There was a Hustler magazine open on the bed. I closed it and covered it with the blanket before the paramedics arrived. The silence of his absence was deafening.

I was already a realtor when I found out about my dad's first family and those half-siblings. Someone from my dad's first wife's family came to my office and dropped off a family photo, which included my dad. I can't describe the feeling I had upon seeing it. It was something more than disbelief: "But, no, it must be real, that's *my dad*," and "We look nothing alike, yet we both look like Dad." By then, I was too consumed with being Realty Lady to follow up with my potential new family. It's not like they were prospective clients. I did discover that Dad's first daughter was twelve when she died, the same age I'd been when he died. An interesting coincidence and though I don't feel an ethereal connection, I have always felt that I have an old soul. Hmm . . .

After Dad died, MLM wandered through life as a shell for six years, punishing herself for not saving him—she was First Aid Attendant of the camp and paramedic in Campbell River. When she couldn't take it anymore, she tried fumigating herself in the garage. Yeah, that's how I was told I found her, but I've tucked that memory somewhere deep and safe, thank you very much. Still, it probably does explain why I started biting my nails and losing my hair shortly after. Bald spots always go super well with fake Esprit sweaters. (Not.) *Reminder:* If you can't laugh at this stuff, you'll go bat-shit crazy. Humor is the feel-better option, I assure you!

When suicide didn't work, MLM took up stealing from K-Mart, hoping to get caught and jailed. She got community work instead, which turned out to be a blessing. She loved it. And though her guilt was still great, she found a new reason to live. Looking back, I probably wished I'd been reason enough, though it didn't register at the time. (I so promise the rest of this book is full of light-hearted fun and laughies!)

The good news for me was that because MLM loved working with these handicapped people so much, she made a career out of it by opening our home to them. In other words, we had two or three "challenged" adults living with us at any given time. Whether it was Sharon repeatedly saying, "Mickey Mouse, Mickey Mouse" when she got excited, or Ronni hunched over with cross eyes, crooked teeth, and the occasional excessively long string of drool, I became super popular at school. (But not really.) Despite my natural teenage mortification, I loved these ladies because they were like innocent children: completely lacking in malice and full of unconditional love. Okay, so sometimes I did get them riled up as I imitated Ronni and yelled, "Sharon farted! Mickey Mouse!" while they chased me around the yard, but there *was* a lot of laughing involved. (Oh, so *now* you're starting to understand.)

To cope, I discovered liquid courage (*read:* alcohol) and after I switched high schools and gears in grade ten—perhaps getting tired of the shy kid inside me—I allowed (maybe "forced" is a better word) myself to be outrageous and fun by showing up to class in random, crazy costumes with my best friend at the time.

For example: "Let's go as Backward Day!" We would wear our clothes, you guessed it, backwards and were forever known as "The Spin Twins," since she is also a redhead. Such a performance was contrived. I was still that shy kid on the inside, but I faked it pretty well. Then, I got all fake-Benetton-labelled snobby and started hanging with a new crowd, chasing boys in Janet's yellow Honda Civic. But that nutty freedom didn't last long. "High" school disappears in a flash and then real life begins.

I have a half-brother, the second product of MLM's military marriage, who's eleven years my senior. He replaced my Superman after Dad died and taught me about goal-setting. When I was a teenager, we would talk over coffee and he would tell me about the twenty-one habits of success, quoting Brian Tracy as I scribbled notes with a four-color option Bik pen. I'd conduct board meetings with my friends in my bedroom, going through pros and cons and action plans. My list-making and OCD started early—I must have grasped both as a means of self-control.

My half-sister, eighteen years older than me, had already left home and married by the year I was born. When I (re)discovered her—she moved back to our hometown years later—we didn't click immediately. I'd been the apple of my father's eye and she'd been the seed product of an unaffectionate Englishman. Though we didn't share hair bands, it turns out we had a lot in common! We ended up forgiving each other our pasts (without being asked) and became real sisters for life.

My other half-brother, Fernando, lies in Heaven. He started out as a genius—no really, like Doogie Howser, only sporting medical *and* law degrees by *sixteen* years old—but, while he was still a teenager, he was hit in the head playing baseball and developed an undiagnosed blockage in the brain. By twenty-two, he became mentally handicapped. He lived with the beautiful Carmelita until she died at seventy-two then, lacking the will to live, committed suicide by starving himself to death. (I'm not making this shit up.) *What???* My mother read this and tells me he died because this shunt that was inserted between his brain and his heart came out while he was carrying a heavy sofa chair up to his apartment. *See, all these years I thought he killed himself!* Seriously. (OMG. This whole book could be a fabrication. Read it anyway, it's entertaining.)

Neighbors found him days later, naked in the bathroom, clothes left as a trail of evidence that started at his typewriter. MLM tells me his final, typewritten words were: "Naked we come, naked we go. Praise be to the name of the Lord." (But in Spanish.) I'd only met him a couple of times and though there was a language barrier, I could tell a part of him knew what he'd lost.

After high school, I traveled for six months through Mexico and met my mother's Carmelita and Fernando, *obviously before he died, duh*, but by then he was in his forties with a bum leg. I stopped in unannounced to see them. My grandmother was old and old-fashioned and no longer looked like a movie star. She gave me a curfew of dinner time, but I wanted to go out and explore the world, or at least Mexico. After a week of restrictive habitation and difficult communication—I spoke no Spanish and they spoke no English—I continued on my journey. She died two months later, possibly while I was trying on leather sandals in Guanajuato. She was seventy-two.

After Mexico, I worked a few odd retail jobs in Vancouver, B.C., where I couldn't afford food let alone expression of personality, and where nothing of much consequence happened.

At twenty, I moved back to my childhood hometown and dated Pete C., a guy ten years older than me. He dumped me for an older (than me) woman. *After this rejection, there was no way in hell I was going to let that happen again,* even though I wasn't even in love with him. Hello, tender ego and abandonment issues. After this, I went straight into land pimping, i.e., selling real estate. (Pete did let me sell his house for him.)

After I was rejected from one firm for being "too young," I studied what the top agents in the country did and copied them, taking my skills and determination to a competing company who didn't actually care that I didn't have a car to transport buyer clients in. (I borrowed MLM's.) Part of what I learned from those most successful realtors in the courses, seminars, books, and the like was to "call until you get one," in other words, never give up. I became known by other realtors as a barracuda. I was relentless and driven.

The other thing I learned was to don a look that was business sophistication. Even though I was slightly choking under the buttoned-up collar and becoming a seriously tense shell, far from the formerly fun and *real* me, I was already on a roll, or perhaps "in a role" is more aptly put.

At twenty-three, I met Good Man, sixteen years my senior, and eventually moved in with him back in my birth town after this story began.

The Comox Valley, as it is officially named, and Campbell River are some of the most stunning places on earth: majestic mountains covered in dense evergreens (the ones that haven't been logged) that reach up to skyscraper heights; rivers, stream and ocean surround a recreational outdoor paradise that includes mountain biking, hiking, kayaking, skiing, golfing, and more; and where you can snowboard and golf in the same day. Seriously. Charming communities where everyone knows your name, or will within a short time—*the very reason I ran away!*

After many years of eighty to ninety + hour work weeks and 150+ sold properties a year (over 300 in our best year), I eventually became the bitter broker—selling real estate and *selling out.* And don't get all "Well, suck it up Big Bucks" on me, because I did make some bad investments, aside from the closet full of couture. Now I can't retire. At least I have the shoes. I may have sold my soul, but my soles are happy! (There was an old lady who lived in her Louboutins?)

***

[1]Sometime after my dad died, Her Husband passed as well. By then, I was a rebellious teenager in a town one removed. I didn't have to see them. I realized years later, after Choices (a "heal me" course I'll describe later), that I wasn't actually as angry at Her Husband as I was at The Wife. She ought to have protected me. Though I didn't think what Her Husband did was all right by any means, I still felt sorry for him somehow. He always seemed a quiet man under the thumb of his towering, overbearing wife, and I know what it feels like to be bullied and alone. Long after he died and I thought I was all better, I went to confront The Wife and forgive her. I showed up at the same mobile home where she had lived and the abuse had happened. But instead of accepting my good deed, she called me crazy and denied anything happened, so I swore at her and stormed out, forever hearing the aluminum door slam shut behind me. I wasn't healed yet. *Obv.* I never saw her again; she eventually got Alzheimer's disease and died in a care facility. I did eventually forgive her. I think my heart simply softened over time. When we suffer, we cause others' suffering. May they both rest in peace. (This footnote is way too fucking long.)

PART TWO: (I KNOW YOU ARE BUT WHO AM I?)

ELAINE KAUFMAN, WILL YOU PLEASE STAND UP?

Elaine Elizabeth Kaufman, EEK, came to be just *prior to* my crazy quest for self in Seattle. I launched this new life after first taking a writing course via thefilmschool, four years after my divorce. I'd renounced television and movies along with my marriage, having spent a great portion of our time plopped in front of the TV, but at least I had some experience. (Good Man's favorites: *Die Hard, Conan the Barbarian, Top Gun,* and *Shrek.*) My favorites: *Liar Liar* (I relate myself to a female version of Jim Carrey) and *Silence of the Lambs* (there's no relating here, it's just weird). I know that probably says something about my self-ascribed falsity and paranoia, but I'm totally sure this will come in handy at some point. *Sideways glance.*

Thefilmschool gave a three-week course. I figured I could afford to take time off and I'd been yearning to try my hand at writing for years. I'd only ever journaled, daily, since I was seventeen–the physical diaries as of this writing now sit in a security deposit box under lock and key and vault and armed guards.

One of the first things we do in the *writing* course is something called *On Your Feet,* led by Tom Skerritt. (Yes, of *Steel Magnolias* and *Top Gun* fame, and incidentally one of the founders of thefilmschool. I know!)

I'm thirty-nine at this point, a series of wrong-for-me relationships since splitting with my ex-husband in my recent past, including the one that landed me here in Seattle, when I come across this screenwriting class advertised in a local paper. Though it's not my style of writing, at least the class is only three weeks long. I would need to get back to Canada to be Realtor Lady in an acceptable amount of time. Though I'm more interested in short story writing, à la Alice Munro, I sign up. I figure stumbling across this writing opportunity must be a sign from God. *Fair warning:* I can pretty much turn a pile of sunbaked dog do into a sign from God if I need it to justify I'm-going-to-do-this-anyway actions. I don't notice the *On Your Feet* course title until much too late. God is funny that way. In *On Your Feet*, terrified writing students (*read:* introverts) get out of their comfort zones, off their laptops, and on to their feet to, yes, *act*. We are given bits of popular scripts and paired up, and instructed by the Master (Skerritt), "Take ten minutes, then we'll start." I want to throw up or run away, à la track and field day, but I've already run away to Seattle, so I guess this timid "adult" is about to get untimid. My first "role" is the bedroom scene in *The Graduate* and I'm Mrs. Robinson. Seriously, this calls for a double swear: Fuck fuck.

I don't get my turn the first day, or the second, so by day three I know I have to take my turn—our little duo is all that's left—and though it feels like caterpillars are crawling around in my empty gut—I had enough foresight not to eat—I act. Somehow, I remember my lines and I forget the audience. After, I take what might be my first breath. I wouldn't say I loved it, and I'm definitely no Meryl Streep, but I feel proud of myself for doing it. Yay me!

Then we share parts of our own scriptwriting projects, acting out others' script bits so as to experience a unique point of view. Since I don't actually have any script bits, I'm to borrow someone else's who's actually serious about screenwriting. That's when I'm cast as a burgeoning screenwriter's fictitious narcissistic character named Elaine Kaufman. I find out after several blog posts as EEK that a real Elaine Kaufman did in fact exist. She lived in New York and worked as a restaurateur until expiring at the ripe old age of eighty-one, a month before I added Elaine as the alias to my blog adventures. A sunbaked dog poop sign, I say!

To give perspective, I'll include a snapshot of where—and who—I am as our journey begins. I should also note that this story is non-fiction, unlike that dude's memoir. You know the guy. He went on Oprah twice: once to promote his "true story," another to admit he was a halfway non-fiction fibber. (Though, after a few rounds of MLM read-throughs, I'm beginning to wonder if I even know the difference. Whatever. They're my memories!) In order to stay honest and respectful (at the same time), I've given my characters—who are all real people in my past or present—new names, new nicknames, or new careers. Basically, just enough to protect identities and save my dimpled ass from lawsuits. Also, some condensed dialogue so you get the gist of it, for compacting or comedic purposes, and two conversations plus an email exchange I fabricated based on *what was most likely to have happened or could have happened or maybe just should have happened.* If you're in this book and I've misquoted you, I don't apologize. If I've misrepresented you, then I do apologize, but only a little. (All my early, crappy stuff is utterly true to the best of my memory. And if I am an innocent, half-way, non-fiction fibber, I can only hope I'll get on Oprah! Online.) Some of these "characters" I've known for years, some we'll meet together along the way. My story starts in Canada.

After my divorce, I dated a massage therapist I'll call Junior—he's over ten years younger than I am and an early riser, so to speak—and ever since, I can't sleep past five a.m., if that. I must say I kinda like it now. (The getting up early and the morning wood.) Once I'm awake, I can't linger in bed. I get up, drink a Nespresso, work out, write, peek through my custom blinds I never open, eat a bowl of old-fashioned, steel-cut, slow-cook oatmeal, run a Facebook circuit, shower, trim those nasty and frizzy and rogue pre-gray hairs (on my head), check for Charlie (my chin hair), put on my game face, which includes a lot of cosmetics, and go to work. With almost twenty years in the real estate biz, it's no wonder I'm crazy.

Even though I can work from home, I go to the office since it feels more official. I check emails, reply promptly, review marketing plans, adjust advertising accordingly, view houses that people want to sell, provide pricing evaluations promptly—sometimes I get the listing, sometimes they hire someone else—process paperwork, make phone calls, take phone calls, and ask a lot of questions, such as:

- "Do you live in the area?"
- "Do you have a house to sell before you can buy?"
- "Is it listed?"
- "Are you working with a realtor?"
- "If I could show you how I can get you more for your house than you can get on your own, would you consider talking with me?"

I view the house, complete an evaluation, present the report to sellers, and answer their questions:

- "What kind of marketing are you going to do?"
- "Do you do Open Houses?"
- "Can we do a one-month listing?"
- "Will you cut your commission?"

Then we either complete the listing paperwork or I get the "We'll think about it" line, which means I'll inevitably see it listed online with someone else in a few days, usually at a higher price than I've recommended, the same price that will later get reduced and sell and the "value enthusiastic" realtor will get paid.

Welcome to my world.

REALTY LADY REALITY: LIVING THE
PROFESSIONAL LIE/LIFE

I get a call from some potential seller clients, Miriam and Roger, who want to sell their custom-built, "ultra-ecofriendly, highly efficient, no expense spared," three-bedroom home. *Translation:* It's worth more to them than the market will bear. I ask the requisite questions:

"How did you decide to contact me?"

"What's important about the realtor you hire?"

"Who else, if anyone, are you talking to?"

"What motivated you to consider selling?"

"If you couldn't sell, how would it affect your plans?"

These, among several other questions, allow me to determine their motivation and emotional needs, before I end with: "Tell me about your home and what you love most about it."

Miriam and Roger were recommended to me by two sets of past clients, because they want honesty and a decent marketing plan, and someone who will fairly represent all the no-expense-spared features of their *very special home*. They're not talking with any other realtors, *which really means*: they're not planning on talking with any other realtors unless I suggest an insulting list price for their home, *which really means*: a realistic value, in which case no matter how many rave reviews they've heard, they will kick me and my finely-clad ass to the curb. Why are they selling such a fantastic house? To "simplify [their] lifestyle so [Miriam doesn't] have to work" and if they couldn't sell?

Miriam asks, "Oh. What do you mean?"

Roger gets on the other line. After a quick greeting, I continue. "If the market won't bear the price you want, will you stay where you are?"

Miriam draws in a deep breath, *very audibly*. I wait. Finally, she says, "Well, we really want to sell. But we're not in a rush. We're not desperate."

I can tell by her change in tone this is anything but true, no matter what the reason.

I say, "Of course, no one wants to leave any money on the table." I speak slowly and calmly. "Miriam, Roger, I want you to know that from what you've told me, I'm almost a hundred percent certain I can sell your home."

Miriam exhales a sigh of relief.

I add, "I'd like to explain a little bit about how I work? Is now a good time?" (I'm already twenty minutes into the conversation.)

They confirm.

"We'll set an appointment for me to come out to the home ("home" is a purposeful word choice: personal, bearing emotional attachment) to view it when both of you can be there—because you'll both have valuable and individual input about the best features, which will help me design a marketing plan to attract that particular buyer who will likely appreciate those same things as much as you do...Does that makes sense?"

They agree.

"Great. I'll take detailed notes so that I don't miss anything, but in the meantime, I'd like to give you some homework. It would be helpful to me if you, and Roger, would go through the home together and make notes about *all* the special features it has, whether they can be seen evidently or if they're hidden, like the hot water heating system you were telling me about. Will you do this for me?"

They will.

"If you have time, it would be great if you could dig up the survey certificate or plot plan, heating bills—they're a selling feature—and any other documents you, if you were a buyer, would appreciate. Will you have time to do this?"

Miriam says, "Yes. We have photos of the construction. Would that be helpful?"

"Definitely! You can either email them to me or, if they're already in an album, we'll leave it out on display with the brochures I'll have done up. Would that be all right?"

(So far I'm using "The Assumptive Close." Also, since I'm outing myself in public, I might as well offer this as a reminder: the more yeses you get early on, the easier it is *to get even more yeses*. If you'll notice, this conversation is not manipulative, it's simply professional. I'm looking for what is important to the client *and* information about the house that will be important to the buyers. Realtors should take notes! I could give seminars!)

"Okay. Once I've had a look at the house (notice how it is now a "house": a commodity with which they'll be ready to part) I'll come back to the office and do *my* homework. I'll prepare a market evaluation. I'm going to give you a range of three values: the wholesale price, aka the sellers' *have got to sell it now* price, or at least what I would expect it to sell for within thirty days; the retail price, which will fit with current general market conditions and may take sixty to ninety days to sell in this market; and the test-the-market price, which is the Vegas gamble. You get to pick the price. Fair enough?"

Miriam asks, "What about marketing?"

"Good question, that's next. So is that a yes on you picking the price?" (A true professional steers the ship.)

Miriam apologizes, "Sorry, yes!"

"Fantastic! Okay, the marketing plan: I'm glad you asked. Once we determine an asking price that you're comfortable listing it at, we'll go through a marketing plan that will target buyers that are the most likely to pay top dollar for it, in other words, those who will appreciate all the extras you put into it. Sound good?"

Miriam concurs and I continue, "Roger?"

Roger affirms, "All right. That sounds reasonable."

"When we've gone through the pricing and marketing strategy, then we can determine if we'd like to work together. Fair enough?"

Miriam, surprised, says, "Oh."

"I'm certain I'm going to love your place, Miriam, and I already know I like you—it's important to me that I have a good working relationship with my clients—but I also want to make sure that I can be genuinely enthusiastic about the price that you choose or I won't be able to fairly represent you. But, if that's the case, I can refer you to another great agent."

Miriam says, "But you came so highly recommended, we really want to work with you."

"Then I'm sure it'll all work out. Let's have a look at the house to get started. Does tomorrow at 3pm work or is the evening better?"

(I've now spent over an hour on the phone getting information and building rapport and trust. Most knucklehead realtors rush out to the property without even qualifying whether or not this is a *qualified seller*: one who is ready, willing, and able to sell. I'm not being pretentious. *If you're wasting your time, you're wasting your other actual qualified clients' time!*)

I arrive to view the house with hair coiffed, make-up perfectly applied, wardrobe impeccably professional, and car polished—I am Realty Lady. I ask more questions, take notes, get documents, book follow-up appointment. (Another two hours invested). Then I leave, do more research even though *I already know the likely sale value within 1% from my initial phone conversation*, a knack I've honed from years of experience (I've sold over 1000 homes by this point), I put together the evaluation and marketing report, and return to present it.

I won't bore you with the details (or give away all my Realty Lady secrets), but will sum up as follows. We're sitting at the dining room table with my presentation displayed between us. I give them the news.

"Your property is likely worth $550,000 in this market."

Deflated, they slump. They'd hoped for at least $600,000. "But we've got so much into it . . . and we *need* to get enough to get another place, the market [where they're moving] is higher."

I say gently, "Need doesn't create value. You're not going to overpay for your next home if that seller *needs* more than it's worth, are you?"

They're quiet. (*Never speak first.*) They frown and finally nod.

I continue, "However...because it is such a special home, and since you're not in a rush, I think we can list it higher."

They perk up a little.

"We can go with a test-the-market price to start. If it doesn't sell within your time frame, you can always come down. But only because your home is so unique. Yes?"

They agree.

(*Note to realtors:* It is always best to come to agreement on price before moving on to the marketing plan! The marketing plan is ultimately incidental in the sellers' mind to value. Nail this down first. If you can't agree on price, no matter what your ad plan, you will likely fail and be the bad guy. *I know this from personal experience!*)

At this point, I've now got over five hours invested. Either they will list with me and I will spend a ton of money on marketing and it will sell, or it won't. I don't get paid unless and until it does. (This is why it's best to pre-qualify the potential seller client and situation ahead of time. *Realty Reality Land:* Is this risk worth your investment of time—away from family and other clients—and money that, no, doesn't grow on trees, and is all virtual nowadays [very virtual for some untrained realtors]?)

We list the house on the high end. Roger and Miriam get three offers of $550,000. Each time I tell them, "Roger. Miriam. I know this is less than what you want. You have two choices: take the bird in the hand or wait for the bird in the bush. It might take 'X' months at this point to get the bird in the bush. I still think we can, but it's your call. What will make you happy?" That's what's most important to me (truth), which is a risk because they could change their mind at any point and take the house off the market or get frustrated by the process and switch to a different realtor—again, *I know this from experience, people!*

They reject each offer. Each time the presenting realtor tells me I'm crazy to think they'll get more.

Several months and a lot of "vendor appeasements" and reassurances (and extra marketing costs) later, I put the sold sign up. They get $582,500. *Boo-ya!*

It doesn't always work out this way, though. I certainly wasn't always this professional and I've been confident and overly enthusiastic on value when "the market" didn't agree with me. (Yes, "that" realtor.) I wasn't successfully selling every listing I took, whether by listing at my recommended price or the sellers' price. Such is the nature of real estate sales. There were listings I ought not to have taken.

I didn't work with buyers much in my last several years, but I did use a similar pre-qualifying procedure. I learned after much irritation—really, it's a wonder I'm not an alcoholic like, *cough,* half the realtors I know— that the first thing to agree on is loyalty. If I'm the one showing you properties, *I'm the one who's writing the damn offer.* (It's shocking how many buyers *"accidentally"* write an offer with another realtor after viewing properties for weeks and even *months* with a realtor who supposedly has their loyalty.) The last few years I wouldn't work with buyers without meeting in advance for a mutual interview and agreeing to a (legally non-mandatory, *though it ought to be*) signed Buyer's Agency Agreement. (And for my next book . . . *The Bitter Broker.*)

THE FINE PRINT (*READ:* THE REAL NON-REALTOR ME)

Things to forewarn, err, inform you about me:
- Since I'm half-Mexican and half-Danish, I can be spicy, hot-tempered, loud, and direct (though this is *sometimes misinterpreted* as bossy). (*Sideways glance.*) That is, once I get past my shyness.
- As Realty Lady, I'm not shy. At. All. (Go figure.)
- I'm an environmentalist, but not a hard-core, die-hard fundamentalist. I only gave up gum-chewing and plastic bottles this year. I still eat meat, preferably fried in bacon fat.
- Speaking of food, I eat No Nut Nut Butter and wheat/gluten-free everything, all of which sits in my perfectly-arranged cupboard. I'm not actually allergic to peanuts or wheat or gluten. But I am a little paranoid and who knows when I could develop a peanut or gluten allergy! Plus, I'm a control freak, which leads me to my next point...
- I am orderly to an anal-retentive degree, which some call OCD (Obsessive Compulsive Disorder). You should see my spice cupboard, closet, "junk" drawer, and dresser. For example, all my panties are folded into triangles and stacked in color-coordinating piles. I used to watch the numbers on my odometer, and if they didn't feel quite right, I would drive around the block to arrive at a new reading, but I did limit myself to only a one-block loop. Also, I count things. Like, if I'm eating almonds, I'll have three or five or ten or fifteen, never twelve or nine—that might put me over the edge.
- I use consumables to their last drop, or swipe, or ooze, or squeeze,

or squirt, or smear. Because makeup lasts so damn long, it's the most satisfying to use up. And, yes, makeup is anti-environment generally speaking, but I buy organic, bunny-friendly. I don't rush when getting close to the end of something—I squeak the last vapor from everything that applies—though I'll admit I don't cut the toothpaste tubes open like MLM does. As she says, "Waste not, want not."

- I think myself attractive while also thinking myself entirely imperfect. I'm 5'6", weigh between 125 and 135 depending on the time of month and whether or not I hold the towel bar while stepping on the scale, have long red hair (my trademark feature), dark brown Latin eyes, and freckles everywhere, even on my lips (on my face!), which my physician had me all worried about because that can sometimes be a symptom of some disease that I Googled and researched until my eyes had spots to match the rest of me. Don't ask me what it was called. He says I don't have it. I don't believe him, which brings me to my next trait...

- I'm a little paranoid and have trust issues. Gee, I wonder why. Yet I also can be a little too trusting. I suspect every guy I date of being a serial killer and I once thought a friend stole a pair of shoes from me that weren't even her size and I believe a construction crew installed hidden cameras so they could watch my naughty, bean-flicking (read: masturbatory) activities. Which I do under the covers ever since. I also believe people's stories, even when they seem farfetched, i.e., "You own a hippo? Is that allowed in the by-laws?"

- I'm an optimistic pessimist, a positive-minded faultfinder. And a hypocrite, though I prefer to think of myself as open-minded and flexible.

- My home in Canada holds my heart. I love my house. I love love love my house. I had it built by my ex-husband, Good Man the builder, shortly after our divorce a few years ago. It quickly became my safe haven, sanctuary, nest, the very symbol of my independence. I often lay on the couch in the corner, reading, listening, thinking, napping. Blinds shut.

- I've embellished my bathroom mirror with positive self-help quips and tidbits in four colors of dry-erase marker. After a couple days I forget they're there, but totally believe they're subliminally sinking in nonetheless.

- I often entertain the fantasy that one day I'll marry The Gerry, a moderately famous actor my literary attorney advises me not to identify. Who has no idea I exist. We may have a child in this fantasy of mine even though I don't technically want kids. Which is true, but The Gerry is that kind of irresistible. Oh, The Gerry. Sigh.

- I own every Brigitte Bardot movie ever made. In fact, hers are the only movies I own, unless you count Sex and the City, which is more like a staple for any self-respecting, fashion-following vamp. Ah but Bardot... Bardot was the consummate woman-child, gifted and tormented by her beauty and the façade created for fame, hoping that one day her life would become more meaningful than her appearance and the public's perceptions of her. I have to say I relate, though not about the beauty bit—I'm not that narcissistic—but the creating an image for success part feels fitting. Eh, shrug.

- I possess several different and distinct personalities, though that could be part of the Cybil Gemini in one or more of them. Good Man once counted eight. I only count seven but at least I'm aware of them (us?) all:
    1. Realty Lady (uptight, professional)
    2. Woman-child (silly, goofy, vulnerable)
    3. Crazy-ass bitch (the pick-a-fighter)
    4. Sex Kitten *wink*
    5. School Teacher (more in attitude than in style)
    6. Life of the Party (add alcohol and tickle trunk of costumes, à la Mr. Rogers)
    7. The Recluse (hiding out for days, à la Elaine Kaufman)
    8. Redneck Redhead (possibly the real me)

As you can imagine, having all these ladies at my disposal comes as a real asset in real estate sales (always in the best interest of the client, of course). The downside is in the not knowing which one is really me. Holy shit! What if they're (we're?) all me?

- I have a cantankerous, contentious relationship with God. He knows it, for He knows all, apparently. I may still harbor resentment for His taking my dad from me, even though there has to be a silver lining somewhere, damn it. (Lord, please forgive me for the swear. In Jesus' name, amen.)
- I love brand name shoes. I own over fifty pairs. I had to sell some to get down to fifty. A leftover psychological need for validation now that I can afford the real deal labels? I kiss them good-bye before shipping them off to the next happy eBay owner. Always recycle, right? Is kissing one's shoes a "thou shalt not worship false idols" sin? (Probably.)
- I love fashion. Style is an artistic expression of my personalities even though I used to be all classic-style, beige on beige, and small stud earrings, in the name of work. Being half-Mexican, though, I practically popped out of the womb donned in bobbles and bangles (it's a heredity thing). Some days I might wear a baby pink frilly dress with ballerina flats and my hair in a pony-tail (woman-child), other days you might find me in an ensemble of a carefully-constructed color palette, a what's-trending-now gingham skirt and sheer floral flowing blouse with heeled boots and a hat. (I have at least twenty hats.) The fashion styles don't always determine the personality of the day—unless it's recluse, then PJs and matted hair it is.
- I have a cantankerous, contentious relationship with food. I work out so I can eat. I love bacon so much it must be a sin, and my love

of cheese is not far behind. I get this from my dad. Danish farmer. Butter eater. Sometimes, I eat cold butter straight up, just like my dad once did. (It's a heredity thing.) But joking aside, because I'm also a little vain, I moderate my indulgences. Okay, that's probably not true. I'll work out more, which means I'm actually the opposite of moderate: excessive. Damn it, I fail again.

- I love my family but will mostly leave them out of this book for privacy's sake. Except for MLM, a shining star in my life (even though I may present her otherwise at times). She inspires me in many ways and is a big part of why I am who I am, and I kind of like me, in a non-narcissistic way.

- I can either be super shy or super outgoing. Both are genuine parts of my personality. Warning: [SOILER ALERT]. I was so shy as a kid that I peed my pants in class in grade seven because I didn't want to have to raise my hand to go to the bathroom. When my adjacent classmate and BFF noticed I'd leaped up and backed out of the classroom—naturally and thankfully, I was at the back of the room—she pushed my puddled chair in. Of course, Mr. W noticed and all eyes turned on me. My mortification was only mildly reduced by the realization that everyone would think I got my period. Whew! Thank you, Michelle, for helping me hide the source of my shame.

- The music I dig depends on my mood. Right now I'm listening to Develop Creativity Self-Hypnosis, i.e., wailing whales. I don't buy the gimmick, but then again, here I sit writing. What I'm not big on is rap, top 40, and country, unless it's Johnny Cash, and only because my dad had him on eight-track cassette.

- I believe to the core of me that love is the answer. I will give anyone a hug or a hand if in need. I feel most compassionate toward those who are most shamed and shunned by society. And even though I sometimes come across as snarky or catty, that's just my writing voice, people, my writing voice!

And without further ado, here we go . . .

PART THREE: HBUAB

Handsome but Unworthy American Boyfriend

HOW IT ALL STARTED (SORT OF): SO, I'M NOT GOING TO BE RICH & FAMOUS?

As mentioned, an intensive, three-week scriptwriting class at thefilmschool with Tom Skerritt started this whole fiasco four years ago. It wore me out. Twelve hours a day and six days a week, plus homework. The days were divided into sections with five different instructors, who taught five distinct storytelling techniques. Skerritt taught the acting class; John Jacobsen instructed on storyline, plot, theme, and structure; Stewart Stern (Academy Award winning writer of *Rebel Without a Cause*) led us through verbal-visual-imagery-free-flow writing; Warren Etheridge explained character arc and theme development; and Rick Stevenson carried us through an intense and emotional "tell your own personal story" journey. We quickly learned to bring tissues for his class.

"I peed my pants in grade seven."

"Grade five for me."

Another brave storyteller out-shames me and I'm thinking, "Wait, we paid money to tell our pee stories?" I'd better come out the other end of this an emotionally stable, award-worthy writer.

Thefilmschool left me with the realization that I needed to write (as in I found my passion) *and* that I suck(ed) at scriptwriting. There's so much structure and rigidity in it, and I'm a little looser than all that, with writing at least. After the class ended, I struggled to write something in a format of which I could be proud. But I couldn't write anything at all! So I changed lanes and tried writing short stories, dramatic pieces that evolved from my broken heart and crumbling life. The stories needed work, but had depth and potential, unlike some of the boyfriends who came after my marriage.

Three months later, with too many blank pages staring me in the face, I took an online fiction writing class so I could refine the short stories. Prior to any actual refining, I sent one off to Tom Skerritt. He liked my writing enough to meet with me! Holy Moly Molly! Ah, but wait...It turns out he wants me to write real estate stories, a web series script actually. But at this stage of my real estate career, I'm burnt out and feeling like biting people or punching them in the throat, so all I can think is, "Fuck no." I write one story anyway: it's a true story, it's funny, he likes it. Hey, Mikey! I want to send Tom more while I've got his attention, but then I get writer's block, either from lack of enthusiasm or lack of writing material. Did I use up all the humor of my past? Could that be?? More likely my career has traumatized me into selective amnesia, not unlike my childhood. Real estate is a racket, I tell ya!

So, a month ago, in June (no need to keep up on dates, there won't be a test), and eight script-barren months since the initial scriptwriting course, I take another scriptwriting class in Seattle, a short, three-hour, evening interactive session. The instructor is Pilar Alessandra, who is up from L.A. and sponsored by thefilmschool, but not officially affiliated with it. She walks us through each step of the script writing process. There's no crying or tissues or "my sad sob story's as awful as yours" exercises. There's simply a logical line of questions that lead to an outline and then a fill-in-the-blanks format.

Something clicks this time. I think I finally get it. (I'm OCD, remember.) After that I'm up writing at 4am every day for a month. I make an outline and get a fourth of the script completed. I finish the script—a typical romantic comedy about a chick struggling for authenticity and independence, and yeah, there's a real estate component to it, too. But no way, the main character is so *not* me. *Cough.* I sign up for the mentoring offered by thefilmschool, then send the script to the copyright office, and to one of the mentoring instructors for a critique. After pulling the trigger, I wish I hadn't. Oh shit, it's so bad. There's that gut-wrenching, flushed-faced feeling again. But I figure I haven't peed my pants and he must have seen other terrible scripts, and he's there to tell me how to fix it so all is not lost.

I'm supposed to be enjoying the process, which I am, but I'm also goal-oriented and need to see some sort of tangible return, a side effect to years in business-minded mode. I've compromised my thoughts enough to be okay with not making a profit, but I really do want to see something I've written get produced. This writing thing could turn into an expensive hobby.

By mid a-year-later, some of the other students from thefilmschool class are already living their dreams, writing and seeing their work turned into real reel. I'm proud of them and I admire their creative talent and drive, *but what about me?* A friend from the class, who lives in Arizona, flew up to shoot her film this month. Doesn't that just blow you away? In some vacant office space, I'm sitting with her and her director and his girlfriend, who will be in the film, as eight-year-old girls parade through auditions, some nervous and some confident.

In between auditions, my friend, Reel Lady, gushes, "You wouldn't believe the organizing and fund-raising. Oh, and networking and promoting and schmoosing I've done so far."

Confused, I reply, "You obviously enjoy the process."

She continues, "God, the days are long and I've done so many rewrites and scouting for locations and finding the right crew who will follow *my* vision and work within a very limited budget, but yeah, this short [film] is my passion. Actually, it's also a resume of sorts, you know, for bigger things."

And she's enthusiastic and in it for the long haul, and in this I discover something: *I have no interest in the film industry.* These people live and breathe film. They are encyclopedias of knowledge on all aspects and all people of and in the business. Yes, I can learn all that, *but I don't want to.* I'm already doing something I don't want to be doing and making fat coin at it. So now what the hell do I do? Do I write for the sake of writing? *Really?* Writing for the sake of writing seems so...*unproductive.* Yes, I'll still enjoy writing, but . . . but . . . *sigh,* am I going to have to re-read Eckhart Tolle's books *again*?

But wait! This stuff comes later. We're *way* jumping ahead right now. Maybe we should start at the (other) beginning of this game-changing time...

Here's where this not-half-life crisis really takes flight...

***

PUSHING FORTY: WELL, PARTS OF ME
CERTAINLY ARE

January 2011. Comox, B.C. Canada
   I don't have a lot of time left.

Actually, I have about thirty minutes. Then I'll be off to a prospective client appointment. Mid-thirties couple, two kids, one dog, maybe a hamster, who want to sell their Comox Box and get a spot with "some land." They've already told me about the very special hardwood floors they installed when they renovated, so I know they'll want more than it's worth. As they tell it, "We don't want to give it away," which means I'll be the bad guy and there's a 50/50 chance I won't get the listing, and even if I do, the house will probably be overpriced and not sell and expire and—how does it go?—some other realtor will list it at the correct price and *then* it'll sell. Fucking land pimps. *But there is that slim chance I'll get it and sell it.*

I'm tired. I'm thirty-nine and a half and on the forty side of that half. In four months, I'll hit the next big decade. The thing is I'm actually looking forward to turning forty, because in my mind I look way better for being in my forties than I do for being in my thirties. Perception is everything. Appearance is everything. So, why did I suddenly get tired at thirty-nine? Why can't I shake this exhaustion? It can't possibly be these fifteen-hour days. I'm used to that by now. Aren't I?

I'll tell you what else I know about forty. I didn't make it here without a single gray hair. I have only the one but why the hell couldn't the damn thing wait a few more months? It's right on the crown of my part. I was going to move my part to hide it, but I have silver-lining syndrome (and soon to be silver part syndrome)—I'm always looking for the positive behind the seemingly negative, even though I'm a walking living(!) oxymoron at times. Perception is everything? I decide the single gray hair confirms I don't dye my hair, evidence of the one physical thing—my hair color—I've learned to like about myself. Sure, redheads are all the rage now, but it wasn't a day in the park when I was a kid. Actually, it was, but I was bullied and teased a lot in that park. As long as I only have this one gray hair, I'll be fine. But I've long suspected it will recruit friends. I can see which ones they'll be by their squiggly, erratic growth—even though I trim them, they're relentless little bastards. And not unlike the short and curlies you might find elsewhere, if you know what I mean. Not that it's fashionable to have much, if anything, down there these days. And how old do I have to get before I can change that trend? Do women in their fifties and sixties still wax their bikini lines? I cannot imagine little gray-haired ladies getting Brazilians, or those poor gloved-up aestheticians parting the folds. And what's wrong with a little trim, anyway? Am I the only one to suffer an ingrown you-know-where hair? I know I can't be, since my aesthetician gave me a handy little device, factory-assembled for just such a travesty.

And, speaking of hairs, why is there suddenly an overactive follicle on my chinny chin chin? What's up with that? All it does is add another minute to my morning because I have to check for the little rascal. I never know when Charlie's going to show up because, unlike most of the men have been in my life, he's unpredictable. He likes to surprise me when I've forgotten about him for a while. All this growth is especially bothersome in the summer months when every patch of fair fuzz is amplified by unforgiving sunlight. I'm not a big fan of summer. Don't get me started on wrinkles and sunscreen and potions.

I could go on about the random fine hairs on my belly, toes, and arms, and I think I'd have a right to. My hair is too light to qualify for laser treatments, which I find completely unfair given the fact I can finally afford the costly option. Can you imagine? Never having to wax or shave or pluck again? Oh, the freedom! But I'll have to invest my savings elsewhere, perhaps in Botox. So far: no Botox. I like my animated facial expressions and am not willing to part with them. This is usually where I would *Cut to next scene: needle in forehead* but no, I won't succumb! (Small voice: *yet.*) Though my twenty-something stylist is already doing it herself. For what? Her face still looks like a newborn's ass! Sheesh. And my editor says, rightly so, that *I'm* vain?? I'm just trying to catch up! Maybe

I'm not vain, only competitive?

So, IPL (Intense Pulsed Light) it is! This laser I can do. Basically, the aesthetician zaps the area—in this case, my face—with a special cold/hot wand that feels like a rubber band snapping on my skin. After a few days, my freckles get really dark and I look like someone has thrown coffee grinds on my face. Even make-up doesn't cover the so-called fix. But this destruction only lasts about a week and then my skin flakes like a leper. Alas, after it's over with, I look at least six months younger! Okay, so I only started this treatment and I'm supposed to do it three times, and then once or twice a year for maintenance before I'll really know. (Let's see, if I do this every six months for the rest of my life and my stylist does nothing, then in twenty years we'll look the same age.) But, at least there's no knife, so it doesn't really count as another cosmetic surgery. *Right?* It's what I tell myself.

I went through a phase of fake acrylic nails, but now I think they look tacky and rank right up there with the so-called "tramp stamp." These days—or years—I have to be careful *not* to look like a cougar. I've hit the right age bracket and am almost fit enough to pull off some of the outfits, but Lord, stop me if you see me even look sideways at a straight-brim ball cap. That's going too far. In fact, any article of clothing containing skulls and calligraphy is going too far for fashion of any kind, though it does seem to be popular. *Hmm.*

I'm not all that fit though I look pretty good "for my age." I hate that comment, even though I'm the one saying it and I say it a lot. Why can't I look "pretty good," period? That's it. I'm taking responsibility. Anyway, I have a wee little belly now, because man, I love food. I'm already working out like a demon. Please don't take food from me now, too. Right, right, moderation. Fucking moderation. Fucking slowing metabolism. I'm sure glad this aging thing gives me the "comfortable in my own skin" Girl Scout patch. It actually really does, or I'd be upset all the time. What I used to take for granted I now shrug off nonchalantly, only carrying the mildest bitterness for the young, careless beauties stealing the decent, and therefore rare, single men in my age group...but that's another story.

I think I was mid-twenties when MLM first suggested I get a nose job. She was over for a visit—I was married to Good Man at the time—and I'd been talking about breast enhancement. Back then I sported a B cup, which also meant a complementary muffin-top from being above my "best weight." And though Good Man didn't care, I did.

"Mom, what should I do? If I lose the weight, then I lose what little I have on my chest." When I look back, I'm not sure if I was hoping for support, not for my chest—I hardly needed it there—or *dis*couragement, but I got what I wasn't expecting.

"It would give you better proportion." But that's not the part that surprised me. After she said that, she started dissecting my face. "He could make your nose a little bit narrower at the same time. You will be sleeping, anyway. And maybe put the tip up a bit. You could have asked when you had the accident." (I'd been in a car accident and my nose was broken, whereby it got fixed—as in put back to where it was originally, as in no cosmetic changes made.) She demonstrates on her own Roman nose, turning to the side slightly and pushing her nose into a pig snout.

"I think I'm okay with my nose," I say uncertainly.

Later, I use a hand mirror and the bathroom mirror for maximum coverage. I examine every angle of my now not-perfect nose to determine if, indeed, I am okay with it. I'd never had an issue with my nose. Several other areas, yes: my arms are too long and/or my calves are too short, my little fingers are too little, my head is too small or my ears are too big— "There is a surgery for that," MLM tells me—my toes are stubby and my face isn't symmetrical (I don't think she's noticed this yet), and there's my freckles, for which MLM recommends the Obagi Blue Peel, an acid procedure that removes brown spots and "imperfections" like "your large pores, Dolly."

"But my freckles are pretty faded from the IPL..." I trail off.

She means well, she wants me to be happy (and pretty), I know this, yet somewhere deep down inside I want her to say, "You are perfect the way God made you." And mean it. I want to be able to tell myself the same thing. And mean it. One day I will. For now, I've got to run, to tend to some short and curlies—the ones on my scalp.

*

What have I learned? That with aging comes a sort of acceptance of certain physical changes. But if I'm not quite caught up with that, then "polishing the stone," as MLM likes to call it, can provide a good bridge. If I so choose. Which I so do.

Homework: Pick, pluck, cut, snip, and zap my way across that bridge to self-acceptance at my own damn pace.

***

HANDSOME BUT UNWORTHY AMERICAN BOYFRIEND (HBUAB): TRAVAILS IN ONLINE DATING

"What do you mean?"

"I'm just not that into you."

Stunned silence followed by indignant confusion, as he tries to keep me from walking away. "You're kidd—"

"You lied. I don't date liars. Or insecure men." (This statement becomes rather ironic later on.)

I'm already on my feet, but from all my years in real estate, I can't help but stick out my hand for a hand shake. He doesn't flinch, but looks at my hand as though it's dipped in fresh dog shit. He marinates in rage. I shrug and leave.

I should note that I put Vancouver, B.C., as my place of residence on my profile. Slight five-hours-away fib. (This isn't even the ironic bit. Just wait.) But I couldn't risk my real estate clients finding me parked out on a dating site—some of them did anyway—when I should be selling their houses. Plus, it was downright embarrassing. I'm just not that kind of girl: the dating site girl. Add superior-minded and judgmental (*read*: insecure) to my list of should-leave-behind traits. But I'd hoped to meet someone in Vancouver, anyway. Despite my redneck potty thoughts, I am a city girl at heart, after all! Or at least I want to be.

I get a few irate texts from FitforYou turned Shorty Pants:

"Wow. You must think you're all that"

"You're not much to right home about"

"What did I lie about?"

I resist chastising his improper word usage and reply: "Your height," then I can't help but add, "but thank you for confirming I made a good decision by leaving."

After this experience, my motto is First Stop: Phone call, then Straight to Skype.

Golfer006 and I chat on the phone one night and although I'm not keen on his sort of whiny, slightly Southern drawl, I set that aside because he addresses me as, "Baby Doll."

"So what's the '006' mean? Shouldn't it be 007?"

"That's my handicap. You golf?"

"Is that a good score?"

He laughs. "You don't golf."

"Where's your accent from?"

"South Carolina. A good old-fashioned Southern boy."

"Hmm, I'm not sure I like it, your accent."

"Really? Most women do."

"I'm not most women."

He chuckles and says, "I can see that."

I ask him all the requisite questions, most of which would be considered too direct and obvious had I met him on the street or in a coffee shop, but we did meet on a dating site so pre-qualifying should be expected, plus I'm using my Realty Lady interrogation skills to weed through the throw-backs.

"What do you do for work? Do you like it?" He brokers manufactured parts of some kind, he loves it, he makes good money.

"When were you married?" Four years ago.

"How old is your daughter? Does she live with you? How often do you see her? How's your relationship with her mother? Do you want more kids?" His daughter is ten, she stays with him on the weekends, he takes her to gymnastics on Tuesdays, he gets on "okay" with her mother, he doesn't want more kids (he got snipped to make sure).

"What kind of car do you drive?" He drives a *two-year-old, black Range Rover.*

"What are you looking for in a woman?" Someone reasonably fit and healthy who "will let an old-fashioned man take care of her."

And...Where do I sign?

I tell him, "I should note that *two-year-old black Range Rover* can be found as a dealmaker on my "Dealmaker/Breaker List." (Shallow, I know.)

He laughs. "What else is on your dealmaker/breaker list?"

"Lying. You fib, I forfeit." I share my Shorty Pants experience.

He laughs again, though with an almost untraceable smidgen of hesitancy. "What else?"

"Financial independence. I don't mean rich. I guess I mean financial security. You aren't being chased by creditors, are you?"

More forced chuckling.

At this point, I should have been listening better, but we'd already talked about fashion and his penchant for Armani suits. Any guy who buys Armani suits is financially responsible and secure, *right?* (Oh, but just wait.)

We schedule a Skype session. Remarkably, I'm not nervous and take this as a sign—then again, I do take everything as a sign. Anyway, I can't remember what we talk about because he's much more handsome on screen. We cover more of the fundamentals: Would I move to Seattle? (*Hell, yes!*) Do I want [my own] children? (*Not necessarily.*) Does he still believe in marriage? ("I'm a Southern boy: of course.") The basics check out.

We Skype every night for a week, then I'm off to New York City for a week with a girl friend to visit another friend and, I'll admit, to meet *The Italian.*

I met The Italian on Facebook shortly after my divorce and in the midst of one of my numerous break-ups with Junior. I'd liked his (The Italian's) page—he's a writer in New York City—mostly because he's a looker. We began emailing in between both our respective relationships, though maybe it was more like in between my relationships, because I'm not sure he is quite so angelic. But now that I've *virtually* met Golfer006 aka HBUAB (Handsome but Unworthy American Boyfriend), who I'm certain is MyFutureHusband, I neglect to contact The Italian when I land. I'm falling in online love, or at least a strong measure of infatuation and lust.

While I'm in the big city, HBUAB is long-distance, text-attentive: *"How was your day?" "Did you meet anyone famous?" "Are you still my baby doll?"* I embrace this affection, though looking back, perhaps that was just more evidence of his controlling, manipulating, and insecure nature. Ah, there are those three fingers pointing back at the pointer, which must have meant I possessed those possessive qualities myself. (I'll admit now that I did. *Shit.*)

Shortly thereafter, HBUAB schedules a trip to Victoria, B.C., three hours from Comox and the Capitol of our Province, also the capitol for romance (my unofficial label for it). He'll fly in direct from Seattle on a water-landing harbor plane, the very one I'll end up on in not too long. I'll pick him up and we'll go to a late 1800s heritage-home bed & breakfast. We've spent enough time Skype "dating" to know we won't need the two double beds option—unless, of course, he smells funny, the one thing the Internet can't foresee, or rather foresniff, even though I tried to bypass this obstacle by text-requesting HBUAB with: "Please send one used gym shirt in a secure plastic bag." (He didn't send the shirt.)

I listen to Nirvana on my drive over out of nostalgia—the band hails from Seattle—and to distract me from heart palpitations of anticipation. When I arrive, I wait in the Inner Harbor for the plane to come in and when I see the recognizable white-and-yellow, twin-otter plane gliding down, I rub my moist palms on my legs and get ready to touch this man I've never met. I'm wearing casual jeans, a fitted sweater, light jacket, and no make-up. I hardly ever go without a light cosmetic touch, so leaving the house this au natural is a stretch for me, but I want to make sure this guy likes the bared me. Though, I did get a spray tan. (I'm only a little bit orange.) After this initial meeting, I can raise the bar. (*Side note:* Unless you're in your twenties, ladies, set the bar low. Even if you've been drinking. Even if he's been drinking. Beer goggles are only good when you're young and aren't going to visually scare the shit out of the guy in the morning.)

The plane motor echoes across the bay to the Parliament Buildings and Empress Hotel, two of Victoria's 1700s landmark buildings. Seagulls squawk and float by overhead and I worry they'll poop on me, but they don't. I sit on the top of a picnic table to wait, feeling the chill of damp wood through my denim. The plane taxis in. I watch the tourists disembark and cattle in toward the Customs Office, a hundred feet away from where I sit. I don't see Golfer006.

He's the last out of the plane and my first thought is, "Thank You God, he's not short." The rest of him I can't tell yet, but he is more than acceptably fashioned in jeans that are also not too short (pet peeve), dress shirt, and what is later confirmed to be an Armani blazer, finished off with hip, hand-made Italian shoes.

Everyone emerges from the exit spout of the Customs shack and dissipates. Years seem to pass before he appears and walks toward me with a radiating smile and all his rugged yumminess. The man is beautiful. He can tell I'm in awe and looks down to hide a grin. I immediately chastise myself for not at least putting on some mascara - *at least!*

"Hi."

He hugs me but we don't kiss. We just met, after all. *What kind of a girl do you think I am?* There is still a first-meeting awkwardness, at least on my part. "You're beautiful, Anna."

It comes out like warm honey. I melt at the sound of my name in his voice. "You're ridiculously handsome. I can hardly look at you."

It's true. Plus, the sun is shining in my overly-sensitive, vitamin-deficient eyes. He laughs in a way that shows that he knows it, but says, "Nah."

We walk to my car with his bags and I'm smiling and giddy and sneaking glances at him.

He smirks. "Hungry?"

I blurt out, "Always! Do you like hamburgers? Um, I mean yeah, a little."

We laugh and he comes over and takes my face in both his hands and gazes tenderly in my eyes and kisses me ever so gently, then pulls away and looks at me again and breathes, "Beautiful." Then he kisses me again with a little more pressure this time but still soft and wet, and I'm a puddle and a goner and so far down the garden path I'm light years into our future together.

I'm not exaggerating at all, that's exactly what happened. *Gentlemen, take note:* That is how it's done. End of story, you may proceed to remove her tighty-whities.

Basically, after that, he had me. Things moved quickly and I moved to Seattle—well, part-time anyway. At the time, I was still more actively involved in my real estate business, so I would go back and forth to Comox frequently—a couple of times a month at first—while shifting those in-person activities to the two realtors who worked with me. (*Two of the best realtors in the business, by the way.*) I continued to do the marketing and website management, client reports, client follow-up, email and phone conversations, and all other Internet-friendly tasks from afar.

Because this new "system" of working from another country hadn't been tested yet, I wanted to keep it on the down-low. I learned quickly that one of the biggest obstacles to success in real estate sales is *other realtors*. Though most of the realtors I worked with I'd be proud to call my own, more than a few desperate, property-selling vultures will do and say whatever they need to to get ahead. And though I was doing as good a job as when I was a "permanent resident" of Comox, even better in many ways, I didn't need my location to be used against me—indeed, later it was—until I'd had enough proof under my belt, which could only come from continued success over time. (I remember one brazen realtor actually telling me, "If a client tells me they're considering you, I tell them, 'She's never here...'" He picks up the telephone receiver and offers it to me. "Go ahead, call the office. See if you can get her.'" True story. Thereafter, I changed my website, adding my gypsy marketing style.)

For a while, life was normal: HBUAB would go to work and I'd work from home, and we'd go out for fancy dinners on weekends we didn't have his daughter, and order pizza on weekends that we did, and she was as easy as her photo portrayed, and life was blissful. Either that or I was delusional and desperate to get a (love)life. *Sideways glance.*

I have to admit that I wasn't prepared for step-parenthood with all its running around to gymnastics and taxiing friends to the mall, and I'm no good at crafts or homework or baking cookies or braiding hair. Judge not! For, really, I'm *unselfish* for not birthing a child of my own sure to be neglected! (Half joke.) I was kind, if somewhat awkward, and always attended her practices and competitions and asked about her day.

"Are you excited about the tournament this weekend?"

"Yeah."

Awkward silence as she unwittingly tapped away at her laptop doing homework or a school project or who knows what ten-year-old girls do on a computer. I figured she wasn't a talkative child, and whether or not this was true, I could relate to that so I didn't push.

But I wonder if a niggling intuition about my dreamy new man and life also kept me aloof. It started almost as soon as I'd unpacked my fourth suitcase in his West Coast home up in the hills on a small, country acreage amongst the trees, forty minutes outside Seattle in a remote town, more a village (at best).

"I've had enough urban life with my ex. I like the trees," he'd told me. Even though I sometimes wondered if he had buried bodies in that forest, I blew off such a concern as part of my paranoia from reading too many true crime books.

Some nights the phone rang, and I'd watch him answer, agitated and terse.

His answer was the same each time: "Wrong number" or "Not interested." He'd hang up and tell me, "Fucking solicitors. Just don't answer."

It never really occurred to me that no one else ever called him, none of his supposedly "many" friends that I never did meet. Spending so much time apart in our separate countries, I was grateful he seemed to want me all to himself.

And I'd never answer the phone, anyway. I didn't feel it my place, plus I'd spent so many years in sales on the damn phone that I developed a strong aversion to it. But one night he was out in the yard raking leaves and the phone rang with Blocked Number.

Intuition or curiosity urged me to answer it. "Hello?"

An African-American-accented woman asked, "Is this Sara?"

"No, there is no Sara here, wrong number, could you take this number off your—"

"This is [HBUAB's real name]'s residence?" It was half-way between a statement and a question, and it slapped me in the face like a wet tea towel.

"Uh . . . who is this?"

"[Credit Collection Agency]. Sara [last name] and [HBUAB] owe . . ." she goes on, but I've lost my hearing and all the moisture in my mouth.

That's when I recall HBUAB mentioning a Sara, an old girlfriend from way back. "Everyone thought she was stunning. Do you want to see a photo?" I'd said *no* and wondered why any woman would want to see such evidence, but then tossed the thought to the trash.

"Ma'am? Ma'am, you there?" The lady on the phone is trying to get my attention.

I look outside toward HBUAB. He can see I'm on the phone and he's raking the same spot over and over as his old shepherd hobbles around the yard sniffing whatever intrigues him.

"Yeah, I'm here. Um, Sara and [HBUAB] were never married. She never lived here," I offer, unconvinced.

"Well, my records show they were, honey, and someone's gotta pay this debt."

HBUAB has abandoned his rake and is walking back to the house.

"What's your name and number? I'll get back to you." I'm pissed.

I write down Aysha's phone number and hide it in a drawer under the cutlery rack. HBUAB walks in. I'm vibrating with rage and a little fear.

"Who was that?" he asks, already knowing the shit is on its way to the fan.

"What. The. Fuck?! Who is Sara and why *the fuck* are creditors calling for her or her *husband?* Don't fucking lie to me."

He takes a deep breath. "Okay. Okay." Then he tries to hold my hand but I pull away and his posture collapses and tears form and he becomes a child, a vulnerable, insecure infant. "We lived together, like a couple years ago, not here, I swear. I helped her out a couple times but we were *never* married. I'll take care of it, I promise. I'm sorry for this, it's not my fault. I'll fix it, baby doll. I don't want to lose you."

It doesn't sound right but I ask, "Why didn't you tell me?" I'm thawing a little as I watch him crumple.

"I didn't want to lose you. I love you so much, baby doll."

"Where is she? Sara. Where does she work? I'm not going to go talk to her but if they call again I'm giving them her place of work."

I cross my arms and wait.

He tells me she's the receptionist at a doctor's office. I don't believe him but I let it go for the moment.

None of it makes sense but by now I'm exhausted. "Make sure they don't call again. I'll be answering the phone from now on."

He's grateful the storm has passed and knows he's bought some time, even if Sara's credit can't buy shit. I let him hug me. I mean, what else am I going to do? I have most of my clothes here and no car. I'd flown down for some reason, which is really dumb because we're in the middle of nowhere and I can't get around unless I borrow the neighbor's mare, which I wouldn't know how to ride, and I highly doubt there's legal parking for horses in Seattle anyway. (Plus, it would take me three hours to gallop there and I'd be all sweaty and horsey-smelling.)

That night he makes his famous skirt steak salad, completing the evening with candles and wine and music by Radio Head and Cold Play and reminds me about his childhood: parents in prison, emotional torture and physical abuse and foster homes.

"You gotta remember, baby doll, this was in the South a long time ago, it's not like it is now, or here." He gives me some specifics and I cringe and cave and "I understand" and "Okay" and "Don't lie to me" and promises and empathy and forgiveness and under-the-sheets time.

The phone is quiet for a few days. Then one day, I arrive home from a walk before he gets home from work to find a Court Order taped to the door. I unfold it and see Sara's and his name.

I call the credit agency and give them Sara's place of work and phone number. "You said it only has her name on this debt, right? So why do they keep harassing [HBUAB]?"

"I'm sorry, ma'am, I'm not allowed to share that information."

I hang up and say aloud, "Stop fucking 'ma'am-ing' me, damn it."

When HBUAB gets home, I tell him what I found and what I did.

He's calm but I can see his mind calculating. "I'll go to the courthouse in person tomorrow to get this shit taken care of. Fuck. I'm sorry, baby doll."

The next day, he picks me up to take me out for lunch. I look at him questioningly across the center console.

He says, "It's all taken care of . . . "

I relax and we go in to Hillbilly Ville.

Here's how it broke down:

1130am Mexican restaurant. He orders an enchilada. I order tortilla soup.

1215pm Mexican restaurant. We finish, he pays, we exit. We get in the Land Rover and pull out to the street.

1230pm on street near Mexican restaurant. Two black, Suburban, police vehicles pull us over, they handcuff, arrest, and haul off to jail HBUAB—my boyfriend.

1245pm on street near Mexican restaurant. I drive the Land Rover as the police escort me to HBUAB's house, since I don't know where the hell I am, having never driven anywhere here.

0100pm HBUAB's house. I pack whatever I can physically carry into suitcases and garbage bags, leave the rest, and get in the Land Rover.

0130pm in Land Rover. I head to airport using long-distance roaming and iPhone mapping, and call for flights en route.

0145pm SeaTac Airport. I get to the airport to find the only flight is to Victoria, B.C., 3hrs from home. I book it. I call MLM for pick up. I call BFFs for support. *Laugh.*

0200pm SeaTac Airport. Wrong airport.

0215pm following taxi. Taxi escorts me to correct airport.

0245pm Kenmore Air Base Airport. I arrive at Kenmore. I don't have $50US to pay taxi driver and he doesn't take credit cards. The driver takes me to the bank. Bank doesn't do exchange and my debit card doesn't work. Driver takes $38US + $40CAN.

0315pm Kenmore Airport. I haul 100lbs of luggage, leave extra in Land Rover parked in a lot a block away, and pay $100 extra for being over the 25lbs luggage limit.

0330pm Kenmore Airport. Flight delayed. Fog. May cancel.

0345pm Kenmore Airport. Flight cancelled. I rebook flight for next day 2pm to childhood hometown, but leave from different airport an hour's drive away. I call MLM and change pick-up location. I text BFFs: *LOL??*

0400pm in Land Rover. I retrieve Land Rover from the lot, collect 100lbs of luggage, process credit return, say *fuck it*, drive to UPS Store (using iPhone mapping), pay $200, and have all luggage shipped home (to arrive the following Tuesday).

0430pm in Land Rover driving. I call police department. HBUAB is still detained. I tell them I have his vehicle ("I'm not stealing it") and that I'm going to a hotel in Bothell near the third airport I'll see here. Police tell me when HBUAB is released he can report the vehicle stolen. I step on the gas.

0500pm Bothell Kenmore Airport. I arrive at correct airport (just to make sure).

0530pm Bothell Kenmore Airport. I book nearby hotel. I gas up Land Rover (I know, I'm way too nice but it's over an hour away from his place now . . .). I buy Cracker Jacks. I go to hotel.

0600pm Country Inn Suites. I call police department again. "What do I do with his truck? Who will feed his dog if he doesn't get out?" I give them HBUAB's address and location of "very friendly dog, please make sure someone feeds him."

0630pm Country Inn Suites. Golfer006 aka HBUAB aka Felon Boyfriend calls. He will feed dog. I feel empathy for him but I do not tell him where I am.

0645pm Country Inn Suites. I email The Italian, and ex-boyfriend, Handsome Millionaire (HM), in Vancouver. (HM texts back immediately: "Do you want me to come pick you up? I can leave now." A four-hour-each-way trip for him if there's no border wait. *Aww.* I reply: "No, but thank you.")

0700pm Country Inn Suites. I call MLM and eat leftover cold taco soup. I feel numb.

Sometime much later pm Country Inn Suites. I watch TV, stare at ceiling, and fall asleep.

Side note: The staff at Country Inn Suites is very understanding. I leave HBUAB's keys at the front desk so he can pick up the Land Rover and tell him I'll let him know "where they are when I'm on the plane tomorrow." At 430am, he texts me: "Medication in Rover." Fuck. I give him the location, he calls the hotel, who tell him I'm not there but his keys are for him to pick-up.

*

I have no fresh clothes, make-up, or toothbrush. I have a bag of T-shirts, my two favorite pairs of Gucci sandals, my jewelry box, and my laptop. The rest I'll get next Tuesday—unless it is detained by Customs. At least I have my Guccis.

I cry for a month in my Comox box, barely leaving, not eating, and writing from the dark place in my shattered heart. MLM checks in on me. There's nothing she can say, so she strokes my hair and cleans my floors and sits on the sofa reading her Bible. And I cry some more and fall asleep, and she covers me with a soft blanket. Her presence gives me the strength to take one more breath, and then one more after that. I wander about in a daze through the holiday season and hide out. After a month of moping, I pick myself up and say, "Mom, let's go on a holiday," and she says she doesn't like to travel.

And I say, "Mom, we're going to Israel," because I'm still good at sales. She buys a suitcase the next day and off we go on a whirlwind Walk of Jesus tour, on which I get baptized in the River Jordan (MLM prayed on my weak vulnerability, literally) and I come home cleansed and almost a woman again.

And then one day in February, he shows up on my door, unannounced, thin, and haggard.

He'd already sent me a thousand emails, since I'd not answered his million phone calls, explaining the hows and the whats and whys. And now he's here as a last resort.

We sit on the sofa and I feel desperate to hug him but control myself.

"I was making fat cash but Sara liked to spend it just as fast. And when the market turned, I was left in the lurch trying to catch up. I always thought if I worked hard I'd catch up. You told me financial security was number one for you, so I had to make a decision. Lose you before I could win your heart or maybe never lose you if I could catch up. I was catching up, Anna."

"But why didn't you tell me before it got to where it did? You had so many opportunities. Why didn't you fess up? I gave you the chance, I said tell me anything and everything and I'd forgive you."

"I know, I know. I was afraid, I guess. You can be very intimidating. You mean the world to me, and you had that rich boyfriend. I thought I could get ahead of it . . . never have to disappoint you. You wouldn't have wanted to be with a failure."

Well, how am I going to say *no* to that? *I mean really.* (Irrational rationalization to follow...) I *had* been pretty brutal about the financial security thing. And he *did* drive seven hours to get here with no guarantees. And I haven't eaten in weeks and I do miss him so much and everyone is flawed and I *am* intimidating and critical and doesn't everyone deserve a second chance? Plus, our abandonment issues unite us, right? *Right?* I totally fold.

We get back together. I go back to Washington. *We* move to a more affordable townhouse in Redmond.

*

What have I learned? No one's perfect? Everyone makes mistakes? We attract our emotional equal? Ah, fuck, the truth is I have abandonment issues, even as lame and overused an excuse as that is, plus I apparently over-empathize...Okay, *fine*, I'm attracted to emotionally-damaged men with serious childhood issues. At least my heart is kind, even if that's kind of fucked up.

Homework: Stop being a critical bitch. Give a guy a break and the space to be honest (i.e., make sure if HBUAB fibs again, there's no way it's my fault—*not that it is at any rate*). Take detailed notes anyway. Make sure responsible people with tracking devices know my whereabouts while in the USA. Research "implanted human tracking device" options. (This does not count as cosmetic surgery enhancement.)

* * *

VALIDATION VS. VANITY: ARTFUL OR JUST PLAIN LYING

So, yes, I'm back with HBUAB, who I threw in the gutter like a crumpled potato chip bag for being needy, fraudulent, and, well, needy, as in requiring constant validation. *Sideways glance.* Yes, fucking projection.

I say to HBUAB, "You're so vain. God, you use more hair product than I do."

Then I go get my face lasered off.

Anyway, had I not clung to him for the life of me, unwittingly lied to myself and my friends about him, looked to anyone—really, *anyone* who would listen—to validate my copious reasons for leaving him–"He's so vain. He lied to me."–then getting back together with him–"Everyone deserves a second chance. *Really, what could he do?*"–well, perhaps I could point at him with *all* fingers (though that would look ridiculous).

In acknowledging my own humiliation for believing his lies and then forgiving him anyway, I must admit I have sought out validation in my own ways over the years: to confirm I'm pretty, the best, right; to get noticed, acclaimed, Facebooked; to appear enlightened so I could preach my grand values and principles, and, well, you get the point. I am vain. Or am I seeking validation?

Back to the topic at hand: I gave him shit the other day for being vain. Yes, this from the IPL gal. Shameful, I know.

Another example: We're walking in downtown Seattle looking in shop windows, when I say to him, "You fix your hair every time a pretty girl walks by. Why do you need that kind of validation?"

"I don't." He's sincere.

"And why do you have to check yourself out in every reflective surface?" I chastise him.

"I want to look good for you, baby doll. Don't you want to be proud to be with me?"

Damn, he's good with his tongue, err, I mean, words.

"I guess," I say somewhat reluctantly, though acknowledging that he speaks a *semi*-truth. At least I am quick to correct my judgment and thence allow for a little vanity, but definitely no *validation*. He is *vain*. And my need for you to accept this falls under *validation,* so please disregard. But he really is beautiful to behold, so I guess I'll let it slide.

Now we know the rules, though we've also agreed there are no rules: It's okay to look good, but it's not okay to look for how other people look at how good one looks. Clear as mud(mask)?

In the end, I'm not perfect, and neither is he, but we seem to be perfect for each other at the moment—two adult-children with validation and vanity issues. So pass the Haagen Dazs because my Southern boy don't mind the belly, odd chin hair, and occasional in-grown, as long as no one else sees them. He read the last chapter; we have no secrets now. God bless America.

*

What have I learned? Whenever I point my perfectly-polished finger(nail) at someone else and shout, "Vain!", I might as well be shouting at a mirror. D'oh!

Homework: Stop shouting. No one wants to hear my judgmental ranting.

***

TO BOOB OR NOT TO BOOB: THE LOW-DOWN ON THE DOWN-LOWS

On a jaunt back to Comox, two of my BFFs and I get together for a potluck dinner, and a little show 'n tell and feel and squeeze and drink and laugh. My two BFFS—who will appear again—are the tall brunette Marthalicious, nicknamed as such for her homemaking, baking, sexiness, and crafting talents; and Leggy Blonde, nicknamed as such for her legs up to here and hair of sunshine, she's also got orderliness up to there, and quirkiness off the charts.

I'd been introduced to Marthalicious through a member of my real estate team who had helped her buy a house, and thought we'd hit it off. Since I'd been consumed with the belief that so many women have trouble finding real friendships because girls can be catty bitches, (or, extremely shy with the ladies), I thought I'd better put my theory to the test.

I went for coffee with Marthalicious one afternoon, and we become fast friends, spending the better part of an afternoon rambling like what I imagine two old college roommates who had known each other for forever would ramble like. What did we talk about? Hell if I remember, but I'm sure we conjured up a plan to change the world. (Though, perhaps our discussion of properly-layered jewelry won't do much to feed starving children.)

Bubbly Marthalicious speaks with genuine warmth, has an infectious laugh that gets louder and comes with vigorous hand gestures when vino is added, plus she's a damn fine cook. (Though she won't go near mushrooms—they revolt her. In fact, sometimes I like to throw the word "mushroom" around just to watch her face contort. Even though she knows I'm joking, she can't help her distaste. It's cute.)

Leggy Blonde and I met through real estate as well—she has her own marketing and event coordination business. Professionally acquainted for years, we hadn't gotten the opportunity to show our true colors until, one day, we ended up at a career mixer and, after a few mixed drinks and some crass humor and banter over a mutual OCD tidiness quirk—"Oh my god, you should see my junk drawer—compartmentalized!"—we took our working relationship to the next level: friendship. Leggy can't cook but she can organize like a mother-... She went to prep school where she cheered. She's gorgeous, but humble and sensitive, too. Funny story: One time she leaped from my still-rolling vehicle to help a homeless dude who, from out of nowhere, fell in front of my SUV when trying to run across the road and pull up his pants at the same time.

On this gathering, Marthalicious makes a veritable smorgasbord of gourmet delights whilst the remaining two culinarily-challenged bring wine. The show 'n tell...well, we'll get to that.

After stuffing our faces, we carefully tread gossip because we have new rules about what's acceptable to voice aloud and what's not. Generally, we've agreed that anything is acceptable within the circle of trust, which includes us three. I shall endeavor to abide by our guidelines and keep said gossip confidential, though I will say it generally encompasses workplace affairs and, more important, bad hair days.

"Did [so-and-so] get her lips done? I can't tell."

"I don't know but [what's-her-name] got a little too much Botox..."

"No way! She gets Botox?"

"Oh, yeah!"

"Hey, so before we get to our thing, do you think [so 'n so's] boobs are real? They're huge. She always looks like she's going to topple over."

"Real."

"Really?"

A couple of glasses of Malbec later and it's time for the main event, which is not the *Dirty Dancing* DVD playing in the background. However, the movie does keep the door open to the whole plastic surgery conversation as we discuss whether Baby should or shouldn't have gotten a nose job. *Consensus*: She looks better post-nose job, but is no longer recognizable as herself. It's a toss-up. Still, we agree that attractiveness is more important than fame, and vanity is permitted in small doses (and noses), thus it's a good thing she *fixed* it.

The conversation turns back to us. Of the three of us, only I have had "enhancement" surgery. Sadly, the very name of it suggests a natural body part's inadequacy, in this case—you guessed it—the breast. Or breasts, to be more precise. Considering the fact that I'm the only one of us who hasn't given birth, the surgery puts me in the lead in the vanity race. *Or does it?* Perhaps not. Because, come to think of it, my ladies (my girlfriends not my mams) were blessed with more than a handful of great Ta-Tas from the get-go. Really, I was just catching up!

Leggy has a new obsession: with whether or not to get hers "done," as if her breasts were a kitchen renovation or cracked driveway. What you must understand is that Leggy is beautiful. Tall, slim, tan, busty, *lovely*...basically, if I was a jealous person, I would for sure be jealous of her. A catty compliment, but that's how we females roll. (Incidentally, despite my insecurities, I'm actually not jealous of other women's beauty or bodies. Go figure. Get it? *Figure?* Anyway, moving on.)

Leggy was lucky enough to have kept her lovelies after giving birth to her daughter—for a long time after—but now that she is nearing forty, she claims they are no longer the pride and joy they once were. She came to realize this one day when her seven-year-old daughter casually observed her mother as having "long boobs."

"Long Boobs? Long Boobs!"

So started the self-examination—not the medical hand-examination for unexpected lumps and bumps, but the excruciating visual inspection in front of a mirror (all angles, all positions). The goal being to establish the cosmetic value of her natural wonders. As a result, Leggy determined she needed a comparison to set her mind at ease. Texts were sent. She decides to engage real subjects (us) to compare her Ta-Tas to: another set of real boobs (Martha's) and a set of fake boobs (mine) to determine if hers fall short, or rather, long.

As a rule, I'm not one to display my goods. I don't bear cleavage and I consider myself a classy girl, minus occasional redneck swearing and trashy trucker talk when my temper flares. In case you're the 1% of the population who doesn't "get it" (as in, why would I "enhance" myself if I never intended to show them off?) (and yes, I did make up that statistic), well, quite frankly, I did it when I was in my late twenties and simply unhappy and more than insecure about my size A cup, B if I could stand the muffin-top spilling over my jeans that came with the extra pounds required, which I couldn't, as you might have guessed. (*Also note*: It was one of the best things I did for myself!) I felt instantly womanly and proportioned, plus MLM encouraged me to "be happy with myself," which meant going ahead with the surgery. Afterwards she approved of my new goods—"They look natural, Dolly. He did a good job." But, I digress. Anyway, even though I don't like to show them off, I decide I'll play along. Leggy is one of my closest friends. It's for a good cause, after all. After enough chat (and wine), I stand up to get it over with, flashing my Ladies (breasts not girlfriends) to the attentive audience members in the comfort of Martha's cozy living room.

"Turn to the side. I want to see the profile, too." Leggy says.

Martha giggles. I feel like I'm back in the clinic, minus the papery robe and fluorescent lights. I obey.

"Can I touch them?" I nod. Leggy makes contact, though only after I drop my sweater so that I'm covered, of course. It's all very clinical, I assure you. My girls pass inspection. But everyone must take her turn. Fair is fair. Marthalicious goes next. She has great, natural boobs. As she has also given birth, we are duly impressed. Finally, Leggy takes another swig of Malbec, fumbles with her clothes, and hops up for the big reveal. I can't help being cheeky.

"Turn to the side, please."

Hers are nice, natural breasts, not the rocks in socks we expected from her self-deprecating comments. *Was this a set-up?* But, I'm to provide my honest opinion. And my honest opinion is: I'm on the fence. They're good as is, but they'd be fine augmented. Would I do anything if I had her boobs? I'm not sure. I'm not her. I didn't have kids. I got mine done because I had none at all, really, and didn't like that. There's something to be said for all-natural, it's true. If I could have been happy with myself, no matter their size, then I would definitely have preferred to stay the way I'd been born. But, don't get me wrong, I don't regret it. No way, not one bit. I love my augmented assets! And that's what's most important. Not what anyone else thinks, not what anyone else does, but what I think and do. Because I'm not seeking *validation*, and I'm not *vain*. (Fib.)

Later that night, as I'm getting ready for bed, I do a visual inspection of my naked self. Standing in the stark bathroom light in front of the mirror, I assess my body. I start at the top and work my way down.

Well, I like my hair. The color is good—deep auburn, the color Carmelita had once been acclaimed for. I hear MLM in my mind: "She look like a movie star." I smile at this, even though I've washed my face of any movie-star makeup. My face isn't so awful, except the freckles. Why do age spots and freckles have to look the same? Why does an age spot have to have a negative connotation? I frown at this thought and immediately notice a furrow between my eyes. I relax but the crease eases out less quickly—it's been etching its way into a habitual indent.

"Shit," I say out loud, and massage the crease into an angry red mark, which makes me frown again. "Shit, damn."

Thanks to genetics my lips are fullish. Thanks to braces three times, my teeth are relatively straight. Thanks to over-the-counter product, they're reasonably white. My face isn't totally symmetrical, but it's not obvious. Except in photographs. This bugs me. I try to "correct" this flaw with angling and posing and makeup.

MLM thinks my nose is too wide. What's-her-name got a nose job. I like my nose so I didn't. I abandon the rest of my body evaluation, put on cozy PJs, and hop into bed, satisfied I've given myself a self-critiquing break.

And that's the long and the short of it.

*

What have I learned? Most women have some sort of self-image issue. Self-esteem kind of unites us in a way, plus, it's a great excuse to break breadsticks, drink wine, whine, and build each other up

Homework: Reach out to my "ladies" (either definition) when I'm in a lull. Be grateful for what God gave me (and for giving cosmetic surgeons the skill to "polish the stone").

***

115, 115, 115! AND OTHER LIES I TELL MYSELF

Still back in Canada, HBUAB and I talk on the phone about the lousy Seattle spring weather: rain and more rain. He can't wait for summer: sunshine and beaches.

He asks, "Do you want to go on a holiday before summer?"

I murmur, "Oh, hmm, well..." and fade out, trying to quickly change the topic. "It's my busy season for real estate..." I add cheerfully, "I'll think about it."

"I'll think about it"—remember the real estate stats: 75% chance that the ultimate answer will end up being no. Runners up are: "We're not in a rush"—they'll call every other day indicating otherwise—and "We don't want to give it away"—87% chance they're desperate to sell for financial and/or emotional reasons. (I totally made these statistics up, but they're good educated guesses. I'm pretty sure.)

HBUAB continues cheerfully, "Where would you want to go, baby doll? The Caribbean has nice beaches. You can sit under an umbrella. My treat."

I can't help but spit out, "Can you afford it?" and immediately regret it, knowing he's a sensitive if ex-accused-criminal. Things have been a little tense since the whole "getting arrested for lack of funds and fraud arraignment" debacle. (Though, apparently, he got off since I don't think he's calling me from jail.)

He sighs heavily. "Yes."

I flinch. "Okay, well, let's see." I try to sound interested when giving my non-committal answer but it ends the conversation.

I weigh in with myself. There's no way I'm going to the beach! I convince myself of my reasons for not wanting to go. (Notice and appreciate the honesty, but try not to feel sorry for my patheticism, which is not actually a word but should be.)

I'm a redhead, which means:

- I burn—after peeling, of course.
    - o The vat of SPF 100 I slather on myself burns my Naired ass, making sand stick to me for days.
    - o I can't get a hold of the sun umbrella shaft, because it slips through my sunblocked grip.
    - o I freckle.
- I wrinkle as most do.
- I have more hairs on my body per square inch than non-redheads do.
    - o Do you know how hard it is to eradicate all that hair?
    - o Do you know how unforgiving natural sunlight is to said hairs? Can we say spotlight?
    - o Do you know that Urea 20 lotion does not work to alleviate the fine in-growns I get whilst trying to get rid of said hairs? Either I'll have a fuzzy fanny or a bumpy butt. Keep in mind HBUAB is far-sighted, meaning he can't see much of anything within two feet without his glasses on. He is not allowed to wear his glasses during our daylight intimate encounters, though he couldn't care less—and who else is going to get within two feet of my ass on the beach anyway? Nonetheless, he is only allowed to wear his glasses at night, as long as he only wears them with candlelight trickery. He is très sexy in his glasses.
    - The glare hurts my eyes. I could get a foot fungus from sharing sand.
    - My arms get sore from holding the book up and/or my neck gets sore from holding the book down.

Here's the truth: that twenty-something babe bouncing around with her Frisbee/volleyball/anything/nothing looks scrumptious in her itsy-bitsy-teensy-weensy-hardly-there bikini. I used to look that good, but now I don't. Add fifteen percent to your best body weight and see how you like it. (Exactly.) If you don't know HBUAB, then you don't know he is a hunk and could be with said hussy, or any veritable array of similar facsimiles. He doesn't, which still doesn't make sense to me. Perhaps I've spent too much time around my CWAD (Chick with a Dick) BMFF (best male friend forever), an eternal bachelor who has corrupted my opinion of the male psyche.

CWAD BMFF and I have known each other for over ten years at this writing. He is, in fact, my ex-brother-in-law, my ex-husband's brother. Good Man is sixteen years my senior but CWAD is only three years my senior, which immediately put us on the same plane generationally. Either because there was never any organic chemistry or because I was married to his brother for such a long time, we didn't go through any sexual tension—we were always in the "family category"—he's kind of like a distant cousin. (See, wouldn't that would be creepy? I'm not that redneck. No offense to rednecks.) Eventually, CWAD left the hospitality industry and went into real estate, which gave us more in common and solidified our "family category friendship."

He's an Aries: introvert or life of the party, stubborn but loyal, and outwardly disastrously disorganized. He's had a few serious relationships and a lot of "experience with the ladies" from his early career as a bottle-tossing à la Risky Business bar star. And he possesses a never-ending repertoire of relationship advice and philosophy musings, which matches nicely with my interest in the same. We're forever evaluating and re-evaluating what makes people tick, especially in the male-female arena. He's a steadfast friend but only when it's convenient. (I once asked him to take care of a small, potted plant while I was away and he huffed and sighed as though I'd asked him to detail my car with a toothbrush for the rest of his life. I even delivered the damn thing to his door.) (Note: the plant died. Our friendship didn't.)

One day after eavesdropping on my business call with CWAD, HBUAB asks (out of the blue), "So, do you think you'd be okay with me having a female friend?"

I know him well enough to know where this is going. I take a deep breath. "It depends. If it's your ex-sister-in-law who you've known for forever and there's never been anything between you and she's genuinely friendly with me, then I'd probably feel pretty okay about that... Especially since I'd always be welcome in your time together." You get it.

He drops the subject, but his point is made, which I justify to mean he loves me and is extra protective of his baby doll—and not that he is jealous, controlling, possessive, and can't be trusted. Instead, I chalk his insecurity up to his understandably tender ego.

Though I avoid mentioning the extent of my conversations with CWAD from that point on, I don't fib about them or avoid talking with CWAD. He's my BFF and male psyche sounding board, and it's in HBUAB's best interest after all! Plus, this call is an emergency.

"HBUAB wants to go on holiday."

"Great! Where you going? San Quinton?" He laughs.

"Be serious. I'm fat. I can't get into a bathing suit."

"So, what? He wants to be with you." This is not the right answer. I say so.

"Well, you're not fat, but you're not going to believe me, anyway. (He's right.) So, go."

"It's our busy time."

"So, don't go. What do want me to say?"

He's in a no-win conversation. I feel lost.

"Sorry. Thanks."

If I ever want to go to the beach with my man—I don't, but apparently relationships are full of such ridiculous compromise—then I must get over these little irritations. The first step is to feel as great about myself as I possibly can, which means I need to get in shape. The best possible shape I can be in for me, at my age, while still eating, sort of. That's all I can do. That way I will feel sexy and confident and know that I have the hunk. Who is far-sighted. Suddenly, not such an advantage for me.

Oh well, screw it, I'll go anyway. But, there will be no bouncing. I have my limits.

For now, I bid you adieu, for I must make a green salad with tuna and a slice of lemon. Hold the lemon!

*

What have I learned? If my cowboy wants to go to the beach, I will gladly join, right after I give him the ride of his life.

Homework: Practice my rodeo show.

***

IDENTIFYING THE IDENTITY CRISIS: HELLO, ME. WHO AM I AGAIN?

Okay, so I'm struggling of late with turning forty. (yes, still.) If you're on the other side of this aging line or you're just too well-balanced (good for you, weirdo ← compliment, sheesh), trust me. Forty is a big thing—or at least it seems that way. There's actually a term for it—mid-life crisis—and Hollywood acknowledges it with movies like This Is 40. I'm trying to positive-think myself into feeling positive about it. I've pushed on myself, if no one else, the benefits—singular?—of this next so-called milestone: looking better for being in my forties than for being in my thirties. I know I said that already, but bear with me. Being comfortable in my own (lasered) skin doesn't come easy for me, no matter how many optimum points at Shoppers' Drug Mart I earn from investing in youth serums. (maybe because it isn't my own skin?) I'm trying to "own my power," whatever the hell that means. But as the saying goes: trying is lying. I know I said that already, too. Damn it.

I think fundamentally I want to like myself as is, but when I look in the mirror I don't see the photo-shopped flawless perfection I see on happy faces in magazines. If I can get to that kind of perfection, I'll be happy inside like all those models look on the outside. Maybe then I'll be like Carmelita, the effervescent goddess who floats in MLM's memory, unflawed, whole, and un-dissected. (is insanity still insanity if the self-accused is self-aware?) I know the absurdity of it all.

But getting old is about more than face, *right?* I've been eating better. Truthfully, my stress has left me with little appetite. Thank god for small miracles! I've lost five pounds from exercising like a banshee—every day in my living room with p90x and leg weights and Windsor Pilates, and stair-climbing my way to buns of steel at the rec center. My ass still isn't where I want it to be, which is where it never was even when I was twenty, so I could be asking a lot of it. And I've been counting my blessings—my friends: Martha, Leggy, CWAD, who are always there for me when I feel lonely or bored; my family: the whole of them, simply for existing since we don't spend much time together being busy in our hectic lives; and to a lesser degree, my boyfriend: HBUAB. Lesser because he is a main cause of stress for me, what with the distance, driving, and *doubt.*

Traveling back and forth to Seattle gives me ample time to over-analyze our relationship, evaluating the pros and the cons, with the prevalent thought being: is he a con? I wonder if he's caught up on his bills. Will I ever know for sure? Will there be other surprises? Will financial disaster befall him, and therefore us? How can I protect my own finances (*and my shoe collection*)? If I stay with him, the only way I can stay in the U.S.A. is if we get married. Or become a brain surgeon. How risky is that? (either option.) Will I make any friends? Haven't so far. And either HBUAB has none or he's hoarding them from me. Good thing he says, "but I only want to spend time with you, baby doll." *(Yeah, yeah, I know. Shush).*

And do I really want to be a step-mom? I'd thought I wanted to be a mom, but it got to be too late, and then thought this step-mom thing might be a satisfying second prize. But the more time I spend with her, the more I remember my ex-step-daughter. Good man's youngest daughter lived with us full time and was ten years my junior. I grew really close to her, only to lose her along with my marriage. (her loyalty to her sad father was understandable but still came as *a major loss to me*, which might explain why my heart is guarded with my new possible daughter-to-be.) And what might my life look like living full time in the states? What would I do for work? Real estate is eating away at me as is and I'm well-established. Too many thoughts, too many fears.

I think constantly about how I want to make a career change. Just writing that gives me anxiety. I've been "the famous realtor, Anna J," as many locals still call me, for twenty years next February (less than a year from now). Real estate is how I'm known, it's how I know myself, it's my identity, my *validation.* It's one of the reasons MLM is so proud of me. Every week when I see her, she asks for more business cards.

"When I show them your card they say, 'Oh I know who she is,'" she tells me proudly, pulling out my well-worn, photo-on-the-front business card. "and they say, 'Oh, she's beautiful!' and I say, 'I know' because you are, my darling." And she means it. *Sigh.* I love my mom.

But even validation from MLM doesn't keep me from longing for a change of pace and place. There's a dichotomy inside me. On one hand, I'm addicted to the recognition, on the other, I need anonymity, I want to be a regular person and go unnoticed sometimes. Or perhaps I want to be seen for the real me, not the professional persona people can't seem to see past. (*I don't allow them to see past.*) It's my own damn fault, I know.

I was a natural at real estate from the beginning—at twenty, in my first month in the business, I listed six and sold three homes by transporting buyers around town in my mother's Honda Civic hatchback. And either because I didn't think about it or because I was young and fearless when I started, I never doubted my success. Now, I'm a total scaredy-chicken about my next big thing. My heart thumps in my chest when I think about doing something else. (silver lining: extra cardio?)

How will I succeed as a writer? The concept is abstract. In real estate, it's simple, if not easy: keep calling potential clients until someone says yes or fuck off, and after that the logistics are basic. As a writer, I have nowhere to begin. Who do I call? What do I write? Where do I submit? Will anyone want to read what I write? *Will I have to take out swears??* What's the plan of action? What if they hate my writing? What if I quit my career just to fail? What if I look like a fool? Will I need to be "famous" to be successful? Do I want that kind of attention again? What if there are things I don't want to do to be successful, like submit a thousand articles to a thousand publishers? *Then I'm doing more of what I don't want and not necessarily even making a living at it.* God, maybe I should just keep doing the real estate thing! That singular thought is a vice clamping down on my chest.

"I just can't," I say aloud to myself. I'm not sure if I mean that I can't quit real estate or that I can't keep doing it.

I'm in that place that we all get in as we're leaving high school, or college—for those of you smarty pants who attended—where you ponder all the possibilities and decide what you want to be when you grow up. What do I want to be when I grow up? Little voice: *a writer.*

When I set aside the fears, I feel sure about this, and passionate about my newfound love interest. When I'm sitting in front of my laptop and typing away for forgotten hours and days, caught up in the words and the visual story unfolding in my mind, the intense feeling comes—that *flow* that artists speak of. Then there is passion and joy and life energy inside me and emanating from me. In those moments, I'm even okay with being a non-award-winning, mega star writer—*wait, am I high?*—yes, as long as

I can still afford to buy cheese—whew, perfectly sober. (I'll give up Jimmy Choos for cheddar. In fact, I already have!)

I guess I've been thinking about the idea of writing for a living since 1999, long before the screenwriting class, when I wrote a letter about my career confusion and submitted it for publication to Chatelaine magazine, the equivalent to US Vogue—well, *not really,* maybe more like a cheap version of Glamour, well, even that *might be* stretching it, but whatever. I was published! Ironic, isn't it? I can't remember the letter verbatim, it was more a passing interest then, but it talked about following one's heart and pursuing passion with courage and all that wistfulness. I knew even then I didn't want to be in real estate forever, but I thought chasing dreams were too self-important, somehow.

I tried to keep my career searching anonymous, which is another piece of the pie. Because my day job is high profile I have to keep things separate. *Case in point*: I didn't include my last name in the published piece—only my last initial—and it happened that I found out it was published because some astute clients brought it to my attention. They were happy for me. (*they also bought their house through someone else!* Exactly.)

Why didn't I do it *then*, when I was first thinking about it?

When you're a real estate agent, there is no "outside of real estate." I know realtors who tell their clients, "I'm booked at that time" or "I've got an appointment then, would 8:00pm work?" When those so-called "appointments" are actually family time. I know of clients who have moved on to the next realtor when the one they call first says, "I can come after my son's soccer game." Her son doesn't know it's an eight-thousand-dollar soccer game for her. That's often how the game is played in the real estate.

No, there's no way a writing career and a real estate career can co-exist—unless, of course, one is writing about real estate. Then there is clout and acclaim, which could add value in clients' minds. But no, thank you. Hell, no! In fact, I could re-brand myself as hell no! Lady, and although I'd feel in control and empowered, I'd also be riding to appointments on a moped, as that'd be all I could afford, what with the thriving business that being hell no! Lady would give me. Damn it.

Looking back, it was an ideal time to do it. I had a husband who suggested I go for it, and the financial freedom that would have allowed me to do it stress-free. *What a dumbass I was.* My higher self argues in my head that it simply wasn't the right time to write. I believe this simply because I believe all things happen in the right time, according to the will of god or universe or fate. I argue back with my higher self to then get her *"ass down here and live my life for me then, thank you so much."*

I took a self-help course when I was twenty-five called choices seminars. (I super recommend it—it totally saved my life—but I must warn you: bring a shipping container of tissues!) At the time, I was a mental and emotional mess. Yes, worse than I am now. I'd already started in real estate and had success. I'd met my husband-to-be, who was head over heels for me. I had no obvious reason to be unhappy. Maybe because the surface of my life seemed great, it shone a light on my chronic discontent. At the time I was irrationally irritated, often yelling at Good Man without just cause.

"Why can't you put your boots in the fucking mud room? I've asked you a thousand times. Why is this so difficult?"

And once he'd learn to put them in the mud room, I'd find something else to pick on him about. *I know, I know, what a bitch.* Of course, it was never about him. I was miserable and needed an excuse to be so, and he was a willing target. I grasped onto a proverbial father figure to take care of me, and he did take care of me, but because of my unreasonable fears and constant anxiety that he'd *leave me or die*, I would push him away. And eventually I did leave. I feel guilty for what I put him through, and am thankful for his endless patience and love. Truly, he deserved better. *Hug for Good Man.*

In Choices, I discovered that Good Man's unconditional love for me triggered my crazy card because of my childhood issues that I'd never dealt with, even if I acknowledged the events themselves: being shipped off to the wife and her husband (abandonment), being molested (abuse), the wife "catching him in the act" and inspiring me to become a closet dweller for "being a bad girl" (shame), not understanding that I wasn't a "bad girl" (self-loathing), watching my dad die (abandonment again). And after that, watching MLM deteriorate, losing all vibrancy along with her will to live, (more abandonment). When I went into real estate, it was the one thing I had some manner of control over, *because one can only re-re-organize a cupboard so many times.*

Choices taught the precept that everything in life is a choice, including what we think and feel. Here's where implementation is a bitch, again. At the time, I didn't want to feel hopeless and fearful and angry *all the fucking time.* The most difficult choice to make can be just that: changing the way you feel about something. (Oh, pardon me, changing the way *I* feel about something.) I understand the concept intellectually. I get it. But it's the *doing* part that gets me. Damn doing!

So now, present tense, I'm using a choices mantra (if better is possible, is good good enough?). To move forward on one small thing: I've decided to start with deciding. I'm turning forty, I'm getting older but have too many working years left and I don't want to have those be unhappy working years, so I've decided to do what feels right in my gut, even though it's as scary as finding your first gray pube, *not that I'd know*—this will be my last year in real estate, at least as Anna j the realtor. *Rapid breathing.* Maybe I'll write a sitcom about my experiences, or a series of short stories about them, but after February of next year, I'll be referring back to real estate from the other side. *Passing out...*

I didn't do it in 1999. I didn't have *Tom Skerritt telling me that I'm a natural writer(!)* For all I know, he could be telling all his writing students that. *Shrug.* Whether or not that's true, it's the encouragement I need to push me to make this decision to take the leap of faith. I don't know what I'll write, I don't know where I'll write, I don't know how it will play into my relationship with HBUAB. All I know is that I am both exhilarated and terrified. I am trusting that God will hold my hand, whether I succeed or fail. Dear Lord, if I fail miserably, please turn me into Anne Frank so I won't hear or see the laughter. On second thought, maybe just give me her strength so I can get over it and quickly. Yeah, um, let's go with #2. In Jesus's name, amen.

If I end up in Seattle full-time—if HBUAB and I can ever get on the same page long enough for me to really consider marrying him, which he's been desperately pushing for since the beginning (his own need to possess, control, and not be abandoned or maybe to secure my stellar Canadian medical system, *hmm*)—then there will be a whole other set of scaries that come with changing locations and vocations.

Though he lives in Seattle, and I do love love love Seattle, no doubts about that—arts and culture, food, outdoor recreation, interesting people, diversity, lack of obvious pretension, *anonymity*—HBUAB and I have our own real problems, like any other couple. He is also having a difficult time with my identity crisis, like my PMS irritability that sort of doesn't go away, like, *ever*. I'm afraid if I give up my day job I'll be broke, and poor, and a nobody—a nobody with a dream, but still a nobody. And even though I crave anonymity, who wants to be a nobody? That which does not kill him makes him stronger...?

All of which brings me back to *me*. I mean, I would have to rewrite my identity. I define myself by what I do, who I do it with, how much I make, the recognition I get, my friends, my hobbies, appearance, vehicle—the list is lengthy, so pick anything and stir this shallow soup that's me! Everything runs the risk of changing, because *everything about me and my life is somehow related to the fact that I'm in real estate.* Fuckstick.

I've met all of my friends through real estate, whether they're realtors, clients, or business associates. As a writer working from home, how would I meet anyone? *Lest we forget, I'm not a joiner, people.* I like my friends and share a connection with them because we can relate to each other about work challenges—cranky clients, deadlines, juggling personal lives around writing offers or showing homes, happy first-time home owners—but would we still relate if I was out of that racket? And my friends make decent coin. We go out for dinner at least weekly without worry of who's picking up the tab. I have no guarantees of any income as a writer, and haven't saved enough to live comfortably sans income, so will it be awkward if I'm the one person at dinner not eating? *I'll tell you right now, it would be awkward for me, because I like to eat and I'm no mooch.* (Pet peeve.) I can just imagine me saying, "I think I'll skip to dessert."

There'd be knowing glances and someone would buy me dinner, but eventually the invites might stop, and then someone would let it slip that I missed a girls' night out, and there'd be awkward pausing, and "Didn't you get my text? I assumed you were busy writing..." trailing off along with my social life. *Oh my god! They're ditching me, too??* And they all drive shiny new cars like the VW Touareg SUV I drive, but that would have to go, too. It's not environmentally friendly, anyway. But would that matter?

For now, I embark on a new adventure, regardless of the cliff it represents: who do I want to be if not me? Perhaps a better question is: which version of myself do I want to flesh out? If I'm done with the professional Realty Lady, which other me do I want to be? Certainly not the bitchy one, or the fleshy one (sex kitten). I feel deep down I am redneck-roots-woman-child, whatever that means. I'm still figuring that out, but it's somewhere between responsible and care-free, independent and take-care-of-me, and sexy and confident and fun and alive, with a hearty dose of I-grew-up-around-naked-lady-wallpaper!

As a person who revisits the past more than a fat kid revisits a snickers snack bar, and as a person who worries about the future more than a debt consolidator in Detroit, I don't live in the now. Sorry, Mr. Tolle, even if I do have both *the power of now*, and *a new earth* on cd *and* in hardcover book, I simply don't do it. It doesn't come naturally to me. I'm an "analyze, make a plan, write it out, break it down, post-it up, review it often, take action" kind of gal. But, for once, planning is a bit hard going. And writing? It isn't exactly a 24"x36" poster kind of job.

All that being said, I'm going to try something completely new: *trust.* Trust that now that I've taken the first step, I've made the decision, then god—universe, energy, higher power, inner self, fate, destiny, law of attraction, whatever works for you—will take over and allow opportunities to unfold for me that will push me in the right direction. Really, that's almost a cop-out because I don't believe in wrong directions, only *varied learning experiences. Raised eyebrow.* And, if I believe that, then what the hell am I afraid of?? Exactly! Right on! I mean . . . *write on!*

What have I learned? It's my own damn fault for creating such a believable character (Realty Lady) in the script of my real life story (though, that is me, too!) And I can create a new "me" character (Writer Lady) in my new story!

Homework: Pre-script my own character, as in my life. (Watch ratings suffer. Try not to care. *Panic.* Get over it. Eventually, accept new "eccentric" labeled me, which might be better than the ones that will precede it: "mad as a hatter," "she's gone off the deep end," "crazy lady," and "we need a new realtor.")

***

CUT TO NEXT SCENE: NEEDLE IN FOREHEAD

As soon as I said I never would, I knew I'd do it as soon as possible. *Botox*. I really don't have that many wrinkles, what with all the laser treatments and products promising a youthful radiant complexion. I used to roll my eyes at the ads, but now I've got a pad and pen handy should my lapsing memory fail me before I get to the drugstore for all these antidotes to aging. My current concern Botox can fix: the default furrow. The one located right between my eyes. It comes from being cranky in the face (*read*: hot-tempered), not from stern concentration. I could blame it on writing real estate reports during the wee hours, or squinting at my beau, or even genetics via MLM, who used to be spicier than a jalapeño sandwich. Her and my dad's feuds were famous around the logging camp. She once swung a 2"x4" wood beam at him, hitting him in the shoulder (he didn't flinch), when he got jealous of and beat up some other logger for admiring MLM. It doesn't really matter from where it came. What matters is that it's here on my face. And I don't like it. This has nothing to do with authenticity, it's purely vanity. What can I say, I'm not perfect—*as in one of my major flaws is superficiality!* Why couldn't I have gotten the greedy, or mean-spirited, or even truly catty card? If I was catty, for sure I'd be able to at least relate to more women, no?

Not only will a furrow age a woman, an *angry* furrow will make her look ugly *and* old. And that's not catty, that's truth. There's a difference between looking old and looking angry, which is just ugly. And ugly is, well, ugly! Not only that but angry-ugly is also unfriendly, unhappy, and uptight, and as long as I have to be Realty Lady, secretly morphing into Writer Lady, I don't need anyone to think I'm not feeling friendly and happy and relaxed. That could have adverse effects on my work effectiveness and, therefore, income, which I need while I carefully plan (*truth*: aimlessly fall into) this transitional time in my not-half-life crisis.

I had coffee with my two BFFs, Marthalicious and Leggy Blonde, the other day. Leggy suggests the Botox bit "with a little Juviderm on the side." (Juviderm is a "filler" that will plump up sagging areas, like around the mouth, for you purists.)

"Shit, now I have sagging areas??" I whine.

She sideways-glances and I'm not sure if that means she thinks I do or if she doesn't want to admit that she'd like to try this hokey-pokey, plump-us-up herself. I squint and lean in for a closer look at her smooth, sagless face. I have to say, if that's what she did...well, she looks really good, totally natural. If you didn't know her, you would think she looks rested. Knowing her face as I do and having an eagle eye for such details, I can see the difference—it looks smoother. Even I can hardly tell. I'm noticing how good she looks lately, and I'm wondering what her au natural source is. But there isn't one, damn it all to hell! There's no new man in her life and success at work can only lift your spirits—and flatten your wrinkles—so much, so I know she must have been in for something. I want some of that something! (*Side note*: Leggy turns forty only three weeks after I do and here she is getting a Juviderm jumpstart! No fair.) (*Another side note*: This information about Leggy is totally unconfirmed and I have been known to theorize on what may be only slightly exaggerated and, yes, even unknowingly untrue. I apologize to said BFF if my observations don't match reality. If so, please chalk it up to almost-forty hell-on-Earth and appreciate the compliment!) (*Additional note*: I have since found out that the above story regarding Leggy is a badly-made observation and that said BFF didn't have anything done! *Conclusion*: Lose the fellow, lose the furrow. I'm contemplating it. Also, the boyfriend is anti-Botox. I think he doesn't want me to look younger than he does, *but I already am younger than he is*, so that's that.)

But really, for me, I could consider Botox an investment in my relationship with HBUAB. The furrow between my eyes as a result of all the furor and scowling—due in large part, but not limited to, HBUAB—is becoming a permanent etch. At any point in time, he could look at me and think I'm angry with him when, in fact, I'm simply in stasis. *Unlikely, but possible*. If I'm serious about my commitment to our relationship, then I owe it to both of us to appear congenial at all times. The sad thing is that I'm actually buying this bullshit as I write it. Someone pass me a shovel. It's really more about my slight obsession with looking good great *perfect!* Fucking perfectionism.

Things have gotten more interesting with HBUAB. In the month we'd split up, HBUAB hired an assistant, which I took as a sign that things were getting better financially. I try not to notice she is twenty-something and stunning, without a flaw on her face. I try not to care that she texts her boss, my boyfriend, in the *evenings*: "Hit my head on the cabinet door, nearly knocked myself out . . . knew you'd find that funny!" (With attached photo of said door.) Never mind that I'm checking his iPhone when he's taking a whiz. So I try to focus on the fact that the creditors have stopped calling, and he is loving and tender and grateful and I am baby doll. Fucking charming charisma.

But. There is still that nagging feeling inside me. He assures me it will take time to trust him again, that my feelings are completely and predictably normal. With expression of hopefulness and disbelief, I buy it, not because I believe him, but because I *want* to believe him. There is no way I'm going to fail again and go home with my tail between my legs. I'd contributed to his hiding and fears by being all "financial security is most important." I must give him a chance if only to redeem myself in the process. And part of my plan includes not frowning at him day and night in suspicion, hence the Botox.

Reason number two for doing Botox: Everyone does it. Even men do it now. I'm not doing it *because* everyone's doing it. I'm just saying I'm not the only insanely vain person out there. Hell, I'm surprised I'm considering it before my very handsome but excruciatingly vain boyfriend manages to make it to the aging doctor, because he *does so* check himself out in every window we pass, and he *does so* fix his hair when a pretty girl is in the vicinity! Well, at least I'm doing Botox before he does. Come to think of it, he doesn't frown a lot. *Squinting.*

So, after all that, I've decided against Botox. This about-face (pun intended) came about after fretting over HBUAB's waify, model-like assistant. Their frequent business lunches were bothering me, but when I questioned him about it, he guffawed and assured me they—the lunches— were completely innocent.

"We talk about how to make the business more efficient. She's smart that way, baby doll."

Oh great! She's pretty and smart and helping his business grow. Lovely.

There's nothing I can say, so I take a deep breath and give up. If I was more on the ball, I'd be drinking myself into depression-motivated, literary-award-winning writing. Instead, I spy on him. I could be all Angelina Jolie à la anything she's done, but I'm more Renee Zellweger à la Bridget Jones' Diary. And I'm not even simply "letting go," that's different, that's a good thing. Giving up, in this case, is when the heart knows something's up and starts to shut down. I'm not quite at the end, so there's a dance between trying to stay in control and saying, "Fuck it." Plus, there's the whole I'm-a-drama-addict thing. (By the way, all this HBUAB stuff is not exaggerated at all. I say that like I'm proud of it—that's how messed up I am.)

So out of spite, or rebellion, or who knows what, I veto the needle. But I'm thinking about doing an Obagi Blue Peel instead! I know this seems contradictory, but please understand: Part of the Botox bit is directly related to the young bimbo (nothing personal to said bimbo, if you're reading this, and um, thank you), so in order for me to not lose face, I have to keep furrow—or fix it with some other non-bimbo-related repair! (*I realize this makes no sense whatsoever and I'm justifying my actions, but really, who do I need permission from anyway? It's my damn face.* Thank you.)

Back to Obagi: They paint this tinted acid solution on your face and it burns like, well, like acid—or molten lava. Then it froths up until you're blue as a Smurf for seven to ten days, while your skin heals and tightens and peels off like paint on an old wood deck. Then you're silky smooth with tiny pores and look three to five years younger wherever Smurf solution was applied. Plus, you totally feel youthful and radiant. Presto! Then maybe, once I'm done, I'll buy a Fedora and the only thing left is, oh, for crying out loud ...Can she dip me in a vat of this shit, because otherwise *how do I get rid of these creases above my sagging knees now that I'm down to 115 pounds?!* Damn goal weight.

*

What have I learned? Just because everyone's doing it doesn't mean I have to!

Homework: Do what I want to do. As long as no one else gets hurt, poked, lasered, or peeled.

***

A SHOT IN THE PARK: WELCOME TO MY NEW SECRET LIFE

Back in Canada, the nurse reclines the chair and puts an ice pack on the spot where she will inject me with 12cc of botulism. There's a small prick of an ultra-thin needle—"press down on this, please"—and a cotton pad at the ready to stop any miniscule bleeding. Within ten minutes, I'm done and gone. It doesn't hurt at all and I wasn't nervous in the slightest. Within a few days, I look super-friendly again. Ask me to frown, just ask me! I can squint, but only in an ultra "way too cute isn't she adorable" kind of way.

I had thus far resisted "injectables" because my big fat ego liked being (sort of) natural of face—I had to hold on to some beauty claim since I've got implants (such a nasty word, really). But unflattering lighting and shadows and perfectly-plumped friends finally convinced me, just *looking* at them sold me—they look totally natural! It could be that some of them actually *are* natural, which only gives me extra incentive to catch up, or rather down, as in years, appearance-wise. Incidentally, some of them had the same attitude toward implants—as in they like to be all-natural—but after having kids and/or losing weight, some of them are starting to move to the dark side, too. Ah, sweet vanity. Just be subtle about it. There's nothing scarier than one too many facelifts. If it's obvious, it's no longer attractive. If your next face lift gives you a pube-style beard . . . I'm just sayin'.

Truth be told, certainly not by HBUAB (more to follow), it does make me feel more cheerful. Whether it's psychological or physically-activated physiological, it worked: the crease vanished and my joyful spirit re-emerged. Oh, I'm still going through a just-turned-forty crisis, to be sure, so I might as well make the best of it and have it be the best on-going crisis ever!

I thought the first step to making it the best crisis ever was to officially launch a new secret, single life in Seattle! That's not to say I'll be giving up the old, role-identified Realty Lady me back in Canada. I don't have both feet out the door—that would be irresponsible—but I do have my toe dipped in something new and exciting, even if unsettling. Speaking of which, when I look back I can't really pinpoint a time that I felt settled since I was married. Even though I was unhappy a lot of the time, I had a sense of security and predictability that was comforting. After my divorce and a few years of partying like a rock star and ~~dating~~ having sex with inappropriate men (*hmm, prequel?*), a few years of fix-me-ups with men too young for me or merely not right for me, and a few years of constant self-questioning about my career and life purpose, I was on a collision course to a crisis. At least I haven't been bored. That sounds blasé, but it has been quite the ride, so to speak, and if I don't look at it with a sense of humor, I might lose what's left of my reasoning or worse. *Wrist-slashing motion.* (I apologize to anyone reading this that killed himself by wrist slashing. That was insensitive of me.)

Oh, in case you didn't notice, I turned forty. It's done. Past. Checked off. No big deal. The lead-up was crappy, but the arrival . . . *not so bad.* See, there *is* a reason to fear the worst: an actuality less than the worst can turn out to be delightful! Don't try this at home.

Okay, so yes, I decided to go for it. All of it—well, almost all of it. I haven't quit my day job. But I Botoxed that furrow in my forehead *and* I got rid of the reason for it, HBUAB. And because I fell in love with the beauty and promise (and anonymity) of Seattle while flitting back and forth to HBUAB, I decided to do it! To write! I found a little secret get-away for myself, but shhh . . . don't tell anyone.

So now I'm living in (part-time) five hundred square feet in an old, brick building on the ground level, which backs onto an alley, with views of the dumpster and recycling bins. "I'll need you to initial the lease on all fourteen pages, including the mold and lead-based paint disclosure forms, please." I could only reply, "Yes, yes, yes where do I sign?" The good news: I can toss my trash and cardboard straight out my inadequately-secured, single-pane window directly into the bins! And if this little adventure doesn't make me happy, damn it, then the lead-based paint will surely transport me to Heaven (?) before I have to commit suicide, or at least keep me high. Silver lining!

To be fair, my new space is in a great neighborhood, Madison Park in fact, which is a block from a lake with tree-canopied streets and gnarly, uprooted sidewalks and, yes, a Starbucks, where I sit right now. Not just any Starbucks either. No. This is *the* Starbucks where I met with Tom Skerritt after I sent him my script, which he actually liked. Well, sort of liked. Okay, he said it had potential. *Fine, he said I totally need to rewrite it, but still!* He likes it enough that he told me to continue working on it and not to pressure myself since it was my first script. I can deal with that. I decided at that moment that maybe, just maybe, I've got some literary talent. Perhaps, if not for that meeting, I wouldn't even be here, in Seattle, trying to make a living of this, or at least pretending to. It must mean something!

But, it has to be a secret for now, because I will not quit my job as Anna J, Realtor. I can't. I'm not ready. Plus, I now really need the dough to pay for my secret life *and* my overpriced, dank, lead-based-paint palace (*read:* closet), especially since I'm sharing all clients with my team. For those of you who know me and my true identity, your job is to keep things between us. So, starting now, the EEK me lives in Seattle and the professional Realty Lady me lives in Canada, as far as anyone knows, *wink wink*. Just to clarify, I am Anna here, and only blogging as Elaine. And yes, I'm aware this book is published under my real name and I'm out of the (Seattle) (and Crazy Lady) closet.

And yes, I did say that I left HBUAB! *Sigh.* Because the break-up recently happened, um, really, yesterday, or today if you count a "one last time for old time's sake" session, it's too personal to talk about quite yet. (But it won't be in one more page!)

*

What have I learned? Just because everyone's doing it doesn't mean I have to *not* do it!

Homework: Stop being so concerned about what everyone else is or isn't doing!

***

PART FOUR: (AND THEN I LOST MY MIND AND FOUND MY SELF IN SEATTLE)

IT'S TIME TO DUMP THE CHUMP WHEN . . .

Their business lunches became more frequent. That is, lunches had by HBUAB and his young, divine, clumsy, smarty-pants assistant. He claimed he was being honest and said they were innocent so what could I say? Okay, there was probably a lot I could have said, but stress and anxiety squashes brain cells.

Flashback to two weeks ago... (Tom says, "Never use flashbacks, they show the screenwriter to be amateur." Good to know.) I'm going to the gym a little later than usual and text HBUAB to tell him. He says, "Wait for me, don't go yet."

I say, "I'm on my way."

"Can you hold on a little longer?"

"I'm here."

Radio silence.

I go in the gym. *She's* here. I get on the step machine beside her and she's awkward and I look at the ring on her slender finger because I don't know what else to focus on and he comes in and his face looks guilty and my blood boils and I get off the machine and I storm out of the gym and he follows me.

"What's going on?" My Viking, chili-pepper temper is barely contained, though I have no direct evidence of his cheating beyond my red-flagged short-fused intuition.

"What do you mean?" He knows what I mean.

I lose it. "Don't give me that fucking shit! Why is she here?" I know she lives elsewhere and "our" gym is out of her way.

He wants to avoid a scene in the parking lot so he spills it before I escalate it any further. "I offered her a gym membership as part of her employment benefits, but if it bothers you, I'll take her off, no big deal."

"You do that. Go in there right now and take her off. Fuck, now you're *working out with her?* It's her or me. I'm done with this crap!"

"Let me talk to her at least, but I'll do it. She'll be off tomorrow."

The next day he tells me it's done. I wait a day, then hack into his computer, which is now password protected: clue #1! So is his phone: clue #2! I manage to get into his gym membership account to find out she's not only still on his account, but she's there as his +1, his girlfriend! I lie to him and tell him I'd asked the gym and they told me. (Oh, the irony!) He wants to know who told me this because he's going to "get her fired for giving out personal info," but I don't let him get off on that technicality.

"She's still on your fucking account!"

The next day, he tells me she's off. I check again and she's still there. Fucketty fuck fuck. I go to the next step, searching his emails, for what I'm not sure, but I do find it: The original email from her, almost innocently enthusiastic, if not laden with subtle sexual innuendo.

"I'm the girl for you! You have to have me—working for you, that is . . . I have fast hands—can type 60 wpm—a wildly creative mind, plus I won't uglify your office. (See photo). You need me!" (Okay, I made that up because in my rage I can't remember exactly, but whatever she wrote, it was something equally suggestive, I totally promise!) Plus, there's a mildly-provocative photo attached and an I'm-so-sure-(not!)-accidental (*yeah, right*) link to a personal site of not-so-fucking-mildly-provocative photos.

Blink blink. FUME!

After this, I stalk his office at lunch time by sneaking in past reception. (It's a multi-office building leased to various unrelated businesses.) I walk confidently past the receptionists like I belong there without an appointment so they won't announce me, and then I tuck, drop, and stealth down the halls, knowing full well I could get busted at any moment without a reasonable excuse. I'm John Cleese and my relationship is a faulty tower about to collapse.

I've got my ear to his closed office door as business men walk by with knowing grins on their faces. I scowl and squint menacingly at them and they take a wide berth around me. I listen more intensely. All I hear is typing, not the soft grunting I was certain I'd find.

HBUAB answers a call. "George. I'm sending you an email on that shipment. No, no, it should be there by Friday, man. Trucking issues..."

What must be *her* typing continues. I think, well, she can't possibly give him a blow job and type at the same time—shit, unless he's got the phone tucked under his shoulder and that's *him* typing! But, no, typing and on the phone, there's no way he'd orgasm given those distractions. *Unless she's that good.* Fuck!

I throw open the door. Damn it, she *is* typing. Damn it, I look like a fool. Damn it, they *knooow*.

His eyebrows are raised as he says, "Uh, listen, George, I've got someone here. Can I call you back?" He hangs up quickly. I figure I'm busted so fuck it, I say the first thing that comes to mind: "She's still on your account."

She is sitting there, stunned.

I'm livid and too far gone now. "You want to call the gym now while I'm standing here watching you or do you want me to go home, pack my shit, and go back to Canada?"

He tells his assistant what's going on. It's obvious she has no idea, but she does have an opinion, "I'm here to work, don't involve me in your drama. Take me off." She turns and goes back to typing. I can't help but notice she's pretty good on the keyboard and I am a little impressed, and then I catch myself and squint at him again, threateningly. He calls the gym.

After this, I'm paranoid and doggedly determined to discover something else amiss. I do not know why I bother to carry on with these shenanigans other than the very simple explanation: *I've now completely lost my mind.* I check his gym account and she's off of it, but I'm certain there's more to be found out.

One morning after he's gone to work, and I've checked the driveway three times to make sure he isn't coming back, I'm sitting at my office work station—dining room bar table in HBUAB's small townhouse—Googling private investigators. I shit you not! I find a PI firm out of Michigan with good reviews. I use my 1-800 untraceable personal phone number to make my inquiry. A pleasant male voice answers with the distinct name of a private investigator company.

"Um, hi. This is a PI firm?" I ask, shaking my head at myself.

"Yes, ma'am. How can we help you?"

"Uh, well, I need someone to follow my boyfriend. Do you guys have a department in Seattle?"

"Yes, but let's slow down a little. Can you tell me about the situation?"

"I want to know if he's boning his assistant." Now, I'm trying not to laugh, and I can tell by his tone, he is, too.

"We can probably find that out for you."

"How much will it cost me?"

"Our services start with a $1,500 retainer and go up from there." He adds, "Not including travel costs, if required."

I'm sure he can hear my sharp intake of breath as I calculate the shoes I could buy with this retainer. "Okay," I say.

He hesitates. "You know, most of the time we do find something."

I take this honesty to mean he's telling me to trust my intuition, as I'm probably right-on.

I swallow hard. "So how do I submit the application?"

He gives me the details, sends me the file, I call back with my credit card number. I sit for an hour, allowing what I've done to marinate, then I call him back.

"Um, did you process my card yet?"

"No, ma'am."

I take a deep breath. "I don't think he's worth it."

"They're usually not."

"Thank you."

I briefly consider chatting with the pleasant and honorable man, wondering what Michigan is like, but then I shake my head and say good-bye. I search the townhouse, compulsively check his computer and phone when he's in the shower, the only time it's accessible, interrogate him daily and finally find a communication between him and Sara—*Sara??*—about their divorce—*divorce?!* I search the townhouse again, this time reading the documents in the filing cabinet. And there it is: a three-week marriage ending *the week before I met him online.* I go straight to Nordstrom and buy a pair of Frye chunky 4"-heeled loafers, complete with *cute-as-everrr* tassels and on sale, no less. I congratulate myself, figuring I just saved a net $1250.

When he comes home, the divorce evidence is casually sitting on the kitchen counter beside an empty, folded, Nordstrom bag. I don't say anything. I sit stoically watching TV. He picks up the document, looks at it, puts it down, and goes upstairs to our bedroom. I don't move from the sofa for several hours. It's quiet upstairs. When I go up to bed, he's acting asleep. I know he's been crying, it's what he would do. I get ready for bed, crawl in, and go straight to sleep, too spent to feel anything.

The next day he goes to work before I'm "officially" awake. While he's at work I pack my things in a numb, if calm, trance and drive back to Canada. Even given my presumptions—the certainty of knowing something big was coming—I'm in shock. I don't call anyone this time. I travel the seven hours home in silence and crawl into bed and sleep for three lifetimes.

We talk on the phone once after this. He cries and whimpers and explains and rationalizes and justifies. But he knows it's useless. I'm a desert stone. No tears escape me. I am finished. This chapter is closed.

*

What have I learned? A very basic fundamental lesson: no relationship has a chance of longevity built on a shoddy foundation of wet wood, and loss of trust is like mating termites. Honesty, which can require courage, trumps financial security, which can be lost.

Homework: Be honest, trust my gut, and re-evaluate my real dealbreakers.

***

THE AFTER-BREAKUP NEED FOR SPEED: RUNNING INTO RICH MEN

Once I'm emotionally past a break up, which after bouts of bawling, for me ends with seemingly surgical precision, I get back on track. I focus on me. It usually takes sixty days, give or take a day, whether I hike to Machu Picchu, visit the Wailing Wall in Jerusalem, or wail on my pillow. It's a peculiar trait be able to do this—shut down and move on with barely a glimpse over my shoulder, and it may simply be a self-serving (-saving?) coping mechanism, but I think it's better than wallowing and wondering and moping forever. And, in HBUAB's case, I'd already cried over him on our previous break-up for at least the allotted time. One roundabout is all one ex gets!

Settled in my new digs, I'm itchy for adventure, or at least a relief of some excess energy. My ditching HBUAB leaves me with need of exercise, as part of that *"holy shit, I'm single again, how far did I let myself go in that relationship"* kind of way. I check out the 24 Hour Fitness in my "new" neighborhood in Seattle, but it's a ten-minute-traffic-congested-no-free-parking-pain-in-the-ass process to get there and I've used up my energy feeling frustrated along the way. Plus, it's icky.

HBUAB can keep the shiny, new facility, with its slimming mirrors (and plenty of them, which I'm sure he loves), and fresh fruit beverages. I'm not complaining, though, honest. Even though sometimes it seems like after every breakup the girl is left cradling her pillow with a box of tissues and the guy keeps on rolling, looking fresh and loving life, in this case, this time, he's got the shiny gym *and* a soggy pillow and I've got my freedom! But I wouldn't go to that gym, anyway. It's out of the city near our old digs. And I'm not ready, or interested, in exploring other gym options. I need the $$ to pay for furniture first.

I decide to take up running! Running is free and it's a frugal time. (But I'm still not cheap!) I head over to Starbucks, my new safe place, down a double espresso to give me the get up and go to kick up my heels, and make my way to the waterfront. At first I walk, totally self-conscious, feeling like I'm back on the 100-yard dash line, my old shyness lingering at the surface: here, everywhere I go solo feels like the first day of kindergarten, in a "please don't recognize the nerd I am and make fun of my green pants" kind of way. I've never really run before (willingly) and am afraid of looking like a fool, if there's any way one can look like a fool while running. I worry that people passing are laughing at me from behind their steering wheels and know that I'm not really a runner. I can only hope God will spill hot coffee on their laps.

This terror of being seen and, worse, being seen for a fool, has kept me from participating in many things. From preschool age, my parents could not get me to go to dance class, or music lessons, or ski lessons. You get the point. Learning something new has too much room for failure! It would have done me good to be forced, but that's not the kind of parents they were. I'm not sure if this fear comes from being under-socialized with other children early on, being picked on in the playground, or doubting myself while hanging out in the closet for all that time. Wherever it comes from, it clamps my chest and shows itself in my hot cheeks, as in blushing, not hot ass, unfortunately since that's the ultimate goal. But, as a runner, I'm *supposed* to have a flushed face, a small concession that gives me the courage to lift up my feet.

After a while, I loosen up. I begin to run along the waterfront, down a rutted street lined with old oak trees. I pass ancient homes full of character, pausing now and then to check the "Take One" bins of those for sale. Here's a cute little one, 750sqft, not waterfront, no view: $899,000. *A bargain at twice the price*, plus I'm enchanted with the area, even though I can't afford it. I think to myself, "I could so live here. What more would I need?" Seriously, though. Seattle is expensive, at home this cottage would be one fifth the price.

Further on, the homes get older, statelier, pricier. Now, we're talking pre- and early 1900s estate homes upward of five million bucks. A few

94

yards later I come upon a parking lot half-filled with Mercedes' and Land Rovers and Lexuses. Maybe Seattle wasn't the best destination for my secret life as an aspiring author—most writers don't bank like many realtors do. I can't tell what's in the adjacent building, but from the looks of things, something luxurious. The only evidence of identification is the emblem *STC* scrolled on matching marble. *Members Only Beyond This Point.* I go in. Two handsome men my age come out: fit, tan, nice calves, eyes twinkling, laughing as though in slow motion...I'm intrigued, and it takes my mind off my red face and *swass* (that's redneck lingo for sweaty ass).

According to its website—yes, I Google it as soon as I get home—the STC is the Seattle Tennis Club, which "sits on eight acres of oceanfront, has over three thousand members, nineteen tennis courts, a fitness center, squash courts, locker rooms, several dining rooms, banquet facilities, pool, beach, boathouse, and a Pro Shop." Not only that, but the STC hosts the Washington State Open (!), only the most prestigious tennis tournament in the entire state. Blink, blink.

I can't help myself. My mind goes haywire with fantasies of one of those gorgeous men as my own: I write in our fancy mansion in a cute negligee, or better yet, comfy flannel and cozy slippers—hey, if I'm going to have an outlandish fantasy, I might as well make it comfortable. My new writing career plan: Find a handsome, rich husband!

I know I won't find one roaming the streets—these are family homes, and any single men my age in this area most certainly don't still live here (or can't be much more than cougar-bait, no thanks), but they may not have relinquished their exclusive club memberships yet. That's why, if you come to Seattle, you can now find me sprinting laps around the STC parking lot, or maybe jogging, or most likely hanging near the entry posing like a dork in my (soon to be purchased) tennis skirt. Apparently, I don't have to be a member to share real estate with their cars. I run back past the 750sqft ramshackle rancher, its beauty dimmed if not diminished and think, "Hmph, how could I ever live in *that?*"

Truthfully wealthy men making big bucks doesn't really bank with me. Though I joke about finding a rich husband, it's just that—*a joke. Sheesh.* First, I'd never be a member of a club that would have me as a member—*I grew up feeling excluded, there's no way I'd be a part of something that might exclude,* including its *Members Only* men.

Second, I dated a rich man before HBUAB, we'll call him Handsome Millionaire, because he was (and still is, damn him). It didn't work out. At the time, I wasn't sure if he really liked me at all, since he wasn't demonstrative either physically or verbally or financially, for that matter, though the latter part could be because I told him, "Never buy me anything!" (I didn't want him thinking I was with him for his loot.) But after we "broke up"—I wasn't even sure if we were officially dating—he told me he loved me. Uh, too late, lover.

Anyway, since you might be curious, Handsome Millionaire and I met through a real estate investment event. (Lest you forget, I had no other life.) He'd come over from the big city of Vancouver, B.C., for it. I admit that I'd heard he was going to be there and I went to check *him* out, not the project, and see if I might want to, er, *invest in* a new "hot property"— him. Someone introduced us and we chatted casually and professionally, discreetly giving one another the once-over. I gave him my business card and he emailed me the next day: "What's a shining star doing in a little valley?"

We "dated" (*read:* had sex) when he was in town for business, the key being *when he was in town*. I teased him with quips like: "A girl in every port, I bet!" and he'd reply with: "Bite me!"

I was attracted to his sense of humor and intellectual, busy mind, plus, yeah, he was handsome and I am shallow—hey, no judgments, at least I'm honest (with you). We talked about his business ventures, which I found fascinating. On another shallow note: he smelled really good. Again, damn him. On an ironically non-shallow note (on my part): he was as vain as I and used hair product, which I tolerated (barely) and shaved his beautiful, perfectly fluffy man chest (dealbreaker!).

He was (is) a sensitive, kind, and trustworthy man, but ultimately, we had different values about relationships. Respect for privacy on this one, please, for his sake not mine. I could have had the big house and the Maserati and the city lifestyle, but when it comes down to the crunch, money is not that important. Refer to HBUAB, *who I loved despite his six-figure debts.*

Nonetheless, tennis skirts *are* cute. *Blink blink.*

*

What have I learned? If better is possible, is "good" good enough? Sometimes, yes, yes it is. Mo' money doesn't mean mo' better.

Homework: Decide what's good enough and what could be—nay, *will be*— better. Bullet-point a list, graph it, put it on a spreadsheet, color-code it, copy it, laminate it, post-it.

***

ESTATE HOMES AND GARAGE SALES:
SOFALESS IN SEATTLE

After I recover from my run-through of the rich and shameless streets of Madison Park, I realize that it might be time to get some furniture. How else will I invite all my future new friends and rich suitors in? To be sure, I do have a bed, if a blow-up air mattress counts, though that may be a little awkward for whomever might crash on it. In fact, as a side note, I'm kind of getting used to it and am even considering putting up a makeshift curtain to hide it from the rest of the living area. Don't want to offend the guests, assuming I'll have some. Oh, right, I need to find something for them to sit on, as I have no seating save for the charming oak floors.

So, furniture shopping it is! I decide that I'll stay in character with the 1920s building I'm in and furnish the studio with accents of the past, also because I don't want to spend a fortune on my Seattle escapades, plus it fits in with my emerging eco-social attitude, or at least makes me feel less guilty about shoe purchases. So, off California and I go to estate sales.

And who's California? A single, cute-as-a-very-cute button, thirty-something, perky, petite, blonde chick from SoCal. She's next-door adorable. Long blond hair, big sparkling eyes, a contagious smile, and just so happens to be a "good" person—she sidelines as a fitness trainer for the elderly. *I know, right?* All I can hope for is that she'll inspire me to be a better person rather than unintentionally make me feel shitty for being shallow!

I meet up with her by the mailboxes one morning. She looks frazzled and in a rush, which I've learned is her standard morning MO. I'm reserved and a little guarded even though she's been genuine and angelically friendly, and something pushes me to step outside my comfort zone and strike up a conversation.

"Starbucks?" I ask.

She holds up her to-go cup of medium roast coffee and says, "Can't live without it." She laughs. "Got to keep up with the residents!"

I've never heard her call them seniors or oldies or prunes or blue-haireds or anything disrespectful. Mostly she refers to them by name, despite the fact that over a hundred are in her care. "You like what you do, don't you?" I ask. It's more of a rhetorical question, as her love of her job is pretty obvious.

"I love it! And them! They're such special gifts from God. I'm so blessed." Her eyes get misty and her smile widens and my eyes get teary and my heart constricts—her warm spirit *is* contagious. Hey, she's rubbing off already! I'm already less shallow! God be with me! (Is sarcasm blasphemous?)

"Well, you'd better get at it before we both have a cry."

We laugh and though I've only known her a few days and we haven't even hung out officially yet, she grabs me in a quick hug before running off to kick it with those who'll be kicking off soon enough. If I didn't like her, I'd probably have to feed her to rabid dogs. She's one of those women you can't help but like and the bonus is that there's no feeling of competition, only a pleasant pureness that does inspire goodness, if not godliness.

California likes old *things*—seniors, antiques, square dance music, the Bible—but not old men, at least not as potential mates. I tell her I can set her up with a guy back in my hometown (comparatively old at 42), but she informs me she wants "someone my own age."

At the first mention that I need furniture she lights up like she's had three espressos and squeals, "Estate sales! Saturday?"

Apparently, even though she's got enough furniture and enough throw pillows to furnish my entire studio apartment, she's attached to her collection of treasures, many carefully pulled from other people's disposables.

Estate Sale Saturday arrives. I drive, she navigates. Now, even though I've gotten lost every time I've gone anywhere in Seattle—my no-sense-of-Seattle direction is now pre-programmed in my brain—I figure if I'm driving and she's using the "iPhone Google Maps, the no-way-in-hell-you'll-get-lost-plus-God-is-guiding-us" tool, we should be okay.

Not so much.

We are on Mercer Island which is sort of an island but accessible by interstate. In other words, there are only so many places to go here, which I think will work in our favor, but alas, we still get lost. As it turns out, she's been following the wrong dot on the Google Map—namely, us: the start dot and not the destination dot. *We have been driving around randomly trying to catch up to the satellite system.* My directionally-disinclined soul mate! Thank God we know how to ask for directions.

When we find the "estate," we discover a regular, run-of-the-mill, government-job-at-best, family home. (No disrespect to government employees, but I doubt they call their homes "estates," or have things changed?) Anyway, this isn't what I was expecting. I had imagined affordable antiques in expensive stone mansions. Really, an estate when it comes to an "estate sale" is basically a home with an open invite to the public, because someone who lived there has died and left the leftover residents, or loved ones, a houseful of stuff to purge. This is all new to me. Back in Comox, we have the typical garage sales, where people open their garage door and put everything on display—usually on plywood laid across wooden sawhorses or makeshift tables spilling out onto the driveway—but no "estate" sales.

Here's how they work in Seattle. First of all, you go into the house, which is a creepy thing to do considering the fact that someone was using what now sits price-tagged only a few breaths ago. Every knickknack, utensil, appliance, couch, bed pan, beer can, toiletry, pair of dentures, musty t-shirt, broken doll, doily, fifties-sixties-seventies memorabilia, old stuff, and new stuff that looks old is for sale. *Everything.* I'm unnerved by the whole "I see dead people" thing and can't bring myself to touch anything, let alone take anything home with me.

Then we get to the house, err *estate*, which still has the old man in it. He's got to be about a hundred and fifty and has raised age spots and wispy bits of hair clinging to their last days.

Even though what look to be "estate sale administrators" stand by, I speak to the old man directly, feeling the need to somehow comfort him. "Do you have a can opener?" I ask, wondering if he's on his way to his grave or a facility. It makes me sad to think of the latter. My intuition tells me his wife must have died and he can't manage without her. And here is his life on display in disarray atop worn, melamine counters, and everything's for sale: ancient mismatched utensils, tarnished silverware that's been worn prong-thin, a cooking pot set with copper bottoms, incomplete Corelle dish set with red flowers around the edges, half-used tubes of

Bengay and Preparation H and Fixodent, a denture tray, strong prescription eyeglasses, a Royal Dalton porcelain lady figurine with a broken hand, three wooden canes with handles worn smooth (he leans on the metal one), a dainty ladies gold watch with pearlescent, oval face.

I look at his face, etched with time but eyes devoid of solid memories.

His shaky hand pulls open an empty drawer. Confused he says, "No, I guess someone must have..."

I want to give him a hug, but I'm afraid he'll pee on me or I'll scare him or I'll break down and cry. I buy a vegetable peeler. One dollar. I don't negotiate.

I say, "Thank you," and touch his frail arm, lingering a little before my lip starts to quiver and California pulls me away, my now forever sentimental vegetable peeler clutched to my heart. I've not only overpaid, I already have one. Estate sales yield no furniture for me, but I do acquire a greater appreciation for what California gifts her residents with: connection and love.

We drive home in reverent silence, and I'm thankful for the traffic and the gospel playing on the radio, afraid if I speak my voice will crack. Who *is* this chick? Have I (re-)discovered a long lost side to myself? This compassionate vulnerability feels familiar. Shh. Don't. Tell. *Anyone.* It would so ruin my ball-busting rep.

When I get home, I call MLM. She's surprised to hear my voice, since I usually communicate via email to save money.

"Hello my darling!" she says cheerfully, lively—*alive.*

"Hi, Mom. How are you?" My shoulders relax at the sound of her familiar accent.

"It's so nice to hear your voice! I was thinking about you. Did you get my email?" She's still surprised I've called. "Are you all right, Dolly?"

All I can muster is: "Yes, Mom, I just really miss you and wanted to tell you how much I love you. And I think I made a new friend today." My eyes fill and drop tears but I try to hold myself together so she won't worry.

"Oh, my baby girl, I love you, too." And then she goes on a little ramble, updating me on what's happening with my family: my brother is working pretty steadily and my sister is worried about something new—she's always worried about something, "you know how she is," MLM says—and MLM is making cabbage rolls for the church pot luck tomorrow, and life is normal and she feels pretty good, and "You're healthy?" I ask and "Little aches but God takes care of me," she assures me, and asks me if I'm reading the Bible and I tell her, "No, but I'm going to Church with [California]," as a concession and she's pleased, and I'm relieved and sigh deeply and we say our "love you, 'bye's," and I wipe my cheeks and take a nap. I love my little mom.

The next day, I shop Craig's List and find a free table: 1930s maple dual drop leaf with two inserts, again for all those guests I imagine will show up on my doorstep any minute now. The young couple selling it to me are engaged and moving in together. When I arrive at the condominium, I see the male counterpart of the duo on the sidewalk. I know it's him because he's looking at me like, "are you the redhead coming to see the table," but I'm only half-looking at him like, "are you the dude with the table," because I'm also thinking, "damn, this table-selling dude is hot."

Finally, he cocks his head and asks, "Anna?"

I smile in a friendly but not flirty way and remind myself that he's freshly engaged and "off the table."

He goes on to tell me about how he and his fiancé met at a triathlon in Canada, and she hasn't been in Seattle long, and I should meet her, and we'd probably get along great, and I'm wondering why people think that simply because two people are from the same country we all must get along great, but I don't say that because I'm thrilled at the possibility of another new girlfriend in Seattle, because even though I'm all easy-going smiles with the boy dragons, I still feel six-years-old-intimidated by the ladies, and maybe us both being Canadian *will* give us that instant connection, and I *breathe* and *nod,* yes, yes, I can do that!

He concludes with: "I'll give her your number and when she gets back she'll give you a call."

I nod and mentally chastise myself for thinking him physically appealing, now that I'm already forming a loyalty to a female friend I haven't even met.

The table fits in my car and I get it into my studio by myself.

I put my veggie peeler on it as decoration, thinking about friendship and an odd offer from another new girl friend, Little Editor, whom I met in a Seattle writing class—tell you *that* it in T-minus one page.

*

What have I learned? I'm really not a catty bitch and I do have a heart. Hmph, who knew? "God doesn't make junk," as MLM likes to say.

Homework: Hug old people. Their appreciation of the affection is worth a wash cycle.

***

FLIRTING WITH GIRLS: THE TAP-DANCING DRUMMER

Last night I went to the famous Can Can by the famous Pike Place Market with the boyfriend of Little Editor, my petite, Zen Buddhist, self-secure, sort of also shy, Seattle gal pal, whom I met in the screenwriting writing class. This fact alone—going to the Can Can with another woman's *man man*—may have set up the evening's atmosphere. It ends up being a night of strangers and sensuality.

But even before that, the idea of a non-date date challenges my notion about heterosexual male-female friendships. I've always been of the mindset that such a concept is absurd—*they're always sexual tension on one side and/or the other*. Isn't there? Of course, I base my theory on my own experiences. Other than the extenuating circumstances of CWAD, I've never had *just* a male friend. Every time I've been friends with a man in any capacity it has turned into romance (*read:* immediate sex) or the "friendships" dissolved rather quickly. I didn't have the college experience or the "hospitality" type work experience where male-female friendships *seem* prevalent. I've only had the "I like you, I like you, too, let's have sex" experiences, so you can imagine my initial hesitation.

Before you jump to any conclusions, here's how it went down (so to speak): Little Editor ended up unable to attend at the last minute and asked if I was interested in going in her stead. Being rather traditional—old-fashioned even—this swaparoo was a stretch for me as I've said: my mindset flags such circumstances as *inappropriate* emphatically. But today I'm a Yes! Girl and since Little Editor is okay with it, then I can be okay with it, too. This decision comes after impulsively saying *yes!* then *well...* a few gazillion times.

I email her: "I'm not sure about this. It feels awkward. Are you totally sure about this? I mean, not that you can't trust me, it just feels weird for me. Never done this before—gone "out" with someone else's guy. Small town girl, remember? Not that big city girls are—*shit, this is all coming out wrong*—anyway, let me know if you're sure sure sure. Okay, lol. Ttys." And so the email back-and-forth begins.

"I completely understand, but I'm *really* okay with it. I can't go and he really wants to go. It'd be better if he went with someone than alone, though I don't want you to think that's the reason I asked you! Ugh, I'm bad at this, too! Please go."

"Okay. Yes! I'll go, of course. Get out of my comfort zone. Yes! Girl, right? Sorry, about the flakiness!"

"Great! I'll give [Can Can Man] your number! Have fun, tell me all about it."

I reply, a couple hours later, "Aaaagh! Having second (third?) thoughts again. Are you totally, completely, 100%, swear to Buddha, okay with this???"

"Yes! Yes, yes, yes. But if you're not comfortable you don't have to. I think you'd enjoy it, [Can Can Man's] a good guy, he won't hit on you. (Though you are pretty, I'm not saying that. Lol.)"

"This is crazy. Okay, I'll go. All is well. Let's get together and do some writing next week, yes yes?"

"Yes! Or shopping. Or dinner. Or both!"

That settled, I meet Can Can Man at the Can Can venue.

I arrive wearing jeans and heels and a flowing, semi-sheer top over a tank, chic but not too sexy. He's wearing jeans and a casual-collared, long-sleeve checkered shirt, leather jacket, and no discernible cologne, which I appreciate. He's standing outside, and takes a chance that I'm his redheaded non-date for the evening.

"Anna?"

"Hi!" I say, more relaxed and cheery than I feel.

He shakes my hand and I immediately feel better. I don't know what I was expecting, but so far this feels rather normal and non-threatening. After having recently had the other encounter with the table-selling hottie, I'm starting to question my theory on the impossibility of male-female friendships. Maybe there is such a thing. I'll mull it over later.

Right now, I'm at The Can Can. It's dark, dingy, and too warm. It sits underground. When I walk in, my eyes squint to adjust to the low lighting. It's a relatively compact space, maybe six hundred square feet with a 7'x9' stage. We sit three rows back on a hard wooden pew bench. I instinctively grab the round, two-person table with single cross base, subconsciously expecting to find what turns out to be accurate: a wobbly table. Can Can Man takes off his jacket and places it between us.

He asks, "Do you want a drink?"

Now feeling chill, I decide to enjoy the evening. "Sure. Um, I'll have a vodka with water and a slice of lemon, or lime, whatever they have. Please. And thanks."

He nods and goes to the bar. I look around.

The ceiling is low, and it's a cozy setting—from the tables being squished together for lack of space—an even cozier stage, and low quality air. Wafts of Juicy Fruit gum and floral perfume float through the room. The patrons are look-alikes of Frank Zappa, Willy Nelson, Betty Page, an anorexic Jesus (of Narcissist), hippies, groupies, and wannabes. I like it.

I learn that the twenty-eight-year-old (I ask) hippy seated next to me is a violinist. Maybe she lives in a van, though then again, maybe not (she seems to be the source of the Juicy Fruit and floral scent).

She leans in close to whisper over the piped music, "I'm a groupie for the band, Snake Suspenderz."

I'm not sure if the twinkle in her eye means to add humor to her introduction or if she's winking at me, but I tell myself I must be a little paranoid from being here with my friend's man, who has returned with my beverage.

"Thank you, I'll buy next," I say.

He gives me a grin and raises his eyebrow toward my new friend. I laugh, guessing what he's thinking.

Since any leftover ice has been broken by his expression, I lean over to him close enough so she won't hear and whisper, "She's bubbly and friendly."

"She's interested," he says matter-of-factly.

"No way, I'm old."

He repeats himself.

I assume he's being a typical man, longing for typical male fantasies, but then I start to notice the subtle signs: she touches my arm, her hand lingers. I glance at Can Can Man, who's no longer looking at me, but he is smirking.

I tell him, "Maybe she's a touchy-feely gal."

The next time she speaks to me, she leans in close, her hand on my thigh, her breath on my ear. Well, it *is* kind of loud now. *Blink blink.*

She says, "Hey, there's this fair coming up in Oregon County, you should come. It's totally fun. I'm camping alone."

She goes on to tell me what a freeing kind of affair it is to not worry about the confinements of clothing: "Going natural isn't mandatory." She must see my rapid, nervous fluttering.

I stutter, "Um..."

She's now giving me unmistakably sexual eye contact. "Can I get your number?"

I tell her my age.

She doesn't skip a beat. "You're beautiful."

More blinking.

Three shows commence. The first band is my groupie friend's Snake Suspenderz, and consists of middle to senior-aged men, the most notable the lead singer: a 4'x 2'-sized bass-voiced concerto (lead singer), complete with skull-adorned fez, false teeth, and ukulele. The others also look to be veritable members of a circus, playing circa 1930s jazz with a twist. After they finish their set, while I'm in the bathroom, my flirty companion takes her leave. I arrive back to my seat, relieved in two ways.

The next musician, whose name I don't catch, looks like an ancient wizard, his hollowed eyes shadowed by a felt fedora. His long gray beard tickles his acoustic guitar, which he plucks with pointed fingernails as he foot-stomps out folk tunes. The final band is my favorite, He's My Brother, She's My Sister, from L.A., eclectic in its own right, and talented beyond its tap dancing drummer.

Ah, but the drummer...

She stands on a wooden box, which I later find out is her instrument, wearing tap shoes, a short dress—so short it might be a shirt—and short shorts underneath. The lady is a pretty, twenty-something nymphet with amazing legs. Her drums are set up on both sides of her, and she dances as she stomps, her face distorting into what one can only describe as an ecstatic, nay *orgasmic*, expression, her tongue licking her parted lips in an obscene signal of pleasure. No exaggeration. The solo military man sitting off to my right is rapid-fire gum-chewing and I'm afraid he's going to blow. The tactile tension in the room confirms he's not the only fan.

She sways with sensual agility and feathers the symbols, her modest chest heaving with the soft tones of the music, then begins to move faster as the beat builds. At the crescendo, her eyelids become slits and her head tilts back ever so slightly, while her hands thrash the symbols and her feet stomp the box. My face feels flushed from embarrassment and *oh my god am I a dyke?*

I'm suddenly glad it's warm and dark enough to hide my sinful thought. I avoid looking at Can Can Man, though I suspect he's mesmerized along with the rest of us. I wonder for a moment if I should at least become a lipstick lesbian. Yes, she is that alluring. If not for the atmosphere, I'd have felt like an intruder in a private affair.

By the way. . . *dyke*: full on carpet muncher, no dicks need apply, masculine undertones; *lipstick lesbian*: could be bi-sexual, fem-girly slant. *It's only offensive if you consider either term an insult, people!*

When the band ends its performance, the drummer steps off her instrument as though stepping out of a cold shower—what the rest of us now need—and strolls to the back of the room to get a drink of water. We all collectively wipe our brows and relax our stiffened spines—and perhaps *other* parts for the men. I feel lucky to be a woman for once.

Can Can Man turns to me and says, "Well, that was something."

The guy nearest him and I reply at the same time, "Yeah."

We all know what he means. Everyone in the room does.

Can Can Man and I sit for a minute, recovering.

Finally, I say, "Well, [Can Can Man], I can honestly say this was a most *stimulating* experience."

"Agreed."

"Nice to meet you."

We laugh.

"Tell [Little Editor] I had a good time."

He says he will. When we exit, we give each other a wave as we go our separate ways. Strangely enough, I experience no awkwardness with my non-date for the evening, I quite enjoyed his company, and I quite enjoyed the evening. It makes me wonder if, perhaps, men and women *can* be friends.

My assumption that men and women can't be friends without sexual tension is now in question. Or, maybe friendship *is* possible even with underlying tension. And maybe there isn't always that base innateness. Nah, I still think it's there. I've seen *When Harry Met Sally,* and according to Harry, the guy is *always* interested. But maybe friendship is possible, too?

I wake up the next morning on my cool air mattress with a bar stamp on one wrist and ink scribblings of a County Fair on the other. It makes me smile and shake my head.

I'm not going to become a lesbian or a nudist, but I am going to get some furniture and soon, damn it.

As lovely as she was, I hope the violinist doesn't call me.

What have I learned? There's a fine line between being bubbly and flat-out flirting, even when my flirting is with the fairer gender. The right dose will make someone feel good without unfortunate side effects, therefore...Bubbly/friendly: good vibrations. Flirting/teasing without intent: bad dog.

Homework: Know my *flirtentions.*[1] Be a good dog, aka not a bitch.

✳✳✳

[1] My editor says I can't copyright a word. I call bullshit. But because I'm a generous person, please feel free to use any of the words I made up in this book. You're welcome.

THE CASE OF THE SOFA: BRING IN THE
SOPHOMORE

In my ongoing quest to find furniture, I stumble upon a sofa at a
secondhand store that is ideal for a single gal sans kids and pets. It's
whisper white! It has fluffy pillows, it's comfy—maybe I'll sleep on it—and
only three hundred dollars! I fall in love with it. I must have it. It's a
bigg'un, though, and I'm not sure it'll fit through the door of my apartment.
To be safe, I measure it. I go back home and measure the door. It's a one-
inch risk. Men will tell you an inch is no biggy. *Raised eyebrow*. Men lie. I
text my friend and ex-BF, Handsome Millionaire (HM), who is, as
mentioned, tall, dark, handsome, half-Italian, and wholly good with
numbers.

He texts back, "Remove the door and it will fit."

"Oh, for crying out loud. The door is heavy and I'm a girl, after all! Plus,
it's a tight fit."

"I always knew that about you!"

"Inappropriate!"

He's no help after all, but even if I took off the door, it's a close call, and
since the dealer will not take it back—stereotypical "I don't need the-
hassle" gay-guy attitude (hey, don't pretend you don't know what I'm
talking about, girlfriend!)—I have to be able to get it into my apartment,

lest I supply the first floor residents with a permanent hallway lounger. I decide it's not worth the risk.

But that was last week.

After numerous Estate Sales, Garage and Yard Sales, Antique Malls, Furniture Shops, and Craig's List Responses, I reconsider. Everything I've seen is either uber-ugly or ultra-expensive. I tell myself this lovely piece of furniture is now worth the risk and I'm convinced, if properly angled, the sofa might fit without having to remove the door. I have it delivered. The two-man delivery crew manages to angle it in through the building's front door and down the hall. They try to nudge it through my door one way and it doesn't fit. They haul it the hundred feet back to the lobby to turn it around. I smile encouragingly and try a giggle, but it's the end of the day and these guys are tired and I'm sure underpaid. They don't even attempt to return the congeniality when they come back with it turned around. They angle it sideways and on end and, in the end, it doesn't fit. I can tell this is all I'm getting out of them so I say, "Just leave it here..." They're already shuffling back to the van as I mumble, "...in the hall."

It rests there for a day. I decide to use my persuasive powers at the mini-hardware store around the corner. I love this neighborhood. They give me the number of a local handyman. I call and he comes right over within a couple hours. Yay!

He is Paul-Bunyanly-bearded, 6'4", with marine glass eyes, about 230 pounds, and in a Washington Huskies ball cap. The overgrown beard makes him appear older than his twenty-nine years—I ask—and suits him. He is not my type, though, too young by far. (Been there dumb that. No offense, Junior.) Yes, I am age-prejudiced when it comes to romance.

In mere seconds, Bunyan unhinges the door and sets it aside as though it is made of Styrofoam. The sofa still doesn't fit. *Blank, confused expression.* He seems unconcerned.

"The legs have to come off," he declares.

"We couldn't get them off in the store." I twitch, already making mental plans to resell the sofa, I might even make a profit. For mere dollars, I'm willing to engage in such endeavors here in my new identity, whereas back home I pay my assistants to deposit my paychecks. I know that sounds a *snitch* arrogant, but truly my priority in real estate is doing the things I do best and that an assistant *can't* do: dealing with clients, establishing pricing and property-specific marketing plans, strategizing negotiations and drafting legally binding contracts *in my client's favor, people.* If I could hire someone else to adequately input, administrate, and organize the plans I put out for them, then I am using the *time my clients are paying me for* more efficiently. (*Yeah, now who's sorry?* I forgive you.)

But here in Seattle, it's somehow freeing to do the mundane myself. It almost gives the illusion of having more time, not feeling so rushed to get to the next important task only *I* can do. I feel unimportant in a good way. I don't know if it's the normalness I appreciate or my getting to don a new hat, so to speak.

Anyway, two hours later, after a run for more tools, Bunyan has the legs off and the couch in. After all that scuffing, it needs to be cleaned. I guess this is why people buy black leather sofas? I'm wondering how much this couch is going to end up costing me. All this time, I've been hovering near Bunyan, watching him work and blubbering about how I got to Seattle and am going to be a writer maybe a screenwriter even though I don't watch TV or movies so maybe I won't be a screenwriter and isn't it so exciting that I have my own place? and I'm not a big fan of estate sales but Craig's List is pretty good and look at my table! and oh my god the old man! and I show him the vegetable peeler and pause for a moment and start feeling sentimental and then I ask him about his history and he tells me he's lived in the neighborhood all his life and that his family knows Tom Skerritt and I tell him more about my screenplay and how it seems like the never-never writing plan because it's taking so long and Bunyan grunts acknowledgements, or maybe that's the sound of his exertion, and finally four hours later, he's done and stands and wipes his brow.

I ask, "So, what do I owe you?"

His brow furrows with thought as he says, "Fifty bucks."

"That's it?"

"Not your fault I didn't have the right tools."

"Really? Still, no way that's fair."

"How about fifty bucks and you come with me to a Sounders game?" What a gentle(man) giant.

"Deal!"

Now I have a sofa and dining table—no chairs—and a date. I'll spare you the details . . . but I will add my latest enlightenment.

⁎

What have I learned? Maybe all those remove-three-layers-of-my-face remedies really did reverse the aging process a little. Woohoo, a wise investment! It's probably better to lay down the cards right away and risk feeling awkward than slap down my DL in a restaurant and have to learn about how many field goals so-and-so kicked or how many home runs so-and-so ran on a discomfited drive home—*uh, not that that happened, y'all.* Tuck, drop, and roll, baby!

Homework: Don't show my I.D. until after the dinner is paid! JK! Rather, show I.D. at the soonest opportunity. I'm not desperately single, after all. *sideways glance*

***

PUMPED UP OR DUMPED: DAMES OF DESPERATION

Why are we, single heterosexual women, so silly when it comes to men? To be fair, men haven't got a clue about us ladies either, *but—hello!—this is about us ladies*. Even though I'm constantly on the look-out, at the moment I'm not feeling desperate (fib), but I've had several girl friends ask me for advice because they're feeling a little needy. The truth is, I do want a man in my life, too, but I want a good one. Not that they don't. Whatev. You know what I mean.

In the meantime, my new friend, California, is pretend church shopping—actually she's Mr. Right(eous) shopping. She wants a Christian. In my two weeks here, I've been with her to three different churches in the Seattle area. Though I'm high on Jesus points, I do feel a bit Helena Bonham Carter à la *Fight Club*. To be sure, I'm *not* church hopping hoping to find a man. I'm there to find God. (Not a fib.) I don't even want a church-going man—most churchgoing men are far too *religious* for me. I'd rather have a kind man who doesn't recoil when I say, "Fuck" and feels *spiritually* inclined, which is so not the same as religious, but now I'm getting off track...

Anyway, we're about to go to church one Sunday morning when I ask her, "Don't you wonder if Mr. Right is doing the same thing? Don't you think one of you should stay put and let God figure it out?"

California pauses then carries on tossing items from the passenger seat and floor into the back seat, and we get in. She pulls down the visor to put lip gloss on. "I know. I thought of that. But then what if God wants me to go somewhere else?" She tucks up the visor and looks around the car. "Can you see my scarf?"

I lean over and rummage through a pile of bags, cardigans, books, vitamin and water bottles, and a yoga mat to find two scarves. I hold them up, she grabs one and puts it on. "Ah! Thank you!" Then she sighs and says, "Sorry, I need to clean this thing."

She finds a brush and puts her hair in a ponytail with one of the multiple elastics she's got wrapped around the center gear shift. I continue, "Or you could trust. Pray and trust."

She says, "Also, I want to find the right church, the right fit."

I say, "Okay, well, that I can understand."

And off we go with our two missions in mind that may happen to coincide: Find right church and then let the Big Guy find the right man, "God willing," as My Little Mom would say.

Little Editor continues to date Can Can Man, who is not so far a one-woman man. She isn't a one-man woman either. Sort of. But, she *is* getting attached to him.

Maybe because she's an editor or maybe for some other reason, she often shares her feelings via email, but perhaps because of the wine or because it's dark or because of the cornbread—we're at Kingfish Café, a Down Home South kind of restaurant in Seattle—she takes a deep breath and allows herself to be vulnerable face-to-face. (Though she does avoid eye contact.)

"I guess I don't want to share him, really," she says timidly and looks away.

I wipe the crumbs from my lips and reply, "But didn't you go on a date the other day? Like, with another guy."

She makes eye contact briefly then glances away again. "Yes. I know."

"So you want your cornbread and you want to eat it, too?"

She allows herself a chuckle. "It's hypocritical, isn't it? I guess I'm not sure. Maybe if he was sure about me I wouldn't want to date other men."

I wave my greasy rib bone in the air, "This is what happens, in my opinion: if a man, or a woman, you are dating wants to date other people, *you're* not 'the one.'" I wait to be sure I'm not too brutally honest.

She confirms, "See, this is why I respect you, you're so honest."

I continue, "Sometimes too honest, I know. No filter. I can only base it on my own experience, though, really, I've never dated in the traditional sense so what the hell do I know? Honesty doesn't mean I'm right, either. But anyway, keep in mind if you're doing the same—dating other people, or even looking for someone to date—then you're feeling the same, too, in a way. It's kind of like, 'Hey, let's hang out and have sex until we meet the real person we're supposed to be with, but on the off-hand chance you turn out to be that person, let's continue having sex and hope for more.'" I gnaw on my next rib.

She pushes the okra around her plate. "Yes, that's exactly what I'm doing. Playing it safe, I guess. But maybe it's also an emotional safety guard."

"Hmm, yeah, I'll buy that. And that's okay, until someone gets hurt. Personally, I'm not emotionally equipped to date more than one at a time. I don't think I could divide myself like that. I'd feel like I was cheating, which as you know I've 'been there dumb that,'" I say as I take a sip of wine and she nods sympathetically. I continue, "I find a guy I'm attracted to and get attached right away and don't *want* to date anyone else, hmm..." I frown wondering, then continue, "Anyway, that's my issue. You were married for forever, so you need to play the field, plus you've got an agreement."

She's thoughtful. "I definitely don't want to jump right into another relationship, but at the same time, I prefer spending time with him."

I reply, "For sure! I guess I 'dated' '*The Guy Who Tried to Kiss Me in the Parking Garage turned Houdini*,' so I can only imagine. And even then, was it *really* a date? Anyway, I'd be worried about hurting the guy—if there's more than one, someone's going to get hurt." I wipe BBQ sauce off my face. "If they're serious, that is. Don't listen to me, I've never been able to even try it."

"Yes, I feel bad about that."

"God, don't! Apparently, that's the etiquette of dating. I usually just jump in the sack and then straight into a relationship. Though, I think nowadays fornicating while multiple dating is proper etiquette, too. Is it?"

She matter-of-fact agrees, "Yes, that's often how it works."

I shrug and continue, "You've both been honest with each other. You need to do what you need to do, for you. But yeah, if you're playing the field, then fair is fair. Have you talked to him about it? Maybe test the waters. He might be feeling the same as you. If he is, then you could try exclusive and see how it feels. You can always change your mind."

"Thank you, you're always so good with advice."

"Then why am I so messed up?" I laugh.

"I'm going to talk to him, even if I am afraid of what he'll say."

"You'll feel better. Oh my god, I'm stuffed! Another hog bites the dust."

But, hey, I get it. I recently met a guy at a writing workshop, the aforementioned Houdini—a fellow writer, a director even, who's tall, dark, and yes . . . *I should know better by now.* (Here's where I like to preach [teach?]: Never "should" on yourself or others, it's a shitty thing to do.)

Flashback to meeting The Guy Who Tried to Kiss Me in the Parking Garage, aka Houdini: The first meeting is brief. The writing group meet-up takes place at a small local pub in Seattle, somewhere near Pike Place. The place is dark and musty and feels underground even though it isn't. The workshop coordinator asks everyone to introduce themselves, but it's an informal setting and we're all spread around. I spot a fellow at the bar ordering a drink who skips his turn, half listening to the lesson and chatting it up with the male bartender. Either by design or coincidence, it isn't a busy night for business. Naturally, I'm taken with his cocky aloofness.

My turn comes and I feel instantly bashful. "Um, Anna Jorgensen, from Canada." My cheeks turn crimson from the unwanted attention. Nothing exciting happens during the class, other than my stealing glances at the tall, mysterious stranger at the bar. He leaves early without us having shared any words and I don't think he even noticed me. A few days later, the dozen or so participants are emailed a list of each other's' email addresses should we wish to stay in touch or set up writing groups.

Even though I'm terribly inhibited in group settings, I've never been shy about going after a guy I'm interested in. *Head cocked:* Why *is* that? Maybe because I've developed a highly intuitive screening process for only going after the ones who won't reject me, sexually at least. And though, in the past, if I liked a guy enough to fornicate with him (minus a *seriously-this-is-so-Vegas-nightclub-mega-mid-life-crisis* discrepancy) I always ended up in relationships with them, *or could have.* I may need to ponder this more—I may need to become a dating coach!—please stay tuned.

Anyway, I email him: "I'm working on a script and wondered if you might be interested in reading it, or part of it?"

His reply, "I might be interested ;)"

We set up the date and time. I'll meet him at the venue, a chic restaurant/bar near the Seattle Art Museum. I can't be sure if this is a date or isn't a date since the invite was sent via email and all "Let's discuss your project at [his favorite restaurant/bar], I might be interested." Um, interested in what? My script or me? I figure either way it doesn't matter—he *is* tall, dark, and yummy!

In all fairness to him and what I'm about to tell you, I do wear a date outfit—a fabulously stylish number that happy gay hipster at Club Monaco helped me pick out the day before. Yes, I do look good, TYVM, in an "I'm not trying too hard *for a date*" kind of way. My ensemble: a silk baby pink, pleated skirt 3" above the knee, a semi-sheer white silk tank top under a cream cardigan, and white-heeled Prada wedges. Très chic if I do say so myself. (I do.)

When I arrive, he is already seated at the bar and I'm relieved at the added casualness of this space over a table setting, where we might have to make regular eye contact instead of gazing at the sparkling wall of liquor behind the bartender.

"Hi!" I say too perkily.

He stands, kisses me on the cheek, then sits down at the same time as I do. "You look nice."

"Thanks!" I'm still too cheerful.

He's wearing designer jeans, a casual, long-sleeved shirt and his dark overcoat rests on the chair next to him. He hasn't read my script yet, because I haven't sent it to him, but I tell him a little about the premise: "It's about a girl—a woman—looking for authenticity and independence. Sideways glance." He chuckles but barely cracks an uplifted corner of his soft-looking lips.

"So it's about you," he says matter-of-fact.

"Of course!" *Flutter*.

A couple of potent beverages later and I'm rambling about my life in Canada. "...and I have been all buttoned-up and boring and serious and can't say 'shit' if my mouth is full of it—yes, I *know* that's cliché, but it's also *so* true. I drive a beige SUV, *beige*—though I prefer to call it 'champagne'...They'd be shocked—"

"—Who?"

"Who what?"

"Who'd be shocked?"

"Oh! My clients, the public, everyone. Sometimes I want to tell dirty jokes and be goofy and have too many drinks in public and not potentially lose any business or ruin my 'professional reputation' because of it, but that's not how it works—"

"—You have choices."

He's hunched over his amber drink and hasn't eaten, nor will he—it's "not my thing," whatever that means—but I *am* eating, a tuna nicoise salad, which is quite good, in fact, because eating *is* my thing and I'm hungry and this is the strangest date/non-date I've had, but since I've never actually had a date, I guess I really have nothing to compare it to. In the past, as mentioned, I'd meet a guy and, if I found him attractive and he found me attractive, we'd have sex (yes, right away, before any "dating"

117

took place, stop judging, *sheesh*), then I'd swoop into a relationship immediately. (That's not how it's done? *Blink blink head cocked.*) I mean, maybe we dated *after* we were already a "couple" but that's different, no? (Yes, even with Good Man.) Anyway, moving on...

"I don't like my choices." *Pout.* "So here I am in Seattle living a secret life!" *Giggle.* (Note to the ladies: Pouting and giggling do work charmingly but must be sprinkled with intelligent and serious conversation so we don't come across as Twinkies. A *Twinkie* is redneck slang for a bimbo, which is not appealing to a man unless the bimbo quality is only temporary. Which is fine if that's what your goal is. It isn't mine. I really ought to teach this stuff.)

He looks at me sideways and almost smiles, which is as much as I'm going to get out of him, because he's way too mysterious to offer more, which intrigues and frustrates me as I realize I'd prefer a little mutual conversation. Odd but true.

I do flirt and flutter and fawn and giggle at this date/non-date. It's so easy to do. Plus, I'm being authentic: I have had a great time, even if it is martini-induced.

Here's the ending: After two martinis, I'm totally tipsy. Yes, I'm a lightweight—two's my max. He says he'd love to stay and chat longer, and I'm thinking, "Only I've done all the chatting," but he has somewhere to be and he pays for my dinner.

"Okay, but I'll buy next time...if there's a next time," I insist.

"There'll be a next time, but a man pays." He makes no point of eye contact when he says this as he flips bills out of his wallet.

When I get up off the bar stool, I sway a little and put my hand on the back of the chair but it swivels and I stumble and he grabs my arm and I *giggle* and we leave and he walks me to my car in the underground parking garage.

On the way there I say, "No wonder girls don't wear high heels here— all these damn cobblestones."

He offers his arm for me to hang onto. How chivalrous! When we get to the parking garage, we have to hit five different levels since I can't remember where I've parked. (No, I shouldn't be driving home at this point, even though we've been here, what, three, *four* hours? And if that admission makes me liable in any way, I totally made that up.) It's on Level One and when I see it I exclaim, "Yay!" and he walks me over to my champagne-colored VW and suddenly I'm sober and looking for my keys while he stands waiting with his hands casually tucked in the pockets of his long, black overcoat.

Then I find the keys with a, "Ta da!" and he leans in for the kiss, and I shuffle and sidestep and stumble and drop my keys and lean down to pick them up and we bump heads—oh, wait, the dropping the keys bit didn't happen—but I do waver side to side, avoiding his lips and finally giving him a hug—Oh God, awkward moment. *Shit.* And he doesn't know what to make of this, so he gives a stunted laugh and a nod and takes a step back and says, "See yah." *Damn.* I close my eyes for an instant while I catch my breath, and then get in my car without looking back, feeling like a total nerd and say to myself, "Shit fuck damn."

It's not that I *didn't* want to kiss him. I'm nervous, I'm not ready, it's too soon, I don't even know this guy, I'm old-fashioned—minus those few racy years and all those exes, but that's in the past!—I'm old-fashioned *now*, and I'm not even sure we were on a date, and even if we were, am I supposed to liplock on the first go? I'm so bad at this. *Shit. Fuck. Damn.*

Cut to next scene: Radio silence. Did he forget my number? Now that he doesn't want me, I'm certain I want him! *See?!* Where did this crazy desperation originate? I was sort of sane before this date/non-date episode. *Sideways glance.* WTF? And even though I realize I know nothing about this man, except that he's too mystifying for his nicely-pressed, not too fancy suit and overcoat, which means he's too mysterious for me (*read*: ego, *read*: player, *read:* I need an excuse for this rejection), I can't help but feel what my gal pals have felt: *desperation!*

Side note: Every single woman simply must read the book: *The Manual*, by Steve Santagati. *The Manual* explains how bad boys think and teaches how women can win them over, though I'm starting to think they wouldn't be winning at all to get a bad boy. Nonetheless, it gives some good advice on which ones you might want to win over—bad boys with good hearts—and which ones you might want to toss—players with good coats.

So, yesterday, after church and the market, I spend the afternoon and evening alone in my apartment, shopping Craig's List, reading, washing dishes, listening to Hillsong United, making dinner, contemplating my date/non-date and my relationship with HBUAB, and writing. I decide I'm not ready for the dating world. It's only been a few months since HBUAB and I broke up, and although he has many great qualities, we're finished. I deserve better and possess the inner strength to let go rather than hang on like a clingy victim.

I know I'm not ready to replace him. I don't need a player or a bad boy or any man (or County Fair maiden). I can keep myself company. I'm starting to like my own company and space, and even though I have lonely moments, I know I need time on my own. I've gone from one relationship to the next, erroneously relying on initial physical attraction to make everything copasetic. I don't feel the desperate need to dart down to

Starbucks to be amongst people *just in case* a Mr. Perfect Prospect shows up. I may not feel this way every day, but today's a good start. And I'm proud and empowered that I had the self-respect not to give in to a kiss that, in my heart, I knew wasn't from "the one."

That was yesterday, today I'm back at Starbucks! "Single! Single here!" Hey, a girl needs blogging material, right?

*

What have I learned? Some guys are studs and some guys are duds. But we have the power of the pussy and can set our own rules, whether we want to be open, exclusive, or downright prudish. I have the ~~girl~~ *woman* power to decide if, to me, he's a Super Man or a Slimy Dan. I rule!

Homework: What we persist in resists us. Stop trying to push the river. Enjoy my own stream for a while. Make my own rules, ride the wave. And. All. That. Jazz!

***

BOYS, BOTOX, AND BEST FRIENDS

A few weeks later, I walk down to the beach park three blocks from my quaint, old abode, with my "bible" in my bag, which is, at the moment, *The Wizard of Oz and Other Narcissists* by Eleanor D. Payson. Though the park is only a few blocks away and the neighborhood is mostly residential, the oak-lined street at the end of Madison Park Avenue offers more than half a dozen well-reviewed restaurants, a sign of the bustling beachside community it once was that the locals now must feel is their duty to support. I've tried several of them—the restaurants not the locals—my favorite being Thai Ginger, where I now feel comfortable eating alone for lunch *or* dinner (if it's not too busy, that is). There's also a Mexican restaurant, a shop that makes wood-fired pizzas, a couple of pubs, and several delis. I haven't worked up the nerve to dine solo at the liquor-slinging establishments. They're more social oriented and I'd feel all patched-polyester-pants loser in them. But maybe one day. For now, take out only, thanks. I want to know whether or not I need clinical help, which probably wouldn't help anyway if indeed I am a narcissist, because all evidence points to "no cure yet found," and if I'm not, then I need to know how to avoid these non-curable head cases. Oh, how I love human psychology! What makes people tick makes me tick (and twitch).

I plunk down in a warm, shady spot and look around at the groupings of twenty-, thirty-, and forty-somethings sunning themselves and swimming. I'm not a fan of being in the water—too cold, too exposed, plus I almost drowned when I was in Mexico a couple months after I'd met *mi ajualita.* (That's Spanish for "my grandmother," pronounced *mee ahwaleeta.* "Granny" doesn't quite fit. *Holy shit, I just thought of this: I wonder if she was busy saving me. I mean, like, because she died and all and could've been floating around looking for something to do before jaunting off to Heaven!*) Okay, carry on.

It's mid-afternoon and the banter of college youth drifts toward me in spiraling waves and I wonder what it would've been like to attend college. Would I have still felt like a misfit? I conclude, *yeah, probably,* and then decide on the spot that all these college youth splashing around must be exclusionary sorority types with current events knowledge and superior attitudes. I squint at them. Hmph, they're probably all narcissists. I have zero basis for this, save my own insecurity. *Stupid insecurity.* I frown and start reading my narcissist book again. Less than three minutes later:

"So, what are you reading?" a man asks me, his voice breaking slightly with a raised pitch at the end. He sits on the grass nearby.

I smile at him and tell him.

He laughs and I see his small, straight teeth. Maybe late thirties, with short cropped brown hair and thin-rimmed, rectangular-framed eyeglasses. He's slender but not skinny. His ears stick out a little and he has the unmistakable features of Jewish descent.

"Wow, I'm not sure where to go with that. Is it interesting?"

"So far, yes, very. I'm not the narcissist," I add, qualifying.

"Oh, okay, good. I was a little concerned for a moment."

Sense of humor, nice.

"Actually, my last boyfriend fit the criteria to the letter. I'm trying to understand why I'd go for such a guy. That might concern you."

He laughs again, more relaxed this time. "Well, I just met you—actually, we haven't met."

He introduces himself and offers his hand. I shake it and tell him my name.

"This will sound so cliché, but do you live around here?"

"Technically, Canada, but I've got a little place up by Bert's."

And so begins a conversation.

The man is Jewish (by birth, not practice), wears beige khaki pants and a collared, short-sleeved shirt with a white undershirt underneath.

I ask, "You're an accountant?"

He's disappointed. "Photographer. Originally from the East Coast."

I reply, "That's on my list of places to visit." The Italian crosses my mind, who I haven't heard from in a while, then I refocus. "It's brave of you to approach me."

He seems relieved. "You think? I mean, yeah, I saw you here by yourself and I didn't want to bug you but then I thought, maybe you're a nice person and why not take a chance?"

"You don't get anywhere sitting on the sidelines," I say.

We chat for a while, making small talk about our histories, and eventually I get us caught up to the part where I mention Lawyer Man, a guy who just asked me out in Starbucks.

JP perks up. "I photographed the aforementioned lawyer last week. He's married to Charlotte."

"No way?! Naughty Lawyer! I am so blogging this. Hey, I'm hungry, you wanna grab a bite to eat?"

Surprised, he agrees, "Sure. Do you like Thai?"

"Thai Ginger, my favorite! Zagat-rated!" I'm happy to have a dinner companion even though I have no physical attraction to him. (I will note that I've never thus far *become* attracted to someone I didn't have an instant "I want to eat you with a spoon" reaction to immediately, *which doesn't necessarily mean stereotypically attractive!* Though, all right fine, it usually does. All my past boyfriends will love this "compliment.")

"Zagat," he says.

I cock my head curiously.

"It's pronounced 'Zagat.'" He pronounces it differently than I did.

"Good to know."

And despite his awareness of the elite rating system and its correct annunciation, as I suspected, he's a no-go. I can just tell. I know I'm picky. And, as I already mentioned, it's not about how GQ/Men's Health a guy may be, because I've seen a few of those and they haven't affected my libido any more than collecting dead flies from a window sill. I think it's a pheromone/chemistry thing. Plus, I like bad boys—*used to,* used to like bad boys. (Note the one exception in my relationship life: Good Man was a nice guy. Let that be a lesson to me!)

Had there been a positive smell vibe then maybe the dinner interrogation would've been sexy. I get what I like to give: the prequalification dating questionnaire.

"So would you like to live in Seattle?" he asks.

"I love it so far."

"Would you do real estate here?"

"God, I hope not."

"What would you do?"

"Write!"

"Do you make a living from writing?"

"Not yet, but maybe one day. When I grow up." I'm trying to be funny, but he's marching on ahead.

"Do you want kids?"

"Used to think so, but now that I'm past forty, I'm not so sure. I'm far from ready to even be in a relationship right now." I pat my bag with the "bible," reminding him that my recent boyfriend was a narcissist.

He frowns. I'm not sure if he's disappointed in my age or the fact that I don't want to make like rabbits.

I ask, "You?" even though I know the answer already.

"Definitely." Then, "You're over forty? Wow, you look really good."

"Thanks. Botox." And, "How many kids would you want?" Now it's my turn. He frowns again at the mention of Botox.

"At least two. You don't want kids?"

"So obviously you don't have a girlfriend right now." I'm making light and, again, I know the answer, but I'm trying to track my way to solid ground. I add, "Nope, but *you'll* make a great dad one day."

"Not right now, no. I mean, I don't have a girlfriend."

"Not every woman wants to be a mom, JP. And sometimes, for some they miss the boat."

"There's time if you do it soon."

I burst out laughing. "Maybe I can be your wing-woman!"

I feel for him. He's genuine and has his shit together, but he seems so desperate—I've never experienced a man with a clock ticking, and I don't want kids and this fella is ready to settle down and raise rug rats like yesterday. Plus! I simply must want to jump a guy's bones, no bones about it.

At the end of the meal he asks, "So do you play tennis?"

"Nah, too one-sided. I'm OCD, everything must balance." But I feel like I've taken him down with a one-two-punch, so I add, "But I'd be up for a bike ride."

He perks up. "There are plenty of really great scenic trails in the city!"

"Sounds like a plan, my friend."

Feeling guilty for not feeling fertile-friendly with JP, and for looking young enough to be, I pay for the meal.

"I'll get the next one," he says.

"Deal." I nod affirmation.

*

Later that day, feeling fraught for female-female interaction and missing my girlfriends back home, I decide to reach out to my closest femme acquaintances in Seattle. I'm lying on my air mattress, staring at the sunshine as it diffuses through the lavender curtain MLM gave me (at what age *does* mauve become the color of choice?) and contemplating why I thought I had such a difficult time making city girl friends. The only thing I can come up with is that I simply hadn't made the effort. (I can't face the possibility that I wasn't likable. *Sad face.*) It's been easy meeting fellas—all a gal has to do is be open and friendly and make eye contact and smile and, really, most of the time you don't even need to give much of a smile. It must be the same for making girl friends, too, no? *If the answer is yes, why does it seem so fucking terrifying?* Don't answer that, I know the answer: I was an insecure scaredy-chicken.

I decide to make a girl friendship effort and contact the ladies I've already met.

I text California: "Hey, you up for a coffee and chat?"

After ten minutes and no reply, I'm mildly discouraged and wonder if I'm intruding in her busy social life and *feel guilty for possibly making her feel guilty for having to put me off.* I note how I wouldn't give it a second thought if she was a man—well, at least a man I wasn't interested in romantically. I consciously change my thought about it. Maybe she's busy, or hasn't seen the text, or is in the shower, or still sleeping or eating or sorting pillows or shuffling stuff around in her car. *Or whatever.* Don't take it personally. Okay.

I text Little Editor: "Hey, I know it's short notice but I'm going to Vivaci to write if you're not busy and want to join me."

I lay around, waiting for someone to reply, staring at the ceiling as a tiny spider crosses the stucco above me. I read somewhere that we ingest an average of fourteen spiders during our lifetime while we sleep[1]!

I've already checked my emails three times but I check them again. I write a group, girl-power email to Marthalicious, Leggy Blonde, Sultry Sage, P90X (another friend from Canada), and MLM. (Here's where I'm using my literary liberty card and merging a bunch of conversations into one. Okay, so I can't remember the exact communications verbatim, but I did my best. I'm compacting for efficiency sake and such a tactic shouldn't be used against me, though this whole fucking disclosure/explanation kind of defeats the compacting purpose, so in future please note that *I'm representing the essence of my experiences, people!*):

---

[1] I wonder if spiders are mostly protein? Junior once told me that semen is actually carbohydrates, not protein, though I haven't confirmed that factoid and I don't know if that includes men that have been snipped and are therefore shooting sans swimmers.

"Hello Lovelies! Loving Seattle but do miss my girl time. I've made a couple gal pals here, but why is it so much easier to meet boys? Even if they always seem to want the cookie—either for keeps or just when they've got the munchies!! (Sorry, Mom. Don't worry.) Anyway, I need some advice. Love you all lots and bunches. Miss you!!!!

P.S. I'm still working on my screenplay. I have no idea what draft I'm on now but the stack keeps getting bigger—the good news: I can use it as a coffee table! I've met with Tom twice on it and he's great with ideas and hand gestures, but it takes me a few days to riffle through them (the ideas) and blah blah blah blah . . ."

I hit send and feel better immediately. Even this one-way connecting makes me feel better. I check my iPhone and find two messages:

From California: "Today's not good but let's get together tomorrow before church? Do you want to come?"

From Little Editor: "I've got kid duties but let's get together soon?"

I text California back: "Coffee, yes! Church, next time. I'm going to the markets. ☺"

The next day, I go to two different markets—the Freemont Market and the Ballard Market. The Freemont Market has a little bit of everything: used and antique furniture, crafts and artwork, and tons of food vendors, including Maximus the Pig Vendor, who was on the Food Network and that's TV so it must be good. (I can now highly recommend the pulled pork sammich and mac and cheese, too delish!) Ballard Market sells fruits and vegetables, and flowers in beautiful, thoughtfully-arranged Asian arrays. I'll bet you can guess my favorite market—*uh, foodie here!*

At Freemont, I walk around to the different booths, chatting with vendors and keeping an eye out for friend-worthy females. Most of the ladies seem to be with other gals or gentlemen. I'm at a booth that sells antique kitchenware and old jewelry when I spot a like-aged woman turning over an ancient iron pot.

First, I want to say that I have no problem being casually congenial with women when I have no agenda. I chat with female booth attendants and grocery store clerks and baristas with nary a nerve agitated. That's easy. But to go beyond niceties into vulnerability has been another story. A nerve-wracking, nail-biting one.

I pretend to look at an old kettle and muse, "You get, like, three hundred percent more iron cooking in one of those."

She smiles and nods, then puts the pot down and casually moves away.

Do I smell or something? I put deodorant on, real deodorant, not that damn natural stuff that never seems to work. Now I know how guys feel when picking up chicks—awkward!

After trying this strategy out a couple more times—*in my mind*, because fuck it, I can't be bothered—I decide to self-soothe with food. I should weigh five hundred pounds by now, I know, though I don't. Don't hate me. Stress keeps my metabolism up. I sit in the shade on my new (old) ten-dollar chair, mowing down said pork sammich while the blonde lab beside me salivates. His owner, whom I'll call Beer Rep Guy since that's what he is, chats me up. I give him the once-over: he's not much taller than me, in jeans and a t-shirt and ball-cap, has brown hair and nice green eyes, is cute but not devastatingly dreamy, and probably in his early thirties. I feel zero attraction to him. And, yes, I have been told that attraction can grow. I'll keep that in mind. Thanks. (I wonder what the stats are on that. Instant attraction vs. he grew on me like hard-to-get-rid-of crab grass. I'll get back to you on that one.)

I've got BBQ sauce dripping between my fingers onto the napkin on my lap and a mouth full of ooey-gooey goodness when he starts to talk to me.

He says, "That looks way too good."

I answer, mouth stuffed, "Sinfully yummy."

"I haven't seen you here before."

I suck drippings off my index finger. "First time. Love it."

"Yeah, it's pretty good. I live a few blocks away so it's a no-brainer."

I say, "Oh my god, I'd be a house if I lived that close." I puff out my cheeks to illustrate myself as a fatty pants.

He laughs and says, "Well, they're only here once a week so I think you'd be safe. You live in the area?"

I pop a morsel in my mouth and chew a bit before I answer. "Madison Park, but I'm from Canada."

He raises his eyebrows. "I don't hear an accent."

I ask, "Can I?" nodding to his dog. He assents with a nod and I give the dog my last bite. I answer, "That's because I haven't said 'out and about' yet."

He chuckles. "Ah, yes, there it is: 'a boot.'"

I smile. He gestures towards his mouth and I use my tongue. He touches his nose. Since my tongue won't reach, real napkin it is. "Whoops."

He's quiet as I use three more napkins to clean my hands, then he says, "Would have been better with a Dottie lager."

I reply, "Beer?"

He nods.

I continue, "I hate beer."

He replies, "I'm a beer rep."

I laugh and say, "Obviously you like your job?"

He replies, "I get to drink a lot of beer!" He laughs and continues, "Do you want to get something to drink? Not beer."

This time I have to say, "Not right this moment. I have to get over to Ballard to buy apples.

Beer Rep Guy furrows his brow but doesn't say anything. I stand up, deposit my debris in a nearby trash can, and come back to get my new old chair. I stand by Beer Rep Guy and stick out my hand. "Anna. Not sticky, but sweet, I promise."

Surprised, he shakes my hand and introduces himself.

I ask, "You got a pen or a phone?"

He digs out his phone and I give him my number, but not without adding, "but I'm off the market so if we hang out it's not a date," and he laughs and agrees, and we say good-bye and I take my leave. It's so much easier to make boy friends, even if they do all turn out to be temporary.

Since I'm already grocery-stocked by the time I make it to the Ballard Market, I buy my allotment of apples and head home. I check my email. No word back from my gal pals back home. I sit on my soiled sofa, pretending to meditate but really just closing my eyes, acting as if the empty room doesn't see my aloneness. I contemplate calling MLM but don't want her to fret or have to put out extra prayers. Plus, I feel like wallowing a bit.

When I'm done feeling sorry for myself, I take a deep breath, collect myself, and go next door to Red Apple Market to buy cheese, chocolate, and a bottle of wine. I go home, open the wine, run a bath, and chop up an apple and some cheese. Then I have a hot bath, put on my PJs, and crawl into bed.

I say a prayer to God. "Lord, please guide me and take away the loneliness, but not by bringing me to heaven, MLM would suffer, and only if it is your will. In Jesus' name, amen."

I don't bother checking my emails.

The next morning, I wake up refreshed and reinvigorated—I'd only had one glass of wine. Whatever, God gave me a new day and a better attitude.

I fling the covers back and hop out of bed, make myself some coffee at home (for a change), and take a nibble of the chocolate I didn't indulge in yet. I decide I'll work from my second office, Starbucks, today, not to meet anyone but to get "out and a boot." Only when I get there do I check my emails. Here are some *of the essence* excerpts.

From Sultry Sage: "Making real, genuine women friends is rare. You're fortunate you have so many back home. We love ya, so chin up. Keep writing! I'm still with the electrician lol"

From Marthalicious: "Ohhh my BFF!!! I miss you toooo!!! Remember you are an amazing woman and some things take time. You'll meet someone soon! Put yourself out there and if they don't want to be your friend, then it's their loss! Xoxoxo P.S. I'm still visualizing you on the red carpet one day, and me with you!! Hehehe."

From Leggy Blonde: "Oi! Try yoga or a dance class or join a club or something. A writer's group? Or hiking? Check online. Hey, Kelsey wants to get her eyebrows tattooed, where'd you get them done again? Miss you!"

From P90X: "Hi, Anna. It's hard to make girl friends when you're not in a work environment. I'd stick with men, that seems to be easy for you! Not much new here, working steady. Miss you, girl! When are you back next? Let's get together."

From MLM: "Trust your Father knows what is best for you. Sometimes the lessons don't make sense until later. Did you try to make a friend at church? It is like family, all God's children are welcome. Maybe if you try a little you might meet someone nice. And you know you can always talk to Him, He listens. If God is for you who can be against you? Love you, my darling. [Happy face, rose, kiss face, heart emoticons]"

Thank you, Lord, for blessing me with these women.

*

What have I learned?

1. When a man approaches a woman in the park, he's got an agenda: maybe friendship, maybe babies (or at least practicing). It's not selfish to know what we want and go for it—whether we're the man in this scene or the woman—but it is selfish to *not* be honest about our intentions, even if it might hurt the other person's feelings in the short run.
2. It might be easier to filter through men and enjoy their company for the moments I get than to convert them to bone fide boy friends-only.

Homework:

1. Know my intentions.
2. Be honest with myself and others.
3. Stop buying narcissist books—accept, nay, celebrate that I am half-Mexican, half-Danish, and part narcissist!
4. Make friends, any gender. Or not. Or yes. Or—ugh . . .
5. Stop thinking about it. Stop thinking. Stop it. *Noo.*

***

SPEAKING OF "GIRL FRIENDS"

Little Editor texts me an invite to a BBQ she and Can Can Man are hosting at his house. Before I can change my mind, I take a deep breath and text her back, "I'll be there!" I don't feel as enthusiastic as my text implies, but I want to meet new people and I'm willing to marinade in some slight discomfort to do it. Plus, I can always sneak away if I so choose. Which I so might, folks!

His house is a modest, 1960s one-story. I knock on the open front door but enter before being greeted. I'm not heard over the dozen or so people milling about, beers or wine in hand, alternative rock pounding from hidden speakers. I'm not fond of crowds—despite getting comfy making girl friends one-on-one, groups of social interaction do make me nervous—so I feel relieved to see Little Editor chatting with a woman. Her familiar, friendly face calms my nerves. Even after gearing myself up to be Yes! Girl, I feel anxious. I'd self-talked my confidence up on the way over. For clarification, a crowd equals three times more people I don't know than I do. (It's easy in real estate as usually a meeting means me and a couple of clients. It took me years to speak up at a simple office meeting with my peers, even after I'd become quite successful. Yep, I fooled a lot of people, but all that "fake it 'til you make it" kind of worked in a way. At least it did in real estate.)

I feel summery and casual in layered t-shirts, Capri pants, and flats. I'm late and overly self-conscious about it.

Little Editor sees me, smiles, and waves me over. I bee-line directly to her.

"Hi! So sorry I'm late. I got lost, of course."

"It's okay, glad you got here." Little Editor is gracious.

I give Little Editor a hug and she introduces me to Gabby, who has shoulder-length, blonde, wavy hair, is on the petite side, and wearing jeans and a buttoned gingham cotton shirt.

"Hello!" She's warm and inviting and I relax a little.

"Are you hungry? Please eat some of this food, there's so much." Little Editor indicates the table of help-yourself platters. Can Can Man's roommate, Michael, spent the afternoon preparing a veritable smorgasbord of backyard delights: barbequed ribs, garlic mashed potatoes, potato salad, grilled corn on the cob, and marinated mixed veggies. The spread is vast and, by the time I arrive, also picked through and cold.

"Starving! Wow, looks great. You went to so much trouble."

"Actually, it was mostly Michael, he's a chef. Would you like something to drink?"

But now Gabby's gone to the bathroom and Little Editor is interrupted by another guest and I'm feeling out of my element and definitely plan on bolting soon. I've made my appearance, having said that I'd come, and am starting to feel cornered. Or is it isolated? Introverted! Some days Yes! Girl isn't always on social call.

I busy myself with constructing a plate of food and figure I'll avoid appearing socially inept by stuffing my face. When I have my plate of distraction, I find a seat on a plastic lawn chair outside and listen to conversations though I don't hear a word. The only sounds I can understand are the consoling chatter in my own head: "Just breathe. They won't bite you. They're talking about politics. *Oh God, is there something I know less about?* If I don't speak they won't know I'm an uneducated idiot. Slow down, you'll run out of food too quick! *Chew, damn it.*"

The group of five I'm sitting near is engrossed in conversation, something about reform or maybe the Mayor of Seattle's plan to elevate the city's environmental protection plan, or something else I'm unfamiliar with. No one stops to ask me any questions, so I gratefully pick my way through my potatoes. I'm consciously eating slowly so my distraction lasts longer.

What feels like hours ticks by, which in reality is only a few minutes, and Gabby returns and pulls up a chair beside me. I can suddenly swallow a little easier.

In short order, we end up talking about men, a topic I am comfortable with, even if I am a *self-proclaimed* expert.

"The thing is," she asks, "where do you find a guy? I'm not into dating sites." She looks at the couple of guys in the round table discussion who are oblivious to us.

"You're right. I've met a few fellows but no keepers. And dating sites can't show chemistry, so it's a lot of work to sift through. Who has time for that these days?" I ask.

"True. Guess that's why girl friends are so important. When you've got great girl friends, you almost don't need a man."

"I agree. I mean, for me, I don't even need sex. That's not to say I don't like it with the right person, but I don't *need* a man to assist." I laugh, feeling more at ease.

Gabby smiles and nods as though she's evaluating.

I continue, "And ladies have more in common anyway; shopping and theatre—well, some guys like the theatre, but I haven't found them, actually I have, so disregard that—but, hmm, did I mention shopping?" I'm scraping the barbeque bits from my plate and licking my fork clean. "Mmm."

She laughs. "We should go to the theatre sometime."

My eyes light up. "There's an art documentary playing at SIFF, can't remember the name, but I'm sure it's riveting."

She smiles. "Perfect! Are you into art?"

"No!"

"Me neither!"

"Dinner?"

"Let's do it!" Now I'm enthusiastic. "There's this place over in Lower Queen Anne that I'm dying to try. Um, it's close to SIFF, it's French, Toulous something."

"Toulous Petit! I've wanted to try that place, too."

"Let's dress up!" I'm now sitting erect with excitement.

"It's a date!"

A few from the round table stop and look over at us, noticing our existence for the first time, then resume their discussion.

Gabby and I exchange contact information and then she says she's going to head out. "Up early for work." She's a nurse.

Feeling full and fulfilled and wanting to end the evening on a positive note, I hop up and say my thank yous and good-byes to Little Editor and Can Can Man and Michael the Chef and, again, Little Editor is tactful and understanding of my early exit.

I drive home, thinking about my possible new friend while listening to an upbeat, alternative rock station and tapping my fingers with restless energy. Making a new girl friend is sort of like making a new boyfriend, or how it ought to be, I guess. You need to size each other up before you can decide if you want something long-term. It's worth at least a dinner and a movie—or art documentary. And the idea of it is just as enchanting. I can't suppress a giddy giggle at these amusing and happy thoughts. Honestly, I am that lame.

The evening of the potential girl friend dinner date, I get ready as if I'd be meeting a man: I have a bath, shave my legs, put extra time into hair and makeup, all while listening to my favorite upbeat tracks, which include the likes of U2, ABBA, The Bee Gees, and Madonna—yeah, I'm hip (*sideways glance*). I decide to wear skinny pants, ballerina flats—no need to break an ankle on my first girl dinner date—and a semi-sheer, silk floral print blouse that I got at Baby & Co.—my favorite fashion shop, though well beyond my budget (I permitted myself this one indulgence for my birthday back in May and haven't had the chance to wear it yet). I'm respectively attractive without being overdone. The outfit is perfect for a first girl-empowered-us engagement.

On the drive over, I'm excited but not nervous. She's already there waiting outside the restaurant when I walk up.

"Hi! You look lovely," I gush. She does. She's wearing a simple navy dress with small print design and sensible heels. Her hair is down and done. Is she wearing mascara? I can't tell.

She replies similarly, "You look great, too!"

We give each other a hug as though we've known each other since kindergarten and enter the très chic restaurant Françoise. As the name implies, it is loungy with soft lighting and booths on one side and a bar and high tables on the other, more social side. We choose a booth. It's casual but intimate, without linen tablecloths, but with fabric napkins and sturdy cutlery and a candle already flickering. The servers wear head-to-toe black.

Cut to next scene: We never make the movie, err, art thingy. No, we don't roll around in Saran Wrap all oiled up—whoops, redneck relapse—but we miss the documentary because we nibble on salads, drink wine, and talk non-stop for hours. She's fun, funny, pretty, authentic, and gabs as much as I do. Naturally, as is my tedious forte, we talk about relationships.

"I'm so done with men!" I exclaim and take a sip of my Riesling.

Gabby's eyes light up in agreement. "I know. I tell you, some days I seriously considering switching to the other team!"

"Cheers to that!"

We laugh and clink glasses.

She says, "You seem to have an easy time meeting men."

I sigh. "Yeah, I hear that a lot. But here's the thing: they're all wrong-for-me men. The good ones I am not attracted to—or can't find—and the other ones I shouldn't be attracted to."

"Comes from childhood stuff."

I briefly wonder how many women with "childhood stuff" end up switching to the "other team" because of said stuff. Not me! I continue, "I tend to go for guys who are overly vain, critical, and insecure and/or need constant validation. I'm self-conscious saying that out loud as I *might* possess some of those qualities myself!" I exaggerate a sideways glance. "That whole 'three fingers pointing back at me' projection thing." I demonstrate by pointing.

"Really? Are you all those things?"

I nod. "At least a little. I read somewhere that we attract our emotional equal, which means I should def-definitely stay single for a while!"

She laughs. "In that case, count me in—as in *out* of the dating scene."

Since it's all innocent fun, I keep the tongue-in-cheek theme going with, "We're better off to stick with girl power and a little battery power on the side."

"The Dolphin."

"Agreed."

I'm feeling totally relaxed, if a bit tipsy, so I add with dramatic flair, "Well, Gabby, I like you. I think we get along great and really get each other. Would you like to be my girl *friend?*"

She answers with a twinkle in her eye, "Yes, I would."

We clink glasses again.

The next morning, mildly hung-over and groggy from oversleeping, I meet Little Editor at her favorite haunt, Espresso Vivaci on Broadway in Capitol Hill. This section of Broadway offers four lanes of quiet, slow-paced traffic, if there is such a thing, and stores that offer secondhand finds, vintage, and new fashion, several mid-range restaurants, and at least one "adult only" store. The area also sports an eclectic, electric gay flair, as evidenced when a gentleman in clichéd spandex, à la 70s, strides by holding hands with his tatted-up, leather-clad boyfriend.

Little Editor and I sit at the open, garage-style front bar, facing the road with our laptops open. I've already collected my caffeine fix with a straight-up, double-shot espresso.

I point at Spandex Man and tell her, "Oh, that reminds me. If I do two hours of writing, then we are allowed to visit my stylist at Club Monaco." "My" stylist, an out-of-the-closet homosexual around thirty years of age, is into hip clothes.

Little Editor gets excited. "Oh, I like reward systems! And I could use a new outfit. Will you help me figure out what looks good on me? I think I need a new look. Something edgier."

"Ooh la la! I like it. It's a deal."

We delve into writing, skipping the chitchat.

Next scene location: Pacific Mall, Barney's. I'm walking laps in (my soon-to-be) four-inch, black, leather, hidden platform, peep-toe, red-bottom, Christian Louboutin (CL) *To. Die. For.* stilettos.

I face the price tag: "Oh God, they're almost a month's rent."

Little Editor says, "They're an investment, really." *She sideways glances!* I laugh.

Clerk adds, "If you get a Barney's card, you'll get 10% off your first purchase."

I pull out my wallet. "Where do I sign?"

On our way back to our cars, we solve the dilemma of where to wear all our new fine wares: a girls' night out at a gay bar. I'm animated with enthusiasm. "A gay bar is perfect! Then I can wear my new way-too-sexy dress, we can dance, *and* I don't have to worry about attracting Mr. Wrong."

Little Editor adds, "And Gabby might find a Mrs. Right."

Wait a minute. *What?* I stop in my tracks and Little Editor laughs then continues, "She came out. Of the closet." At my confused countenance she tries again. "She's lesbian."

"Shut the front door!" I fold over into hysterical laughter. "Well, that explains a lot." I shrug, chuckle, and resume walking.

The next day, while motivation still breathes, emails are sent, but over the course of a few days and then weeks, no one's schedule coordinates and the event never materializes.

Nonetheless, I have the shoes. And a dress! I only bought two items, but when two items go into quadruple digit dollars, we call the shopping a "get out of my comfort zone" spree. Ugh.

*

What have I learned?

1. I'm not great at group socials but I can gab graciously and genuinely in a one-on-one setting. Ladies aren't that scary once I get over myself already. And! Bravery is more rewarding than straight-up fearlessness. Who cares if I get rejected! Okay, I do. But what the heck, once in a

while a connection may happen and that makes the get-out-of-my-comfort-zone effort worth it.

2. Even if I never wear the dress or shoes, I got out of my comfort zone just by buying them, *imagining that I would wear them.* That counts! When I go on a lesbian date without knowing it, I'm *not* out of my comfort zone because *she* wasn't out of the closet, so that *doesn't* count!

Homework: Challenge myself and step outside of my comfort zone! *Confident single head nod.* I get my chance sooner than later . . .

***

BLIND DATING: ME, MYSELF, AND ELAINE

To make up for the impromptu *way* off-budget shoe splurge, the next day I head downtown to buy a table and chairs I found on Craig's List for dirt cheap—it's the chairs that I'm interested in. I need them to go with that free table I got last month.

I leave the Ballard area apartment building only to find the street blocked off and my car trapped by a human blockade. The crowd of people extends down both sides of the street as far as I can see. There are lawn chairs, sofa chairs, sofas, bunk beds(!), trucks backed up on connecting side streets with mattresses in the back, painted faces, costumes, wigs, vendors selling cotton candy, balloons, noisemakers, young people, old people, black people, white people, rainbow people, straights, hipsters, gangsters(?), firemen.

I ask a gentleman in an orange afro wig, "What's going on?"

He knocks me in the forehead with his fizoo and I smell beer. "Seafair Parade, honey."

"What time does it end?"

"Tomorrow for me." And he tries to blow again but he's out of breath, if not out of spittle.

While I blink the spit out of my eyes, certain I've now caught Hepatitis A-Z, the lady next to him wearing a headband of dual wobbling bobbles and painted face answers my query. "Ten o'clock, maybe eleven, by the time they clear us out."

It's four o'clock, the parade doesn't start until seven or end until eleven, and already the street is completely congested.

I have about six hours before I can get my car out, so I decide to do some situation-inspired, get-out-of-comfort-zone homework and take myself out for a romantic dinner. I search my iPhone for what Zagat says is nearby and find a nice restaurant a few blocks away from the chaos. I maneuver through the stream of colorfully-clad salmon that swell in the street and make my way to LaVita Bella. LaVita Bella, as its name might imply, is Italian. It has a little, open-air, sidewalk patio, enclosed with black, wrought-iron railing that is adorned with potted greenery. It's early so it's not yet busy, which puts me at ease. I enter. The sign reads: Please Wait to be Seated. The interior is unoccupied.

A hostess approaches me and grabs two menus from a side pocket of the host's podium. "For two?"

I swallow, feeling like Dorky Dorkerson. "One, please. May I sit outside?"

She smiles. "Of course."

We go outside where a few tables are occupied with male/female couples. She sweeps her arms around to indicate my choices. "Anywhere you like."

I choose a table at the far end in the corner, where I sit with my back to the restaurant so I can people-watch, though I am off the busy parade street and there's no pedestrian traffic. But in case they do show up, I will have the ideal vantage point.

"Your server will be with you shortly. Bread basket?"

"Oh, yes please!" I'm anxious to keep busy.

I spend an excessive amount of time reading the menu until the server, a pleasant Latin-American (my editor changed that from Mexican, which I'm certain was accurate) man perhaps in his early thirties, approaches with the promised loaf. The aroma of fresh-baked, or at least freshly-ovened, bread stimulates my appetite and soothes.

"Would you like something to drink, Miss?"

I like being "Missed." "The Pinot Noir, please."

"Of course." He leaves.

I delve into the bread and slather it with the cold, unchurned butter from the mini crock. "Oh my God," I say aloud under my breath, relaxing even more. There's a reason certain foods are called comfort foods.

Shortly after, my server returns with the wine and pours it from the tiny carafe into my glass using a smooth twist of his wrist at the last drop.

"Thank you."

He smiles. I order. He leaves.

After a few sips of wine, either by natural or psychological effect, I'm all chill and confident. I think, "Hmph, this is easy." Though, to be fair, it's a quiet evening and it *is* early, meaning the place isn't packed with wall-to-wall romantic couples while I wallflower my way through mild intoxication.

Not having a book and wanting to be present in my own company, a good date if you will, I think about what the proper self-date etiquette is. I determine there's not much to do: eat, drink, swallow, look around, blush with embarrassment, repeat. I can't very well talk to myself. That might draw unwanted attention. I'm too far away from the young couple a few tables over to amuse myself by eavesdropping, so I try to read their body language.

Both look to be mid-twenties. Her appearance is exotic, part Asian, part Northern European, I'm guessing. She's pretty and not overdone, wearing minimal make-up. She has short, brown hair and radiant skin, and wears dark jeans, tank top, and cardigan, and dangling earrings. She's in heels. Her date looks to be part Italian or maybe Middle Eastern. He wears a collared shirt that stretches at the buttons over his belly, jeans that ride down, and new-looking high-top runners. His leather jacket hangs on the back of his chair. From the pauses in conversation and awkward eye contact and forced smile *from her*, I assume this is their first, and likely last, date. Now I'm glad I'm alone.

I drink one glass of wine and eat a delicious garlicky Caesar salad since I won't be liplocking with anyone tonight, and an artisan thin-crusted Salumi pizza. Yummers all around. I think, "I can make this at home," then follow that thought with, "But I probably won't." Another thought I become aware of: "Garlic makes me gassy. And my breath reeks and it doesn't even matter." And, "I may ask myself out again, even with flatulence. Then again, I might order take-out."

I think about why I feel self-conscious eating alone in a public place such as this. Maybe not in big cities, but certainly I don't recall seeing anyone eating alone in my small town, or maybe I've never noticed. I only ever went out for lunch alone there once and three people who knew me asked if I was waiting for someone, even after I half-finished my meal. Is there a presumption that I have no one else to join me? And if so, so what? Why can't I enjoy a meal alone by choice, damn it? I ponder this for a moment. I still care what others think of me, and in this case, don't want them to: 1) feel sorry for me or 2) assume no one likes me. I'm self-analyzing while bobbing my head around in mute self-conversation—I'm sure my face is too animated for being solo—when the server returns.

"Something wrong, Miss?"

"Uh, no, sorry, everything was great."

"Anything else? Dessert?"

But I'm satisfied and satiated and anything more would be overdoing it and unnecessary. "Just the bill, please."

I stroll back toward the parade, feeling the evening coolness in the air and wrap my arms around myself. The glow of summer evening sun lingers and stretches shadows. The side streets are hush, and a breeze rustles leaves in restless birch trees. I quicken my pace, hoping to get to warm-bodied patriots where I can escape the cold. My calm, melancholy mood doesn't match the lively festivities, but I find a comfortable corner to watch the rest of the parade. I barely notice the noisy crowd from my vantage point, where I also watch yummy firemen, a parade novelty now. The parade consists of baton-thrusting trollops—they get a big cheer—and sparkly floats laden with princesses in prom dresses and muscle-bound Marines—they get a bigger cheer (Americans have priorities)—and cowboys, pirates, marching bands, convertible corvettes with waving Corporals, and helium-filled blimps in the shapes of whales and cell phones. It's all very flag-waving and it makes me appreciate the prevalent patriotism, even way up here in Seattle hippie country.

When it's over, the masses dissipate to go home with their families and tuck children into beds or to hit bars with their friends to suck back more brews. I make my way to my vehicle and sit for a moment, reminiscing on my romantic evening with myself. Even though the motivation came by default, I'm proud of myself for completing my homework of getting out of my comfort zone. The shy kid in me smiles and sits up straight. I take a deep breath, let it out slowly, and then head home.

*

What have I learned? If you can't date yourself, well then, who can you date? In other words, who's going to want to spend time with me unless I want to spend time with me?!

Homework: Take myself on a solo dinner date once in a while, on purpose, rather than by default. (Pack dress and shoes in case I get stuck and have an impromptu opportunity! Okay, maybe that's pushing it. Lord knows, no one wants to see a chick *dressed up* for a date all alone, especially me! Can we say: Stood Up Dorkerson? Yes, yes we can. Blink. Blink.)

***

REGIONAL DEFINITIONS: HIPPIES, HIPSTERS, AND HANGERS-ON

Speaking of our Good Lord, last Sunday I worshipped God by going to the park, which totally counts because He made that park! I didn't go to church, but I did watch a service online from the comfort of my air mattress in PJs, and that counts, too. Really, truly, I say unto you, it's a recorded, broadcast—live even. Plus, there was a great band. But, after I got my lazy ass up and dressed, I wandered down to Madison Park and sat on a park bench to watch a couple of pigeons coo and skitter about. God made those pigeons and I did think about that. I may even be ahead of the get-to-Heaven game! (Though why does this jesting feel sinful? ~~Damn~~ Darn it. I repent!)

Then JP calls to invite me for a bike ride, but when he calls again to confirm time, I suggest, "Instead, why don't we go downtown to Zagat-rated bakery: The Essential Baking Co.? It's overcast and I don't want to end up in a typical Is-this-August? Seattle downpour. Good idea?"

He agrees. Even though I'm enjoying my me time, I'm also missing connection, and JP knows we're just friends, and maybe he's figured out he's not interested in me, either. Or maybe he wants a wing-woman. Whatever, I want company so it's a fair trade.

Shortly after, we are people-watching from a European wrought-iron round table on not quite a patio but more of an if-I-stick-my-foot-out-I'll-trip-someone setting. Many of those someones are hippies and hipsters, the difference of which I'm trying to get a grasp on—where I come from there are neither. (No exaggeration.) We have which-ball-cap-and-Mack-jacket-am-I-wearing-today-that-goes-with-this-fishing-rod types. (Small exaggeration.) And that's the ladies! (Very small.)

JP adjusts the lens on the impressive camera he brought while I take a sip of my decaf whole milk latte and ask him for help discerning. A male twosome walks by and I ask, "Hipsters?"

He answers, "Hipster wannabes but not quite. See the shoes?" I notice the regular gym shoes on the one, which doesn't really go with the low-slung jeans and oversized hoodie and driver's cap. I nod, understanding. Before long, with JP's tutoring, I perfect my understanding of the distinction.

"So let me see if I can get this straight . . ." I take a deep breath. "A hippie is slovenly, pot-smoking, dreadlocks-sporting or unkempt-hair-wearing, sometimes bearded, overgrown and natural, out of it, outdoorsy, BOed, what's-work, screw-school mentality." I take another quick breath then continue, "And a hipster is carefully creative, *seemingly* slovenly, often dressed in black, hat-wearing, often a driver's cap, imported-cigarette-smoking, bearded, overgrown and *manicured*, totally 'in' aloof, indoorsy, impeccably-hygiened, what's-work, educated yet too-*cool*-for-school mentality." I gasp for air. "How'd I do?"

JP, who is wearing well-fitting jeans and a t-shirt under a short-sleeved collared shirt, along with gym runners, laughs. "You *are* a writer. That about sums it up."

I add, "Oh, and hipsters wear either clean, new Converse or desert boots, while hippies wear worn-out whatever!"

JP and I talk about relationships, or rather that's what *I* talk about. I figure other people actually have other things to discuss—e.g., work, politics, social programs, health care, music, art; hell, I don't know. One day I will so fucking surprise someone with my intellectual prowess by talking about all those worldly topics *and then who'll be sorry? (Answer:* Probably me.)

In mid-discussion by now, I say, "It's weird how men and women can't be friends. I'm trying to figure it out."

He interjects with, "I think they can. Why would you think they can't? We're sitting here as friends, aren't we?"

"Okay, so if I'm sitting here with a girl friend and a hot guy walks by, I can check him out and she's not going to feel awkward in any way. How about you?"

"How about me, what? Would I feel awkward if you checked out a guy? Not really. I'd check out an attractive girl if she walked by, I'd just be subtle about it."

"Why? Why would you need to be subtle? We're just friends. There's no need for subtle, unless you'd be that way if you were sitting here with a guy friend."

"Out of respect."

"That's unnecessary. How about this? What if we're hanging out together and I start chatting with some guy that I'm attracted to? How would you feel if I invited him to join us for coffee? Any of my girl friends would be cool with that, would you?" (In fact, I wouldn't actually do that, because my girl time is my girl time, but I'm testing him. *For his own good, of course.*)

I can see his back stiffen. "I don't know. How would you feel if I asked a good looking girl to join us?"

"I'd be thrilled! Maybe you'd get a real date and maybe I'd get a girl friend out of the deal."

He's thoughtful for a moment, then his brow unfurrows. "I've never opened up like this with anyone."

"Don't take it too seriously, I hear that from a lot of men. The others— closed, aloof, and uninterested—I tend to find intriguing and mysterious and like to chase. I really should be in therapy. Or a man, maybe. Not be *in* a man. *Be* a man. You know what I mean."

This bothers him. "Why do women like the bad boys?"

"I think everyone likes a bit of a challenge. Good guys, like yourself, need to figure out how to appear a little bit bad. Guys like to chase but so do girls. Well, we *complicated* ones do, anyway."

"I don't like playing games or manipulating women. I don't want to be a 'bad boy,' that's selfish and immature."

I nod. "Or you can wait it out for a nice girl who isn't messed up and will appreciate you for the nice guy you are. I'm just saying, don't be afraid to have an opinion that disagrees with hers. A good debate can be stimulating—like this one!" I take a bite of my pastry.

He sighs. "I don't get why you'd want someone who treats you without respect. And why wouldn't you want to get to know someone before writing him off? There's a lot of people who are together who weren't attracted to each other right away."

I'm getting frustrated too. I pause before replying, "I don't want someone who treats me disrespectfully. It's simply never happened that I've 'developed' attraction. It's been there or it hasn't."

He continues, "But how do you know if you've never tried?"

Now I sigh. "If I say 'maybe,' then I feel like I'm leading a guy on or potentially giving him false hope and he's going to get hurt. Don't worry about me. You walk down your path, I'll walk down mine." I take another bite of my pastry then continue, "Look, if you really are okay with being friends with me, that means being okay with eating this chocolate croissant in the company of me and another man," I pause for effect, "one I might be interested in romantically. That's the bottom line, JP. That's all I can offer."

He sits deflated and frowning and silent.

I swig back the rest of my cold latte and ask, "Ready?" as in "Ready to end this non-date and to put a button on the end of this escalating debate?"

He seems to make a decision then more cheerfully asks, "Hey, have you ever been to Olympic Sculpture Park? It's only a few blocks away."

I smile, grateful for the change of topic. "Let's go."

We walk down to Olympic Sculpture Park, where he whips out his camera and starts clicking photos of the art then asks, "Hey, can I take your photo?"

"Only if it's not a lame pose!"

"Do whatever you want."

I jump up and down, making animated faces and kicking my legs up in all manner of directions. I giggle, hoping I won't have a geriatric moment after all that why-bother-it's-decaf liquid. I'm near a large, orange, metal "thing"—or piece of art. He clicks away until I'm exhausted and folded over panting and laughing, and he's in his element and his face is lit up and finally relaxed.

All the art in the park is abstract, impressionistic, thought-provoking. Yeah, I pretty much don't get it but I can't deny a tangible energy and a general feeling of appreciation somehow permeates my chest, lungs, heart—or maybe it's the sun popping through the clouds in the sky, or the clouds of secondhand, hippy, wacky tobaccky wafting around from somewhere nearby.

Still happy from the leaping fun, I ask, "Oh my God, where is that coming from?"

He says, "Myrtle Beach, I think. Have you been there?"

I scrunch my nose up. "Eww, I hate pot smoke!"

But, being curious birds, we venture down to Myrtle Beach Park. All is now casual and comfortable between us. There's no weird vibe and I think, once again, that maybe male-female friendship is possible. We arrive at a beachfront park similar to Madison Park, a compact grassy area under trees by the ocean shore, and locate the source of the fumes. A hippy festival! *Chillography* is underway. Aha! Dancing, hula-hooping, high

146

hippies, and furbies (animal-inspired, ethically-not-real fur head attire, probably made by children in a "developing" country).

We walk around in silence, observing the slit-eyed stoners saying, "Hey man" and "Dude," and swaying to the beat of the techno tunes being scratched out on a turntable under an event tent. I cover my mouth and nose as heavy billows of pot smoke drift nearby. JP makes a face. Hey, I watched my dad die in a closet after toking up, and even though one thing had nothing to do with the other, I have association issues, *man*. And, yeah, I know a lot of people do it and that's their deal, and their deal is totally cool, but I don't have to like it and I can cover my damn mouth and nose if I want to. No disrespect, dude. *Friendly smile.*

By this time, I'm socialized out. And though JP tried to convince me to give a guy (a Jew) a chance before writing him off and I do like his company as a friend, this day is done. I'm tired, hungry, and a little cranky. My face is long and my shoulders are slumped. He gets a case of Hanger-On-er. I don't want to hurt his feelings, but all I can think is, "Let go of the boat, son. You've already drowned." He puts on an exaggerated smile and adds an extra dose of high-toned cheerfulness.

"Do you want to go somewhere to eat?" His lip corner quivers from the exertion.

"Not tonight." My countenance doesn't shift.

We part ways.

I do not contact him again, not wanting to give him the slightest encouragement, even though I know it's my loss in some ways. But yesterday, as I'm leaving Starbucks, I hear my name—which I admit I love hearing for the first time randomly in Seattle. It's JP. He jogs over out of nowhere, smiling and frowning at the same time. I smile and say, "Hi." No exaggeration, within the first three sentences out of his mouth, he says:

"So, when you said you were off the market, well, what if Brad Pi—"

"Gerard [you know who]," I interrupt.

"Who?"

"Gerry. He's the only one for whom I'd reconsider." I briefly consider mentioning The Italian, but don't want to get into a whole long explanation of how I might be attracted to a man I've never met in person. Plus, I still haven't heard from him.

"Do you want to watch some tennis?" JP asks.

"Uhh . . . "

"It's The State Open at the Seattle Tennis Club. It's the major tournament of the year and it's the only time the public is allowed to set foot on the Members Only property." He's enthusiastic.

Feeling smothered—and tough love kind—I say, "Busy, sorry. Gotta run, enjoy your day."

I leave feeling sorry for him and sorry for me, but at least now I know how guys feel when they're not really that into me.

Cut to next scene: Me, solo, at STC half watching the tournament while texting a pal in Seattle I know for sure isn't interested in getting naked with me. Little Editor: "Want to get together and do some writing soon?" I put my phone away and watch young athletes in cute tennis skirts dart across the courts.

Note: Just in case a single, straight man is reading this: *If she's not that into you, she's not that into you!* Women are like men that way. Men and women are not that different, after all. You're not going to convince her with logic. If it ain't there, dude, it ain't there. Throw in the towel, raise the white flag, move on, *man*. And stop acting desperate and disappointed or she won't even introduce you to her potentially-interested friends. Oy!

*

What have I learned? Girls and boys both need a little challenge, a chance to chase, and someone to imagine doing the dirty with. For this gal, if it ain't there, it ain't there. But I'll admit there's a gray area for a lot of people that, in time, will either put you on base or send you walking home—whatever team you play for. Batter up!

Homework: Write *How-To Book for Boys*. Make sure to include sports quips and tidbits, big font, and racy photos of hot chicks. Fundamental feminists would hate me for that statement, but *as if they'll be reading this "offensive trash."* Lighten up, people!

***

KNEE-HIGH STOCKINGS: A LEG UP FOR THE SINGLE LIFE

Little Editor and I spend an afternoon at Vivaci Espresso, tapping away on our keyboards. I'm working through maybe my fifth (sixth? eighteenth?) draft of my if-I-ever-finish-this-Tom-may-need-to-help-me-from-the-*other-side* screenplay. I'm almost resigned about it. Almost. Some days I'm so frustrated that it's taking so long I want to visit a tall bridge, other days I'm glad to be working through it.

We chat about dinner plans and I suggest, "We could go all business-skirt, sexy-heels, classy dressed-up, and go for a cocktail and then dinner?"

She responds, "Or we could wear our outfits." She means the sexy outfits we both bought during my shopping splurge day.

Now I'm concerned everyone will think we're on a date, but I figure I already went on an I-didn't-know-I-was-on-a-real-date-with-a-fucking-lesbian rendezvous so who cares. "Let's do it!"

Cut to next scene: I can't do it! I'm in my apartment, standing in front of the door-framed paneled mirror I recently acquired, looking at myself in the black dress. I can't wear it just *out to dinner*. Wardrobe change into a black pencil skirt and sparkly top. Though I do wear the new CL heels.

Knee High Stocking is located on a tiny, pie-shaped lot between three busy streets, in a gray building with no windows, no sign, and no parking.

(Little Editor drove.) The door is locked, so we ring the buzzer, which I imagine goes to a dank basement with an old, abandoned well shaft and the psycho butterfly/moth man from *Silence of the Lambs*. A hostess of mid-thirties and stoic countenance dressed in head-to-toe black opens the door wide enough to greet us, but blocks our passage.

"Names?" she inquires. Apparently you must RSVP to get hosed and lotioned before death. I don't mention this to Little Editor since I may need to use her as a decoy when I escape.

We tell the solemn lady our names. She checks the reservation list, then disappears without a word, closing the door behind her and leaving us teetering in our stilettos in the busy street—Little Editor decided to wear her outfit, black-tailored short shorts, sparkly top, heels—and I feel a little bit like a prostitute on a corner, not because of her outfit but because *we're tottering in heels while loitering on a damn street corner in front of an ostensibly non-existent establishment.* She looks edgy and confident and is it my imagination or does she have a sexier sway in her step? Maybe I should've worn the dress. I'm never going to pick up Johns in this office outfit! Oh wait, I forgot for a second we're not actually (high-paid, high-class) ladies of the night. My bad.

When the hostess returns, she wordlessly directs us to enter. How mysterious. How exclusive. *How are we going to die??* Inside the compact venue, we notice it's cozy and it takes a moment for my eyes to adjust to the low light. There are a handful of tables just inside the door that are occupied with what I imagine are coy, sexy (still breathing) patrons, and a tiny bar in the back, which can only be twenty-five feet from where we entered. We are seated at the bar that fits four and has its own bartender. Shiny bottles sparkle on glass shelves behind him, which I suspect are spiked enough to knock us out.

Little Editor leans in toward me and whispers, "You have to be in the know to hear about this place." Aha, I do detect a new boldness in her. *Is she in on the plot?* Nothing exciting happens—as in I don't have to use my Lara Croft, moth-man-kicking warrior skills to save us from becoming lamp shades—other than the flambéed goat cheese and Little Editor using the term *well hung*, which I gasp at and take to mean we've crossed into the next level of friendship: *sex talk*. Well, well, well...

We giggle and snicker and throw a few hushed, tentative comments into dimly-lit ambiance, not caring who can hear us. *This is way better: a girl bonding moment!*

"Does size matter?"

"Yes!"

"But *too* big is no picnic."

"Agreed."

More blushing and giggling and sipping.

Then I pour out my heart to Little Editor. "I don't think I'm ready for anyone yet. [HBUAB] might have been a fibber. Okay, he was a fibber. In fact, he likely still *is* a fibber, but he was such a charming con man—and damn, he was good in bed."

"Damn," she agrees.

"So, if we're going to be single, and by *we* I mean me, since technically you're not, then this is a time to cherish! What happens if, *when*, I find Mr. Right, if he really is Mr. Forever, I'll never get this opportunity again! I need to take hold of the reins and drive that singlehood chariot of fire! Fan the flame of independence, total selfishness, me me me-ism!"

Little Editor says, "True!"

Encouraged, I continue my rant. "This is a time of obligation to no one except for me and, of course, a responsibility to family and courtesy to friends. Enjoy it! Relish it! Even exploit it! I need to re-read *Kiss Me I'm Single*."

Little Editor interjects, "Yes! Wait, which book is that?"

"It's by Amanda Ford, a friend of California's. It's really so good. Something about embracing singlehood and all that stuff I just spewed, hehe . . . What are in these things?" I hold up my empty martini glass, but am too tipsy and giddy to look around for men wearing suspicious arm casts. *Eh, shrug.*

We go to the restaurant, Purple, for dessert. Zagat says it's a singles scene. It's just another dimly-lit, if much larger food scene, with a bar that surrounds a cylindrical wall of wine bottles reaching thirty feet to the ceiling, from which a sommelier dangles off a wooden ladder on a track. The bar seats at least two football teams, though I see no football players or even regular sweet-talking *male players* for us. (*Note to self:* Zagat lied.) It's mostly couples spoon-feeding each other and large groups of friends laughing, probably ribbing politicians, so we choose more cheese, please, and a glass of wine. "Might as well." Now that we're past the sex talk bonding convo, I'm back on the man track. I'm satisfied with the new level of friendship and, inasmuch as Little Editor is out in a sexy outfit, I suspect she's itching to get home to Can Can Man.

"Has he seen the outfit?" I ask.

"I'm going there after," she replies and looks away, blushing.

Our sobering up leads to sombering up, and conversation wanes, so we look around and avoid eye contact and ask for the bill, and it's early so we walk a block in comfortable silence and then I say, "Hey, let's take a foray through the Fairmont," which only leaves us further wondering where all the eligible bachelors hang out in this city.

"I mean I'm not really *looking* for anyone," I half fib, "but I wouldn't mind knowing there might be someone out there for when I *am* ready."

"Maybe I should stick it out with [Can Can Man]," she concedes.

We toddle back to her car and she drives me home. We're both tired and thoughtful, if a little disenchanted. She doesn't say anything, but I can tell she's anxious to get to her man, and I'm looking forward to my bed.

The funny thing is I can't help it. I waver between freedom and liberty of single life and missing the intimacy of having a special someone, like hand holdings and cuddles and pillow talk and being comfortable naked and making [sing:] *l-l-l-looove*. Maybe that's why I seem open to chatting with every man who enters my vicinity before I promptly put them all in the no-entering-my-va-jay-jay zone. But am I really that open? Hell no! I've got a dealbreaker list that lengthens with every chap I meet and is increasingly becoming so vast as to narrow down any real possibilities of an actual union to almost naught. By the time I meet The Gerry, even *he* probably won't qualify! Oh right, I may not meet The Gerry. Shit.

As I'm nodding off in bed, I relive the events and conversation of the night and chuckle at our daringness at the dimly-lit secret bar . . .

After two drinks, we pinky swore to doing more of our get-out-of-our-comfort-zones homework.

"Okay, so I'm to look into speed dating, *purely for blogging material, of course!*"

Little Editor says firmly, "Of course! And I'm to look into Amateur Night at the Can Can! There's a burlesque class downtown. I hear it's fun. Do you want to do it?"

"No more edgy outfits for you, lady!"

I'm not sure of her follow-up intentions thereafter . . . perhaps a career change for her as well? Um, did I mention I have hip issues?

*

What have I learned? Being single is an excellent opportunity to do what I wouldn't do when in a serious relationship! Take advantage, girlfriend!

Homework:

1. One-week pass: unabashed flirting (any gender), check into speed dating, sign up! (Or not so much. In fact: don't.)
2. Review dealbreaker/deal maker list.

***

DEALBREAKERS AND DEALMAKERS: MY IDEAL-FOR-ME MAN LIST

Let's keep in mind how far I've progressed since I started this spreadsheet back in 2008 after Junior and I split up for probably the third, but not final, time. It's sort of sorted alphabetically and sort of by priority: the first section includes the non-negotiables, the second includes the definite dealmakers/dealbreakers, and the third includes the important ideals. I've included the modifications I made to this point. It's in point form, rather than original spreadsheet form, since I've added explanations and/or notes lest you think me shallow, which I am, but not totally, and really I'm getting deeper by the second, and soon I'll be as deep as the ocean, just you watch!

The Non-Negotiables:
1. Affectionate. (This includes hand-holding, cuddling, casual grazing, and appropriate public displays of affection, aka PDA.)
2. Attractive. (To me. Yes, I am referring to the physical.)
3. ~~Charismatic~~. (I'm not sure after which break up I scratched this one out, because Good Man, Junior, HBUAB, and HM are all highly charismatic—and *we know* how those relationships turned out. Shit, The Italian may be the most charismatic of all. God help me if I ever meet him.
4. Compassionate.

5. Confident. (Not to be confused with *arrogant* or *boastful*, traits that are dealbreakers. Still, no girl wants a wishy-washy pussy. Well, this one doesn't. No offense to the all-powerful pussy.)
6. Monogamous. (As in "I only have eyes for you." That's not to say the dude I'm with can't appreciate a "beautiful painting," but I need to feel like I'm the only "art" he wants adorning his "home"– *that's a metaphor for penis.*)
7. ~~Financially independent.~~ (Well, I loved a man who was heavily in debt and would have stayed with him if he wasn't also a *chronic liar.*)
8. Financially responsible. (Then again, I'm not sure I'd like to be sleeping under a bridge.)
9. Financially secure. (I'm quite concerned about the bridge lodging.)
10. ~~Fit.~~ Fit. (Let's be honest, I like a nice bod, but not a guy who is over-the-top obsessed with it.)
11. Fun. (I'm actually not really sure how this made the non-negotiable list, but okay.)
12. Funny. (Def definitely needs to be able to make me laugh. Or at least laugh at me. But not in a mean way.)
13. Good communicator. (Or someone who will nod and say, "Mhm," while I babble on about shoes and bad hair. Though, I do want someone who will share his feelers—that's Anna slang for "feelings.")
14. Healthy. (My dad died when I was twelve. I have abandonment issues, people!)
15. Honest. (Refer to The Fibber.)
16. Humble!
17. Intelligent. (I need high levels of intellectual stimulation. Yes, I'm putting this need partly on my man.)
18. Loving. (Like my dad but less possessive, please.)
19. Loyal. (This applies to more than sexual promiscuity. The right man will know what I mean.)
20. ~~No~~ Addictions-free. (Including but not limited to marijuana, illegal drugs, prescription drugs, alcohol, Armani suits, or anything else I want to add.)
21. Open-minded (I've already admitted hypocrisy, so shush.)
22. Patient. (Obviously he'll have to be.)
23. ~~Romantic~~ (After HBUAB, I have trouble trusting motives of romantic overtures. Some guys might appreciate this being scratched out.)
24. Trusting. (But not naïve.)
25. Trust-worthy! (!!)

Dealmakers and Dealbreakers:
26. ~~6"-8"~~ 4"+ taller than me. (I'm 5'6" and wear 4" heels.)

27. Active. (As in you won't rely on me to entertain you, *though I so will!*)
28. ~~Believes in conscious parenting.~~ (I believe at this point that I'm past developing a maternal instinct. It's not scratched out *because* I want a guy who doesn't believe in unconscious parenting. Just to be clear.)
29. ~~Blue or green eyes. Or hazel.~~ (The simple fact is that I've never been attracted to a guy with brown eyes. It might be a biological aversion since everyone in my family has them. Except my dad. Okay, so that doesn't make sense. Whatever. I scratched it off, so let it go.)
30. Defending (aka protecting).
31. Doesn't do *any* illegal drugs. (Apparently, I wanted to make double sure of this one.)
32. Witty. (Really?)
33. Emotionally aware.
34. Environmentally aware.
35. Goal-oriented.
36. Good hygiene.
37. Good kisser.
38. Good teeth.
39. Independent. (I.e. Not needy.)
40. ~~Nice body.~~ (You see that? *Scratched out.*)
41. Nice smile. (*Eh, shrug.*)
42. Optimistic. (Who wants a Dougie Downer?)
43. Responsible.
44. Secure.
45. Selfless.
46. ~~Social drinker.~~ (As opposed to lush or stick in the mud, but apparently I'm okay with mud, now. Or a boozer.)
47. Some spontaneity.
48. Stable.
49. Strong-willed. (?)
50. ~~Land Rover. SUV. Black.~~ (Ashamed and appalled. *Sideways glance.*)
51. Attentive.
52. Comfortable.
53. ~~Dark hair.~~ (*Hello! Scratched out.* Give credit where credit is due, people.)
54. Flexible.
55. ~~Hairy chest.~~ (What?! Who touched my spreadsheet? I'm so adding this back!)
56. Helpful.
57. Well-groomed. (But not overly coiffed. If you use more hairspray than I do—dealbreaker. Aha! That was a test, and you failed. *If you even use hairspray*—Deal. Break. Errrr.)
58. Laughs. (At self, at me, at others, at life.)

59. Mature. (Ish.)
60. Non-smoker!
61. Not controlling.
62. Not critical.
63. Not into porn.
64. Not manipulative.
65. Not suspicious or paranoid. (Uh, #61–65, *sideways glance*.)
66. ~~Not pale.~~ (For the sake of our children, if we have any.)
67. Personable.
68. Playful.
69. Sexually exclusive*. (I starred this one. Hmm.)
70. Sincere.
71. Social.
72. Straight-forward.
73. Supportive.
74. Sure.
75. ~~Well-dressed.~~ (But not in designer duds you can't afford! Oh, it's scratched out, never mind.)

Important Ideals:

76. Accepting.
77. ~~Ambitious~~. Honorable. (Odd switcheroo.)
78. Caring.
79. Considerate.
80. Easy-going.
81. Emotionally solid. (I know, right? Why aren't some of these in the must-have section?)
82. Good relationship with parents.
83. Understanding.
84. Has friends that I like.
85. ~~Has no female children.~~ (Hey, come on, I've already gone through the pain and suffering of losing two step-daughters.)
86. High integrity. (Honestly, the fact this is way down here in the "it would be nice if" list says something about me. And that something is not good. *Awkward laugh.*)
87. Knows how to cook.
88. ~~Not arrogant / egotistical.~~ (A fine line with confidence.)
89. ~~Not flashy / showy.~~ (A very fine line? blink blink)
90. Open.
91. Passionate.
92. Reliable.
93. ~~Respectable.~~ (*Laughing.*)
94. Respected. (I think I mean respectable. I think there's a difference.)
95. Respectful. (93-95? It appears I'm confused.)
96. Safe. (Seriously? Way down here?)
97. Self-reliant.

98. Sexually compatible. (Whoa! Let's move this one up a notch *or ninety.*)
99. Within five years older. (~~Or two years younger.~~)
100. ~~Wants children.~~ (These eggs have a shelf life. *Insert:* sad face.)

My OCD loves that this list, and indeed, its original four-columned spreadsheet ends up totally a perfect one hundred!

*

What have I learned? I'm as deep as an ashtray.

Homework: Get cat allergy meds. (Especially after the next chapter.)

***

REJECTION, REJECTION, REJECTION:
ANOTHER SHOT OF CROISSANT

Rejection #1. I go to a new-artist-music-poem-reading-painter-painting event thingy with California. It's at what would seem to be a Royal Legion building in Fremont, Seattle, only minus the war stories and purple noses, err, I mean Purple Heart Medals. The building has no windows, only an empty hall that might fit fifty seated (between a few ill-placed support beams) in metal folding chairs that face "the stage" (*read*: the side of the room opposite the entry that has no chairs). On one side of the hall is a concession window where you can buy soda and popsicles. Fluorescent lights could send us running for home but are fortunately turned off, and most of the light seems to come from a track of soft spotlights facing the "stage" area. It's unpretentious. Like.

We're both in jeans—it's casual. Since we're late, possibly because of time spent searching for the right scarf or headband in California's car, most of the seats are taken when we arrive. The audience consists of mixed demographic chatting within respective groupings. We find some seats a couple rows from the front. There's room for two more people on California's side and two more beside me. We get settled in, tucking our purses by our feet when the only hot guy in the joint—rugged with five-day shadow and wearing *Mack lumberjack hunting coat and jeans* (me:

drooling) with perfectly longish tussled hair—appears before us.

Looking directly at California, Mack Jack asks, "May I sit next to you?" He's clearly interested. *Clearly.* His teeth gleam and he laughs in slow motion as little diamonds twinkle off his perfect Chicklet teeth, the whole room joining in admiring appreciative laughter...Okay, I may be going a little overboard because of my rom-com script I'm (forever) working on, but you get the picture. Anyway, this guy is super good-looking in that ideally masculine, bushman kind of way and I don't exist to him.

California produces one of her naturally-occurring, cheerfully-pure smiles. "Sure."

He starts up a conversation with California right off, but the acoustics aren't great so I can't eavesdrop well. Soon the lights flicker. The show will begin. California looks up. I glance over at Mack Jack, who is gazing at California, and I can't help but smile at this. California reads my smile and blushes and gives me a look that says, "I know, right!" as in, "He's cute."

I'd like to note that I am super happy for my girlfriend because, well, because I'm super happy for anyone who finds love, or even attraction. I may be a lot of things but one thing I'm *not* is jealous of other women— i.e., I'm not catty. This is true despite my offering up some sarcasm for comedic effect or more aptly put, *so you won't totally want to throw shit at me.* Hello redeeming quality! Ha! (For those of you who know me, if I'm completely off the mark on this, please inform me of my illusion.) *Unless, she's working out with my man on his gym membership as +1,* then I deserve a catty concession. (But I still wasn't angry at *her*, so there you have it! Ha! again.)

By the end of the night, I'm swooning over the emphatically-romantic poetry performer—it really is a performance, more than a reading, and his words flow like, well, like poetry! And his whole body moves about and he swoops his arms around and his face goes crazy with animation all within the 6'x8' stage he's confined to and what started out as average in the looks department turns to...*nope, it doesn't turn to anything, he's still average to me.* But he is a great performer and writes some damn fine prose. I'm moved and wonder if I should date a poet, but then there'd be all that drama and swooping and swooning and that's too much melodrama when you include mine. Plus, it's a bit too artsy-fartsy-femme for my liking in a man. Unless, he's a burly redneck and his poetry contains a lot of cussing, then it might balance out. I grew up with a bunch of rough-neck, good-hearted, foul-mouthed lumberjacks so I'm a bit tainted in the "what's masculine" department. I abandon that idea and opt for a Fudgsicle instead.

Rejection #2. I email The Director aka Houdini, the guy who tried to kiss me in a parking garage and fell off the planet thereafter, in the off-chance he's interested in hanging out as friends since I know I'm not "romantically interested"—he does have small hands after all, and you know what *that* means . . . *(wink)*.

I write, "Hey stranger, are you going to the Thursday night event at SAM? Do you want to get a beverage before the show?" (SAM, or the Seattle Art Museum, is running old black and white movies for the month of August on Thursdays, focusing on a different theme with each grouping, i.e., Films Noir or Audrey Hepburn films, etc.)

Two days later he replies, "Will attend, meetings beforehand."

I read the email, mildly let down but not surprised. Was I actually attracted to him or was it the two potent martinis doctored up by the bartender, or was it his mysterious Humphrey Bogart intrigue, or was it that plain old "I can't have you, so now I *think* I want you" thing, or is it the fact that *he's a director and I'm working on a simply fantabulous script, loves?* His four-word reply confirms: he's not that into me. *(shrug)*

He's efficient, I'll give him *credit* for that. I take it in stride. We hadn't had any deep conversations—I met him once and he might have spoken seven words, so it's not like I'm losing a longtime friend! No, this rejection is only a bitty bruise on my ego and possibly film-making adventures, if not film-going. No biggy on the latter, I can comfortably take myself to a movie now!

Nonetheless these put-me-out-to-pastures are adding up in pastry consumption—eek!

Rejection #3. I go to my last resort. In complete masochistic mode, I email the ultimate bad boy, the one I chased but never got—so far?—the one who made me clutch my heart and breathe, "Oh my God," when I saw his photo, the one who has the same sense of humor I do, the one who I really thought "got" me, the one I'd adjust my height requirement for—by half an inch but still—the one I'd consider changing my name for. *The one I've never met.* The Italian. We would have had beautiful babies . . . *Sigh.*

I email him: "Look Mister, I'm not going to marry you and that's final. Stop harassing me. *wink*"

He replies the same day: "Lol. You're funny. I'll give you that."

There is a brief and, for an instant, hopeful (on my part) flutter, followed by empty Internet air (*read:* nothing). *Frown.*

I'm sure all this is good for my growth. (My waistline if nothing else.) Maybe my writing will improve, or I'll become a more intellectually interesting person, or I'll learn to paint with my toes, or take up basket weaving produced from my leg hairs—Lord knows they're long enough. For now, I will work my way through a tray of très bon bonbons and fluffy phyllo, because food loves me, no bones about that. *Mmm, pastry.*

Okay, listen, I could say I don't want an alcoholic or a big nose or yellow teeth or small hands or bad fashion or a limp or goatees (five-day shadow: super sexy) or Merrill shoes or a smoker or a needs attention/validation-er, or a Mercedes driver or too poor or too rich or any number of other dealbreakers, *but that would reveal how shallow I really am, now wouldn't it?* Besides, some of those things are not *really* dealbreakers *on the right guy*—except smoking, I'm sniff sensitive, what can I say?—but sometimes it's easier to use something as an excuse because he's simply *not* the right guy, whether I'm rejecting him or he's rejecting me. Yes, I am erratic and picky and at times superficial, but the reality land reduction is thus: *Mr. Right for me won't be perfect, but he will be perfectly flawed for me,* and I'll know him when my sniffer tells me so.

And! If I *am* egotistical (*sideways glance*), then this rejection phase may be a good thing—not to get my head out of the clouds, I quite like it up here. I'd rather go through life enjoying my own company than settle for someone whose company I don't enjoy daily! Here's the thing: Every guy I've slept with since I was twenty has wanted more, either more sex or "Marry me, Anna," *except* Pete C. Remember him? He dumped me for that older woman (mental register: *emotional turning point*) and even though I wasn't in love with him, it did crush my ego. Thus, I'd determined *that wasn't ever going to fucking happen again.* No, I am not a rock star in bed, but I think I subconsciously only choose to go the randy route with guys who, at my intuitive core, I know won't reject/abandon me—at least not before I get out the door first! Perhaps that's why, in as much as my ego would like these guys to want me, *I never actually really, truly tried to get that kind of attention from them,* because I know they'd only be in ~~it~~ me for a good time, not a long time. *Hello! Neurotic-emotional-safety-mechanism-developed-from-childhood-trauma-reminder-aha* moment! (Truly, we could all save a pile of money on therapy by writing our own memoirs. I'm not even charging for this advice. Unless you count the cost of this book, which is a bargain at twice the price, and also worth its weight in entertainment value. Especially if you got the digital version, which I'm pretty sure weighs nothing.)

(*Note:* My editor is so going to be all over me for that last paragraph, so let me add that lest we forget: the side effect of only going for guys I know for sure won't reject me is closing myself off to potential great guys who also might not reject me, and this vulnerable-inability *is keeping me single, people, single!*) (*Note 2:* Um, there's nothing wrong with being single. [That was in case my editor tells me I'm offending all single people, too, now]. I apologize.) (*Note 3:* That was so Canadian.) (*Note 4:* Wasn't there a disclaimer at the beginning of this book about its offensiveness?? I fucking unapologize.) (*Note 5:* OCD requires a #5. I apologize to my editor for all these notes, xo)

The profile of my Mr. Right: a man who picks dandelions for me on his way home, because even a lowly flowering weed reminds him how he loves me. Oh, and a man who makes me throw my head back, place my hand on my heart, and breathe "Oh my God" when *not* having sex and *not* because of his looks. And who's funny as hell with the right pheromones who will *please* take me trout fishing. That is all. In Jesus' name, Amen!

Cut to next scene: Fat old lady eating a doughnut surrounded by cats.

*

What have I learned? Rejection is good for Taming of the Shrewd Ego. Also, if I don't put out until I'm sure sure sure then I don't run the risk of falling for sexual intimacy masquerading as real love.

Homework: Check lease to find out about pet restrictions. Err, I mean, sit peacefully with this feeling of rejection, let it flow through my body, acknowledge it, write a note to it, allow it to be, talk to it (but not in public), then take a deep breath and let it move on and out. Lick doughnut off fingers.

***

PISSING ALL OVER GOD'S CREATION: NAMELY, MYSELF

I'm heading back to the Great White North for a while. I've been intuiting that my team and real estate clients need me. And, no, there is no evidence or cause for such conclusions. In reality realty land, it's more likely that I miss my team (!) and my clients (?!) and MLM and all this endless and continuous work I'm doing on my screenplay (and myself?)—my outward purpose for continuing this secret life in Seattle—is making me a little homesick. Weird.

In an effort to get as much Seattle in as I can before I leave, I Google "things to do in Seattle for singles." I get 1.6 million page suggestions of all manner of events and how-to-make-new-friends-and-influence-people clubs: "Seattle Singletons," "Mutt Mixer Dog Block Party," "Heavenly Hikers," "East Side Chic Chicks," most of which are on the Meetup website. I browse the profile photos and jotted words in profile bios, uninterested despite a few friend compatible and companionable faces. Still, I figure I'd rather go the organic meet-and-greet-in-the-street approach. The truth is that even beyond my normal introversion, I'm feeling like the non-committal, unwelcome mat because I'm already on the ferry in my mind. I "note to self" that Meetup has potential for when I get back, whenever that might be. Non-committal, remember?

I close my laptop and text California, "Hey, would you feel like going for a hike? Heard there's great hiking in the area." (Might as well work off all those doughnuts before heading "home.")

She replies almost right away with: "Yes! Let's get a group together. How's tomorrow?"

"Perfect! Let's do it, meaning: you gather up the gals, since you're the one with friends lol." Some truth in every joke, right?

"Okay."

I could invite Little Editor to come along, but I know California's gal pals are heavy duty into God and I suspect, perhaps mistakenly, that we all might not be a compatible fit. Let that be a lesson to me: if I want to be included, then I need to give others a chance to be included, too. My bad. I close my laptop, ruminating on my female friendships, sip my latte and smile at the twenty-something college student setting up kitty-corner from me. She smiles back. I take note that I don't feel nervous, which makes me wonder. Maybe I use my fear of female friendships as a crutch to avoid vulnerability with women *when it's convenient for me to do so. Holy shit!* This doesn't make me change my behavior, but *awareness is the first step for crying out loud.*

The Hike

California arranges it. Since she is highly holy, her group consists of card-carrying Christians. I include myself as God-fearing because I did get baptized in the River Jordan, though I'm certainly the only one who has to do any major swear censoring. By the way... I love hiking! Yep, totally true. I know I'm all Louboutin and 4" heels and shopping and shallow but one of the other me's (perhaps the redneck?) loves the forest. Yeah, trees and streams and bugs and all nature's great stuff. Maybe from growing up surrounded by rainforest, maybe simply because I feel God is with me when I'm closest to his most natural creations. And, I'm cool with being a cross-wearing soul, but if you're not, that's cool, too. I'm not one of those holier than thou, haughty, preachy, judgmental, right-wing fundamentalists. Fuck no! (*See?*) Live and let live, I say! Oh, and "fuck" is not a blasphemous swear word. It's simply base and offensive (to some).

Ira Spring to Mason Lake Trail is about fifteen miles south of North Bend, a sentimental little town close to where HBUAB and I used to live and he was arrested, *ah the memories,* and far enough south of Seattle that there's plenty of time to chat on the drive down. I ride with California and two other girls, one I'll call Encyclopedia Fitanica and another I'll call Bellevue Heights. Four single women so, naturally, we talk about men.

I ask, "So who's single here?"

Three different voices answer back, "Me."

Encyclopedia Fitanica is in the back seat (California must have relocated the antique mall to the trunk). She's twenty-seven, Harvard-smart (medical research or some such thing), and a personal trainer to boot, so she's super fit. She adds, "Well, I did meet this one guy, but it's early, so we'll see." She doesn't elaborate and California doesn't ask her to, so I don't press.

Bellevue Heights also sits in the back and is 5'10" with amazing blue eyes and, you guessed it, lives in Bling City. (Bellevue: newish, snobbish city; not my fave, obv.) I discover I like her anyway. Hmph, good to know.

I muse, "I thought everyone from Bellevue had fake nails. And everything else." I recover from my unfiltered comment with, "But you look naturally pretty. Do you like it there?"

She doesn't sound offended. "Yes. I know what you mean but that's downtown. The rest of us are normal."

Curious, I ask, "So do you ladies want a Christian or are you open to other religions or even atheists, wait, is it atheist or agnostic? Anyway, you know what I mean."

California answers, "Christian for sure."

I ask her, "Hey, what happened to Mack Jacket?"

She says, "Not Christian." Then she adds, "Plus, he likes to wear women's clothes sometimes."

Everyone laughs.

Bellevue stays on track. "As long as I can convert him I might be open, but it'd be easier if he is already Christian."

I add, "But not a cross-dressing Christian!"

More laughter. This is fun!

Fitanica pipes in, "Has to believe in God. What about you?"

I ponder briefly before saying, "I'll go with spiritual but not religious. I'd like it if he had the degree of godliness I do, as in he's not going to make a fuss when I swear, but not in vain!"

Fitanica adds, "Shit, I swear sometimes!"

I decline from arguing that our respective penchant for profanity probably isn't on the same plane. My educational history: I've got a certificate for a six-month correspondence course for real estate, I grew up in a small, redneck community, and my daddy was a truck driver. Her history: She went to Harvard, grew up in Boston and Seattle, and her father is a doctor. I suspect I sling swears around a little looser than these ladies do. *But what the fuck do I know?*

We share a lot of laughs and I think to myself that these are the ladies to go out with when searching for a soul mate, their first criteria for a man being that he be a God-fearing, Jesus-following, Bible-reading, churchgoing, serious-as-hell Christian. Fortunately, Christianity is not on my dealmaker list, which I figure leaves me a lot of opportunity for leftovers.

The hike is relatively easy and includes a long, steady incline of 6.5miles through old growth Fir and Cedar and a few Sequoia, dense underbrush, sunlight filtering through pine needles, and high-hanging, neon-green, glowing moss. Ferns and wild huckleberry are sprinkled between the majestic old timers and the smell of damp earth makes my heart yearn for home even more. The walk is quiet, save for the crunch of our hikers on dirt, and sporadic snap of a twig and occasional songbird and our breath and sparse chatting. While Bellevue and California take their time, Fitanica and I lead the pack, marching up ahead with little room for oxygen intake, never mind chitchat. I love the woods but I also want to work on my glutes.

Since I'm fitter than I thought I was, I vow next time to bring a weighted pack (with food in it—Bellevue and I didn't bring any snacks, so we mooch off our new friends—and shit tickets—that's redneck slang for toilet paper). Maybe it's from all the bike riding I manage to include in my unofficial exercise program, since I gave up running after one attempt (part of my "start a new project/hobby/idea and bail soon after" trait and another reason not to commit to groups/clubs/memberships/anything).

When we get to Myra Lake, we rest on the rocks and gaze around silently, stunned by the natural beauty. I put my sunglasses on to shield my sensitive eyes (and hide their misty affliction). The water is glass-flat and deep blue-green, a mirror of whispery clouds reflecting on its surface. I squat down and dip my hand in the frigid water. The chill gives me goosebumps even though I'm flushed from exertion. We remain quiet and awe-struck as we snack on trail mix and flax crackers and salami and olives, all provided by Fitanica.

When we leave, I'm still pumped up with adrenaline and lactic acid and OCD get-the-most-of-this-wilderness-workout and maybe even holy reverence. I haul down the mountain solo and unencumbered and desperate to pee, even though I also didn't bring water. Alas, the trail offers no facilities and I don't have toilet paper. Besides, if I tried to go the dude way, I might risk sitting on a poisonous bush and get a rash on my fanny and then someone would see me and Facebook my ass, literally. So I opt to run faster, figuring the sooner I get to the bottom, the sooner I'll find an appropriately-private pee spot and drip dry before the others catch up. Plus, I'll get an overdose of exercise—woohoo! *Cut to pee scene:* My bladder wins out, or rather leaks out. I clench tighter but I'm running and jarring my peanut-sized internal water bag and too damn dumb to pull over and pull down the gear and be all earthy bush-woman, or at least woman urinating in the bush. *Where's a damn panty liner when you need one?* Maybe I'll dry out by the time my companions arrive? I run faster. Fortunately, God has a sense of humor and makes me hit the ground a little awkwardly as I run, which causes me to sprain my ankle. I hobble the rest of the way in soggy sweats. *Awesome.* When I finally make it to the bottom with wet britches, I go in the outhouse and trickle the last few drops out then deposit my soaked underwear in the hole. There's not much I can do with the pants. I can't very well walk around without them (this isn't the County Fair), so I lay splayed out on a large rock in the hopes that the sun will dry out the rest, even though I'll still smell a little off.

The girls finally arrive and say, "You hauled! Like the wind." Then we get in California's car. Since they're warm from the hike and the weather is balmy, I ask if I can crack open a window. And they're all, "Yes, please!" And I'm praying that the parfum de piss wafts out with the breeze. If the ladies do notice, they save me the embarrassment and don't say a word. I hope God gifts them bonus Christian points for compassion. Remind me to give California a steam clean car package.

I end the day Calamining my rashed-out cookie on my air mattress and elevating my iced ankle on a mountain of pillows. I pray. "Dear Lord, thank you for making the forest, but please add adequate bladder evacuation facilities when you have time. Also, I have one more day left in this country, so please don't let me crap all over myself tomorrow. If it is your will. In Jesus' name, amen."

*

What have I learned?

1. We don't have to be exactly alike to get along.
2. God is everywhere, but it's easier to find him in the mountains when you're out of cell phone range.
3. If you don't believe in God, that's okay. If you have faith in nature, it's probably the same thing.
4. Kegels only work if you work them. Damn it.

Homework: Place singles ad in Seattle Stranger. "MissFit Christian seeks man w/Rover (not the dog), prefer leather interior. And handi-wipes."

***

THE PACIFIC NORTHWEST: A CHURCH, A GALLERY, AND A VIBRATOR

A Church

California invites me to try out another new church on my last Sunday (for a while) here in Seattle. Because I'm still hobbling, she drives, and we miraculously arrive on time. I wonder if this is a sign. The "church" is in a three-story, downtown, red-brick atrium with high ceilings made of glass and offices that boast European balconettes and face the congregation of casually-clad, mostly mid-thirtysomethings. I'm thinking, "Hell, if this wasn't a church service, I might consider man shopping."

We arrive and find California's whole Christian posse lingering near the entrance. I recognize Fitanica and relax. It's a laid back congregation, at least in appearance. I'm introduced to a couple of ladies whose names I forget instantly, perhaps because I'm too excited. I feel as if I'm with the popular crowd in high school, then realize such a thought could be a sin. Crap, I'm so bad at the "be good" stuff. I repent and receive immediate forgiveness. I'm in the House of the Lord, after all, so there's no waiting in line. (Though technically God is omnipresent, his presence *feels more official* in this room with so many Bible iPhone apps.)

When the tall, dark-haired, well-built, mid-thirties, wedding-ring-wearing man makes his way to the pulpit—I'd noticed him hovering in the foyer to greet guests—I have a feeling I'll be paying attention on this biblical visit. Daydreaming about running fig-leaf-free through lavender fields with The Gerry takes a back seat to a hot pastor. That might be a sinful fantasy, but I assure you there are a lot of "Oh Gods" in this Adam and Eve tale. Anyway, the clan has reserved us some fold-out seats about midway up the aisle of the eighty or so attentive attendees.

Church is weird for me. I love God, I believe in God, I believe in Jesus, I pray, I fear, I try to be a good and loving person. Beyond that, though, I always experience some heavy-duty faltering. I don't read my Bible—though I do have one, thanks to MLM—and frankly, I feel like a fraud.

I look around at all the iBible users with their tagged pages and highlighted passages, trying not to look obvious as I download this children's picture version that seems so much more entertaining. California glances over as I'm shaking my iPhone, somehow hoping that doing so will speed up the download. *Why the heaven is it taking so damn long? Am I or am I not in a place with a direct upload to the Lord God Almighty?* The place seems like a cult of which I'm not a member. Actually, it probably *is* a cult, though even the "Cult of Christianity" would be offensive terminology to most Christians. I don't think it's necessarily a terrible thing, being a member of a "be a decent person and leave the world a better place" organization. But, I refrain from pitching my philosophical propaganda to my new friends.

The Pastor is going through some housekeeping memos. "There's a pot luck after service next week at so and so's house" and a "BBQ picnic Bible Study at Myrtle Beach Park..." I immediately wonder if smoking marijuana is a sin, since it's a natural herb after all. Not that I would toke up, but for those that do, this could be a great marketing idea for the Church. Jesus did drink wine at a wedding, or at least he turned barrels of water into wine, so I assume that's as good as condoning, no?

While I ponder the number of times marijuana appears in the Bible, the pastor moves on. I hear a piano playing and everyone stands up to sing, and a big projection screen pops up out of nowhere and shows karaoke-style follow-along words over images of grassy fields and meadows. If MLM knew what thoughts these images trigger, she'd say the devil was tempting me. He's very good at it, by the way. I resist. I stay present and sing under my breath so no one can hear my off-key voice. I can see everyone singing their faithful hearts out, eyes closed, lyrics long ago memorized. *I am a fraud.* Sorry, God. Sorry, Mom.

Anyway, eventually the pastor gets into his message, and though I most certainly can't quote him or the Bible verses from which he plucked these ideologies, I do like the general gist. Basically, the man is the head of the household, and *yes, at first, this gave me the no-fin-way resistance reaction,* but then he continued with something that translated to me like, "But the husband better hold his wife up on a high, sparkly pedestal and protect her ass and adore her and give her shopping spree money out of his hard earned cash or he's not doing his job right *and* even though he has the *final say* (my back is back up like a cornered kitty on this last bit), he also respects his wife so much that he considers her opinions." I can live with that, especially since I added: "The wife ~~mostly~~ always gets her way." He also says something about giving your neighbor a break and loving God doesn't mean life isn't fun. But, by now, the devil has me and I'm in a grassy field with *my husband,* Gerry, again. Whoops.

A Gallery
JP texted me a few days ago to see if I want to go for "that bike ride we never did?" and although I'm hesitant—I don't want to encourage him—I'm also going to be Canada-homebound for an indeterminate amount of time, so I reconsider. *Plus, why should I deprive him of my charming company on my last day here?* And after all, maybe I'll wing-woman him up a girlfriend, somehow! So we are supposed to go for a bike ride, again, but it gets canceled again. This time I cancel because my ankle is still a little sore from the Ira Springs sprain and I don't want to aggravate it. Tonight I have a date with myself (more later) and I want to wear heels.

I text him, "Can't walk, not sure if I can ride. Another time?"

He replies, "Okay."

I feel guilty for putting him off, even though it's for a legit reason. "I could probably hobble around an art gallery if you're up for it?? There's an exhibit at the Henry."

He replies, "Sure. When do you want to go?"

Cut to next scene: JP drives an older VW Rabbit and he motors us over to the Henry Art Gallery to see "The Talent Show." It's all about self-centered media and social obsession, basically, the N-word (narcissist), so it's right up my alley! The exhibit is actually kind of creepy—photography of man squinting through ski mask, a lot of self-portraits and paintings and private letters or pages of someone's diary I'm not interested enough to read (but are probably a lot like the pages of this book), video segments of a woman's last year with leukemia, which I do watch—and that gives me nightmares later, which *I so kneeeew would happen.* At least the art spurs an interesting conversation with JP as I wonder if all artists are narcissists or simply eccentric. It goes like this:

We're looking at a wall-size, modern, abstract painting and out of the blue I tell him, "I *am* shallow."

"No, you're not."

"Really? You don't think so? What about the Range Rover thing? Me wanting a guy who owns one, a black one, in fact."

"Well, I admit I'm only attracted to attractive women so I guess we're even."

"You surprise me, JP."

"I thought about what you said, and although you do buy expensive name-brand shoes, they *are* unassuming, you know, no obvious labels or monograms. You bought them because *you* like them, not to impress others."

"You've given this some thought." I laugh. "But what about the fact that even though I'm not attracted to *every* stereotypically attractive guy, I *have* only been attracted to GQ specimens in the past, so I have two strikes against me."

"All right, then you're half-shallow."

"I can live with that."

He can't help himself. "But Land Rovers are impractical and unreliable, and they are only owned by narcissists." He laughs.

"Okay, I agree a little bit about the 'look at me' quality of it, but what if it was a 1970s model in mint condition? That makes the owner more artsy-eclectic than just plain vain. Anyway, I get your point and do agree with you, but Land Rovers are the only vehicle made (that I know of) that most closely fit my ideal of rugged, manly, and entrepreneur-esque—but only if the guy can truly afford it, even better if he can afford something pricier but chooses this more modest option, which then could even be considered a *humble* choice. Ha! Gerry drives a Land Rover and fits my ideal of rugged and manly. Sorry." (I briefly wonder what The Italian drives. He creeps into my thoughts from time to time.) "And! It's not about money: Porsche, dealbreaker, Cadillac, dealbreaker, Ferrari, way dealbreaker. Right?"

JP frowns. "You're too picky."

I tell him, "All is not lost. You're looking for love and now you have a girl-*friend* who can give you honest advice about women. First thing: you need to figure out what your own dealbreakers are. You're never going to find what you want if you don't know what you *can't* tolerate. And don't be too quick to compromise. No girl wants wishy-washy *and*, realistically, you'll be frustrated trying to be what you're not. Trust me, I know. Don't go for potential." (I'm good at dishing it out, at least.)

"Actually, I'm learning a lot from you," he concedes. "Some of it I don't like. How's that for not agreeing?"

"An excellent start, JP! Though, honestly, I'm not the best catch out there, so don't judge all chicks based on me. I can see you with a nice girl one day."

"You think?"

"Yep yep, for sure."

He smiles to himself.

On the drive home, I switch topics. "What'd you think of the exhibit?"

"Kind of disturbing, and a bit of a letdown. You?"

"Same same, but at least it was something different to do."

"Some of the photographs were intriguing. Guess it takes all types to make the world go round."

"Makes it interesting, for sure."

He drops me off and we promise one another we'll go on a bike ride soon, but there's no pretense or assumption and I feel free and light and, hey, maybe I have made a real guy friend.

A Vibrator

With one evening left before I go back to Canada, I feel Seattle sentimental and look forward to this solo date with myself.

Choosing caution over chicness, I wear flats after all and a real green dress, not cruel—if you know the song by the Bare Naked Ladies, bonus points for you—and take myself to the theatre. (Oh, I see, the subtitle here made you think of a *different* kind of 'me date.' And you think *I* have a dirty mind! Besides, I prefer organic, as in no batteries required. TMI, I know.) The dress is moss-green corduroy with a halter top, fitted bodice, and full skirt that falls below the knee and has, yes, a fabric petticoat! The play is set in the Victorian age and is called *In the Next Room, or The Vibrator Play*. It's about the first medical use of vibrators for women with hysteria. It's hysterical.

The Allen Theatre was converted from a convention center space and seats about four hundred, though maybe only one hundred of us theatregoers sit spread out at this Sunday matinee. The Allen has a central stage and escape routes for actors branching out from its heart and stepped seating and standard fold-down theatre chairs in static-causing plush velvet. Although the building was renovated only a few decades ago, the coved ceiling and crown moldings give it an air of old world.

I feel completely at ease, and not because most of the other cultured folk are seniors and probably happy to see a young face in the crowd. Maybe they can't see me at all and they're simply suffering from hysteria, or possibly dementia?

The essence of hysteria is based on sexual frustration and the play shows an innocent, new age doctor using "the recent advent of electricity to make great advances in this field via a certain medical device," while his curious wife eavesdrops and later, unbeknownst to her husband, self-medicates. I'm not sure if it's the play or the spot-on acting that has me in stitches, or maybe it's watching these old beans chuckle and elbow one another. Either way, all this laughter is a great release, so to speak. Then, I drive myself home and take off my crinoline and give myself a different kind of release, all organic I might add. *wink*

Today, I sit in Essential Bakery and Co., eating an indecent indulgence (phallic phyllo cinnamon stick) and drinking a latte. I'm going home to Canada today. I'll miss you, Seattle.

*

What have I learned?

1. I like God's idea of a husband, or at least the cute pastor's interpretation of it, or at least my interpretation of the pastor's interpretation.

2. Not all Jewish boys are religious, which has nothing to do with going to the Henry Art Gallery exhibit, but it does relate to religious themes and relationships, which is sort of related to "relations," which is the old-fashioned way of talking about sex and I need it to tie in with #3, so let's say I relearned that I won't be having relations with JP, but we may have a real friend relationship. (Just go with it.)

3. Dildos reduce sexual frustration (according to modern science).

Homework: Either invest in "the advent of certain medical devices" or get a wrist brace lest I develop carpel tunnel syndrome, which would suck, especially the explaining to the doctor part. Then again, do they still prescribe vibrators? And is one covered by my coveted Canadian medical plan??

***

PART FIVE: WINDING DOWN
SEATTLE SHENANNAGINS

MY KNIGHT IN SHINING ARMOR: STEVE HARVEY

It was a day of almosts. I *almost* didn't make it to the ferry to the mainland in time and I *almost* didn't get back into the USA, Home of the Free, at all. *Flashback to yesterday.* I'm nearing the Peach Arch U.S. Border Crossing at 5:30pm PST. I've been on the phone the whole time with my ex-husband, Good Man, who's working on developing a multi-unit project that means over thirty-five listings and I know I'm going to lose cell signal soon. I slow down and pull into the right lane as blue-haired Canadians speed past me in rented motor homes. If the Police are going to catch me talking on a cell phone while driving, I might almost be able to say I was pulling over *for the last twenty miles.*

Good Man says, "Now that the plans are in [to the building department at City Hall], I need a marketing plan."

I answer, "I can do this. How long before you break ground?"

He tells me while I calculate whether or not I'll need to be there for the presentation of the marketing plan or if he'd perhaps appreciate it emailed, to save him time, of course. *Sideways glance.*

I continue confidently, "I can have it ready by the end of the week. I'll email it." I'm using "the assumptive close." That's realty lingo for making like it's going to happen, even though I'm really only hoping and praying

179

it's going to happen.

I stop breathing while I wait for his reply—another rule of realty thumb is you can never be the first one to break the silence. "He who speaks first loses." (That's another sales tip for you.) I'm inching closer to Customs, finger-tapping on the steering wheel, and my cell phone is starting to crackle. He has trusted me to manage the sales and marketing, probably because he doesn't know how much time I'm spending in Seattle.

"Okay," he finally says in a tone that's more questioning than affirmative.

I know what he's thinking—of course I do, we were together nearly thirteen years!—so I fess up, "I'm on my way to Seattle. In fact, I'm almost at the border crossing so I'm going to cut out soon. You know everything I do is by Internet now. And you know, or at least suspected, that I've been back and forth for a while and I'm doing everything I always have been."

I know he knows because CWAD is his brother and works with me on his development projects. And CWAD is so chick that he sucks with such secrets, which in this case is understandable.

Good Man finally replies, "You're sure you can live in both worlds?"

"Yes! Even though I'm taking advantage of these travel escapades, I have been doing this for several months and you know best my work ethic and marketing talents, if I may be so confident."

He sighs and acquiesces, "True." Though I can tell he's still uncertain.

Always quick on my feet, I mention Tom Skerritt in short order, knowing this celebrity is something of an icon to my ex. "Did I mention Tom wants to meet again about my script?" This could be a slight exaggeration, since "wants to meet again about my script" actually means Tom emailed me at least a month ago with: "Hope the writing is going well! Keep at it. Enjoy the process :)" *But that's practically the same thing.* Plus, this helps me pretend that he (Tom) hasn't long since forgotten all about me. (He probably has.) After all, I'm only using his name. Good Man loosens up but I can hear hesitation.

I enlist . . . *Realty Lady.* "Bottom line. The marketing has improved, wouldn't you agree?"

He can't argue. "Well, I guess."

Realty Lady presses, "Is that a yes?"

"Okay, yeah."

"You sure?"

"*Yes.*"

"And sales are up, aren't they?"

"True."

"So I've been *more effective* since I've been gone. Would you be willing to consider that possibility?" I refrain from suggesting he'd probably net a profit by sending me on a paid holiday to Bora Bora, because I don't think he'd buy it, and really, *as if I'd be working on a marketing plan if I was in Bora Bora!*

He concedes, "All right, all right, get going kiddo, email me the marketing plan." (I told you he was nice. Thank you, Good Man, for letting it slide.)

Off the phone at last, I arrive at the border station at 6:00pm PST, to find a cranky, Caucasian, middle-aged, overweight officer frowning at me. He kind of has that serial killer look. I'm a little frightened. Even though he's a little heavy and old for the standard profile. *Maybe he's a retired serial killer turned Custom's Officer!* (After my experience with him, I think I'd preferred meeting up with him in his former occupation.) He moves excessively slowly, not because he can't move any faster, I'm sure, but because he wants to inconvenience me and establish his dominance.

Cranky demands: "Passport."

I give it to him. He scans it in.

"Where you going?"

"Seattle."

"What are you doing there?"

"Holiday."

Looks at his screen. Squints. "What do you do for work?"

"Realtor." I can tell he already knows this.

"You work in the States?"

"Just for my work back home." I pause then add, "I'm not doing anything wrong, am I?"

"I don't know."

I'm thinking unkind thoughts at this point, but am trying not to let that show. My pretend easygoingness with this interrogation seems to bother him more.

"Give me your keys," he instructs. (I hand them over.) "When was the last time you were in the U.S.?"

"A couple of weeks ago."

"Reason?"

"Holiday."

"You take a lot of holidays."

"I try to get down—" I begin, but he's already walked away, "*once a month...*" I trail off.

He chats with a female border guard somewhere behind my vehicle. I know they aren't in a business meeting because I can see from the rear-view mirror that he's smiling and gesturing with his hands. Basically, he's making me wait while he chats it up. He knows this. It pleases him. A while later, he turns his attention back on me, his smile immediately replaced by a frown. He opens my trunk. He finds a foam mattress pad and a vacuum cleaner. (Thanks, Mom!) He walks around the car and opens the passenger door and looks at the passenger seat, where my computer bag sits on top of my diary and the latest book I borrowed from Sultry Sage, *Act Like a Lady, Think Like a Man*, by Steve Harvey. (Thanks, Sultry!) He points at my laptop bag.

"What's in there?"

"My laptop."

"You use it for work?"

"Yes. And writing."

I'm getting a little miffed at this point, but continue to act the chipper little bird, which seems to piss him off more. *But I can't help myself.* He closes the door and I grab my iPhone and wait.

"Put that down."

"Sorry."

He goes back inside his booth, types a novella of notes into his computer, then gives me a slip and directs me to Inspections. I go in, wait in line another forty-five minutes, along with the requisite East Indians, (pardon me, "Middle Easterns"), Chinese (pardon me, "Asians"), and a couple of hippies. Fifteen service counters are unoccupied. Apparently, the guards like to take their breaks together. What a team. Hurray.

A few officers finally come back in and take their places, among them Cranky Border Guard. ("I am Zen, I am Zen...," I repeat over and over in my head.) He doesn't open his wicket until it's my turn. But, alas, the officer about to assist the turban-wearing East Indian couple in front of me leaves his desk and so the couple is redirected to Cranky, who looks disappointed to miss out on torturing me even more, and I can see him stamping the passports of this Taliban couple as fast as he can in the hopes of still having his chance with me. (This is probably the fastest these people have ever made it through since 9-11. *And she so could be transporting a weapon of mass destruction in that stroller!*)

Another officer opens up and calls me over. I suppress a joyful squeal. The new guy—an *African-American*—is as round as he is tall, which is actually not that tall. He wears a nice smile, and appears to be of a kind disposition. I watch as he reads Cranky's recently-posted prose about me and asks me the same questions Cranky did, though in a very different tone of voice. A *kind* tone of voice. I explain my situation. Again. He says something funny. I laugh, stealing a glance at Cranky.

Cranky quickly finishes with his East Indians (their lucky day) and comes over to my officer, whispering something. The officer looks at me, surprised, and then asks me to go sit down for a moment. I do. I watch them have a discussion. Cranky hasn't looked directly at me, not even once, but I can feel his unwelcome attention. I'm called back. My officer looks apologetic.

"Do you have your keys?"

"They're in the car."

"This will only take a minute."

I sit down again. Cranky accompanies the officer to my vehicle. Time passes by. A new batch of risky-looking people waits in line. I'm the only one who speaks clearly-understood English. The officer comes back and calls me over.

"And you're not selling real estate in the USA, right?"

"No way."

"No brochures or marketing material with you?"

"Nope."

"Just clothes, um, and a vacuum cleaner. Lots of people have vacation homes, right?"

My officer nods amicably. "Right."

We look at each other and share an understanding: *Cranky is out to get me.*

"You a fan of Steve Harvey?"

I cock my head to the side for a minute then laugh—a spontaneous, genuine, from-the-gut laugh. They found the book! I immediately look over at Cranky. His forehead is furrowed into a tight knot, his mouth terse.

"Yes. Yes, I *am* a fan of Steve Harvey."

Turns out so is the officer—he used to work at the comedy club where Mr. Harvey got his start and drove him back and forth from the airport.

The officer says, "If it makes any difference, he's a good guy. But that was a long time ago (referring to Harvey)."

"Then he's probably still a good guy. People's characters generally don't change."

I glance at Cranky. He's not looking at me, so I can safely squint at him. I smile at my officer. He smiles back. It's over. He hands me my "get out of Canada free" card.

I walk toward the exit, passing Cranky's wicket. As much as I want to kick Cranky's ass wearing tight leather pants (me, not him) Lara-Croft style, I'm afraid he'll kick *me* back into my own country, so I don't give him the acerbic grin I'd really like to flash him. I do, however, hold my head up high and act smugly self-satisfied. It's now 8:00pm PST.

Thank you, Cranky, for new writing material. Thank you, Mr. Harvey, for writing the book, *Act Like a Lady, Think Like a Man,* and for being a good man so my officer could also be so inspired. Thank you, Sultry, for lending me the book.

In my book, black is the new black.

*

What have I learned? Lying is a dealbreaker. Stretching the truth to clear customs is damn near mandatory.

Homework: Practice my "acting" chops (*read:* fibbing) for my next At the Border scene!

* * *

JUST FRIENDS: ORDERING OFF THE MENU

I'm bored one night and since I've spent quite a bit of time with California and Little Editor and don't want to be "the needy girl friend," I decide to reach out to some potential male friends. Instead of accusing them, I'm giving them another chance! This is my man-aha-moment, and it makes sense: Treat men like the boys we've always known them to be! Yes! Encourage positive behavior with praise, not criticism. If only I'd thought of this sooner. But still, better late than never. So assuming the best—that men are capable of having real female friendships—I text JP, the one guy I was able to guile for a while into hanging out, and whose company and conversation I genuinely appreciated.

I open with: "Hey! Long time no see, speak, etc. Busy?" No reply.

Half an hour later, giving the benefit of doubt with a slight pout, I email him. No reply.

Undefeated, I give benefit of doubt to other duds (no spelling error): "Hey! Long time no see, speak, etc. Busy?"

Dead air.

In all fairness, my phone eventually buzzes as I'm dozing off to sleep. It's JP. "Hi. Sorry, my dad's in town. Maybe next time."

There's not even a smiley face—in the text or on my face, nope, full-on pout now—so I turn my phone off and nod off. *Sigh.*

The next day, I text CWAD BMFF at the crack of way too damn early:

"Hey! Long time no see, speak, etc. Busy? ☺" (Maybe it was my fault for not putting in a smiley face first.)

I wait.

Tap, tap, tap.

Nothing.

I repeat the exact same text but with double smileys.

He replies, "Sleeping."

I frown. "Not anymore!" (Cheerfully, though of course he can't know this.)

"What's up?"

CWAD is clearly a crusty morning creature, but then again, I guess most people don't get up before the sun.

"No one wants to be my friend."

"You're a peach lol."

"☹"

"I'll call you in an hour. I need java."

"☺"

And what about him? The exception to the rule. No, of course not. He's a heterosexual man after all. (Remember, again *When Harry Met Sally?* Yeah, it's still true.) But for 1. He's my ex-brother-in-law and we have been in the like-a-cousin category for so long, it feels wrong; and for 2... There is no 2.

Where am I going with this? Oh, right, here's what I think:

1. Real, true, honest-to-goodness, heterosexual male/female friendships *devoid of sexual tension* are very rare, at least in the age group in which both parties are still interested in sex. *Cases in point:* I haven't heard back from The Director or JP. *Yet, they thought I was ever so interesting back before they knew they wouldn't get a crumb of my cookie,* which is slang for va-jay-jay, which is slang for vagina, which is actually inaccurate since the vagina is only the inside bits, so really it's slang for vulva, which is the whole damn hair pie (which is 70s slang).

2. Male/female *friendships* can also be dangerous. What keeps us from crossing that line when things get bumpy with no humpy at home? I've always been a proponent of propriety and appropriateness. And how do we know what's appropriate? We just do! *Cases in point:* I know a married couple in the industry. Both husband and wife are having an affair—with a husband and wife that started out as a couple friend! When those couples stopped copulating with each other, they started getting it on with their buddies. And though I haven't been in these situations,

I have been led into temptation in another situation, so I speak from experience. Once. But that was enough.

3. Intention is the key and the only person who knows our intention—aka conscious or subconscious agenda, really—is ourselves. So, we need to monitor ourselves. *Case in point: Let's say we hire a cute-ass, go-go dancing, fast-typing assistant who is smart and dainty-fingered and we totally get a boner for her because she's also kind of clumsy. Is it a good idea to go for lunch every day with this employee?* And to help her through "he's not good enough" boyfriend problems? Survey says: *No fucking way.* We know we're doing the right thing if it feels right. Yes, that's it! We can be doing the exact same thing with two different sets of circumstances, but the *agenda* could be completely innocent or completely not. All we have to do is ask ourselves how we'd *feel* telling our better half what we are up to. And if we're reluctant to do that or if we find ourselves looking for ways to justify/explain/rationalize/sidestep/hide/fib/meet-at-the-gym-with-our-partner-who-we-usually-don't-even-work-out-with-at-a-different-fucking-time-than-our-hot-ass-assistant, then that's probably a little internal signal trying to tell us somethin' somethin'. So we gots to figure it out, fix it, or gets out! (Yeah, yeah, easier said than done sometimes.)

I'm thinking about HBUAB when CWAD calls me. "What's up?"

I jump right in, "Why can't men and women be friends?" He cackles but before he can reply, I continue. "No wait, I already know the answer to that one. Let me come up with something new. Was it my baggage or his that messed us up?"

"I've only had one coffee, can you give me a little more to go on?"

"I was thinking about how couples end up cheating and if it's to do with insecurity or what?"

"Uh, I kind of need a reference point."

"Hmm, I'm on a thinking rant about happiness in a relationship. Each party should do his part, if there's problems, work it out and get happy, or get where you *can* get happy because if you're not happy then your partner's probably not that happy either [I sing] *with or without you* [by U2]."

"Which one is this about?" He's trying to follow along but even I can't follow where I'm going with this.

"I'm trying to say that if it's your deal, and by you I mean someone/anyone, then same thing: you're—*I'm*—best to figure it out and get happy—because if it *is* me, then I be taking me to the next deal. And in this case, by *me* I mean anyone!"

I can hear him sip his coffee. "You've totally lost me."

I'm in full rant mode. "There's no right or wrong, by the way. It's what's right and wrong for us and our partner, and we *know know know* what that is because we can maybe get away with justifying/explaining/ rationalizing/sidestepping/hiding/fibbing to our partner, but we can't really fool our self!"

"Did you sleep with [HBUAB]?"

The mention of HBUAB jars me to attention, "Huh? What? No! I'm frustrated that no one wants to be my friend. I'm still having a hard time connecting with female friends here, mostly because I'm not *really* trying but still, and the guys I meet all disappear when they find out I'm off the market, as in not interested in romancing their bone." I take a deep breath and let out a big sigh, then crack my neck.

Now that he's on solid, familiar ground he says, "It's hard being you." He laughs. I sigh again and he continues. "You're an infectious person, Anna. For women, you're beautiful and smart and successful, probably a little intimidating. And guys want a part of that, but they aren't going to hang around while you dangle the carrot if they can be making a connection with someone who will give them the carrot. And I don't mean sex."

In a small voice I answer, "I know. I don't mean to dangle."

"Of course not. You don't have to *do* anything. Women hold all the power. And you have a special way of being arm-candy fluff but also smart. What guy who likes a chick is going to hang around with her knowing he's never getting anything? Of course he'll move on. We've got tender egos." He laughs.

"But I'm fun and funny and could make a good wing-woman," I plead.

"Hey, we're all here just looking for love. Gotta let them move on so they can find it."

I pout. "Well, I don't like it."

"Welcome to life, cupcake." So far still no word from any of my so-called male friends.

*

What have I learned?

1. In my world, tension will always exist between two parties in the same sexual preference zone, unless that tension has been "relieved." (No idea how long, but I could make up a statistic of, say, seven years. Sure, let's use that.) But, no sense in throwing out the boy (or girl) with the

bathwater!

2. When I get off track from my own values, it doesn't feel good. If I'm with someone who makes me feel unhappy a lot of the time, red flag, red flag! Remind me of this, pleeease! (Note: No one can actually *make* me feel a certain way, that's up to me—my perceptions, interpretations, internalizations. Yeah, yeah, yeah. But! Other people's actions so can trigger my internal reactions. And! Those actions/reactions are valid. That's right, fuckers! Uh, "fuckers" isn't directed at you. It's for those who trigger me. Unless, that's you, then it is directed at you!) (But I still love you as a person.) Frown.

3. There are no wrong decisions, only experiences, and everything in life is conspiring to lead me to my greater good, greater happiness, greater purpose. And if I'm wrong, so what! My choice of thought keeps me happy (usually). Yeah, that's it! Pollyanna has left the building.

Homework:

1. Accept my-world male-female dynamic.
2. Reread book: *How To Get Happy, Dammit* by Karen Salmansohn. She's so funny! And wise.
3. Avoid the impulse to ask direct questions about male intentions. Example: Starting a conversation with, "Do you just want to have sex with me?" could be misinterpreted.

***

SELF-DESTRUCTIVE BEHAVIOR: HURT PEOPLE HURT PEOPLE?

Right after my last learning pause on male-female my-world relationships, I'm tested on it. Was it the getting up at 3am, the long drive back from Seattle to Canada, the tummy ache, or the truth in what he said that made me break down into a sobbing mess, toss my neatly-hung dress into the suitcase (hanger and all), and evacuate his home in haste?

"You're really going?"

"You always make me feel so shitty"—*sob*—"why do I keep trying . . ."

Handsome Millionaire (HM), a "devoted subscriber," had read my most recent blog post on male/female relationships in which I complained about how all the men I meet want more than friendship. In response he confronts me with, "You like the attention, that's why you attract it."

"Why do have to be like that? All pissy and angry?" I retort.

"I'm not." He matter-of-factly states. "You like attention and you ask for it, then you come here and complain about it."

He seems confused as to why this isn't obvious to me, but I'm worked up and can feel my internal furnace raging. I'm affronted and don't know how to defend myself and so ensue the (unexpected) tears.

I know he's right. But it isn't *what* he says, but *how* he says it. (I know that's what everyone says, but this time it's really true!) Yes, I admit, I enjoy my own form of validation. But I already admitted that like thirteen thousand blogs ago and he's a damn subscriber! (Remember the "three fingers pointing back" theory? Yeah, that's right, if you spot it, you got it. Tricky theory, isn't it?) Whether or not he knows it, he likes validation, too. Everyone does! And either way, his judgment hurts. He is the only man on the planet who *makes me* cry like this, either because he's the only one who is this brutally honest ([*cough*] like me) or he's the only one I let be this brutally honest, because even though sometimes I want to punch him in his sweet-smelling throat, I actually do appreciate ~~brutal~~ honesty. HM and I dated awhile back, before I dated HBUAB, and we somehow managed to remain friends after we broke up. (Or maybe it's more like friend*ly*, hmm.) Once you get rid of sexual tension—by going there, say—I think men and women maybe can be friends, *as long as the allure is gone gone gone for both parties.* (I *assume* this is the case with me and HM.) So all I have to do to make real male friends is to sleep with every nice guy I meet and then call it quits! If only ~~it~~ I were that easy.

Anyway, I somehow thought he'd be a comforting refuge on my way home to Canada, so I stopped by Vancouver to see him. He still manages to get me riled up to no end, much as he did when we were dating, this time with his discussion about "how stupid you were" to be with HBUAB in the first place. This puts me over the edge. To his credit, it doesn't take much given the emotional state I'm in at the moment: sadly disappointed in the male gender and perhaps myself as well, for believing I could so easily find a real friend therein—or, more likely, it's PMS and *he should somehow know this and appease me with chocolate.* For someone with a genius IQ, this is pretty simple stuff, as in you'd be dumb not to be able to figure it out. (HM, don't get mad at me for calling you dumb, everyone knows it's a joke, or they do now, plus I gave you props for being brainy, so *bite me!* xo)

I go down to the lobby—he lives in *the* residences of this uber-rich building—and wait for the valet to bring my vehicle around. Still sniffling, I find a seat on a marble bench across from the open jazz lobby bar. I'm wearing a hat and an inappropriately warm sweater since I have a circulation condition that would put me in a parka in a Paraguay summer. Mascara sneaks out from under my sunglasses and runs down my cheeks as my chest heaves with sobs that do *not* go unnoticed. Well-dressed patrons saunter and stare. I'm sure they're wondering if they should lend a hand but then reconsider, possibly in an effort to save me from added embarrassment, but more likely to get a good seat near the piano. All I can think is that HM would be completely distressed to be seen with me now. This gives me some satisfaction and I sit up a little straighter.

The valet delivers my car and I get in and drive to the ferry, the last leg of my trip north. (I had planned on camping in the spare room of HM's lavish pad for a night, but, alas, I need the comfort of cozy familiarity and safe surroundings after that conversation.) I do two things to make myself feel better: first, call CWAD BMFF, and second, I text The Italian. Ironically, these actions are practical opposites.

CWAD BMFF tells me what basically comes to "I'm okay you're okay." That I'm not a bad person for enjoying the attention and "it's not your fault you're infectious, it's too bad for the suckers that don't know any better." (*Translation*: Buyer beware.)

"But, it bothers me that he [HM] thinks that of me."

"But even if you do like attention, so what?"

(This is why I need the male perspective.)

Then, The Italian. *The* Italian—who hasn't called, texted, or so much as sent a smoke signal in at least a week. (*Translation*: Not interested. Which I forgive him for only because we still haven't met and live 3000 miles apart.) Just a reminder of the full short story with The Italian, as there's not much to be told: We have occasionally and randomly emailed each other in between our respective relationships and since said relationship statuses have nary been mutually single, *until now*, our communications have been sparse. Indeed, other than my initial lustful infatuated reaction upon seeing his photo all those years ago (and *possibly* using his face as a screensaver for the better part of a year—*in between relationships, of course*), I've hardly thought about him. (That's the honest to My Lord and Savior Jesus Christ truth of it.)

Completely out of character for what he's used to, but not out of character for my nutcase condition, I text him: "I'm mad at you." Followed by another winner: "Why can't we be friends?" and "Stop harassing me!" and a few others I needn't humiliate myself with here.

I'm busy typing my rant when he calls—he must be bored—but we don't get to talk long because I'm now on the ferryboat and reception turns crappy. Before we get disconnected, I am able to throw in, "Even though I'm not going to marry you because there's way too many dealbreakers." I think he laughs before the signal cuts out.

I feel better. Sort of. In a surface kind of way that's good enough to keep the leaking tears at bay, but not good enough to stop me from eating a bag of caramel popcorn (let's see...12g of fat x 4 servings...equals definitely not 115 anymore).

In all fairness, I do know what my blog reads like and book (my editor constructively reminds me on every other page), especially for those who don't know me from my geeky youth. But I do leave some things out, either to protect the innocent or simply for laughies, and HM, who *does* know me (inside and out I might naughtily add), *is* right about a few things. But I'm still disappointed. And if he said it to get my goat, then he's being unkind and greedy! Because he can bloody well afford to get his own damn goat.

Now, if I can *just* resist contacting The Italian again and live off the last echo of his hearty laugh, that might be enough to balance out the thousand calories of popcorn...

*

What have I learned? It's probably not the best idea to cry on my ex's shoulders about my man problems, even if said ex is supposedly a "friend" now, and was hardly really an ex anyway. So, given those details, I say this rule *technically* doesn't count. But since *I'm* not a meanie, I will give him the benefit of the doubt and count our random when-he-was-in-(my)-port sex acts as an official relationship! (*You're welcome, HM. xo* [I can practically hear him saying, "Bite me!" while he reads this, therefore...]

P.S. Thank you for reading this! xoxo.)

Homework: Cry on girlfriends' shoulders. They're softer (dual meaning).

End note: Thank you, HM, for being lovingly, brutally honest. Despite the tears, I appreciate it and apologize for sullying your posh lobby!

*⁎⁎

RETAIL THERAPY WITH BONUS: FIREMEN IN THE PLAZA!

Speaking of friends from Canada, I'm now back in Seattle when Leggy Blonde comes for a visit. We spend our first day (and second and third) shopping or, rather, walking endlessly on hilly downtown streets in inappropriate footwear (*read*: four-inch pumps) to shop for "I'll never live without it" must-haves (*read*: forgettable, "we already have four hundred" similar items) from stores we frequent at home in Canada (Club Monaco, lululemon). We spend the fourth day (and fifth and sixth) walking endlessly in more inappropriate footwear to return said items. By the seventh day, we have sore feet, toned calves, Ibuprofen and Tylenol in our pockets, and have to accept the fact that the streets of Seattle are not meant for heels. (By the way, I have no idea how we got to seven days since she is only here for maybe three. Whatever, let's go with it.)

Leggy *lives* in heels—this bumpy, groovy, brick-paved, cobblestoned city does not match her style. It doesn't match mine either, but I've chosen to walk my own way: dress up in clothes, dress down in low heels. (Except for when Leggy is here so I don't look like a turnip beside her.) But, I have to agree, as far as people-watching for fashionista divas is concerned, Seattle is rather dull. Alas, I swallow my disdain and suggest Bellevue. At least we'll be able to style-watch.

Bellevue Square and downtown Bellevue, Friday late morning: crickets. Where are all the shallow, vain people (aside from us)? The overdone Vancouver-esque girls with the fake nails, hair, and skin that I promised? The overtly-displayed Louis Vuitton and Gucci handbags? Armani-suited men in fancy cars? There's no one to see at all, let alone make fun of, err, I mean *be inspired by.* Apparently, either the economy really *is* down or we somehow missed the witching hour.

We give up and go for lunch at a top Zagat-rated restaurant. It fits Bellevue well: white tablecloths, tuxedoed waitstaff, freshly-baked bread, sterling flatware, $125-per-plate Chateau-Briand. The one and only John Howie Steakhouse, OMG. I chow down the best, juiciest, messiest burger ever. Its fluids run between my fingers and over my hands, and the whole wicked experience costs me less than twenty dollars. (The gloved bus boy discreetly hands me another starched napkin.) I am in bliss.

It's a low-key, girl-bonding, catch-up kind of weekend. We haven't done a night out yet by Saturday and we figure writing material is in order. But, somehow, we can't rev ourselves up. We go out anyway and Leggy, in an effort to be more outgoing and friendly toward men (after a little liquid courage at chez moi), chats up the vagrants on the sketchier streets of downtown. No idea how we got here. These homeless are of the unfortunate class (yes, there's even hierarchy herein) that sport L'eau de Hobo, aka stale urine. (*Note:* Even though I peed all over myself on that hike, *it was only the one time.*) Clearly, she's not trying to get a date, so we call it practice, and I tug her away.

Leggy says, "I'm in the big city of Seattle, shouldn't we be living it up? Where are all the good looking, business-suited men?" (Did I mention she's separated from her beau? No? Well, she is. *Insert:* sad friend and sad face.)

I answer, "At home with their wives and their kids. Sorry."

She's nonplussed. "Try again tomorrow?"

And we both acknowledge that we'd rather be home in bed. Well, she's actually on air mattress and I'm on sofa.

The next morning, we find men in suits, if a Fireman uniform counts as a suit. Said firemen show up with fire truck(!) at the Madison Park Starbucks (for coffee). I'm on them like white on rice, while JP sits nearby with his new belle, who I notice nothing about because her back is to us and I'm focused on the firemen. JP pretends not to see us. *Tsk.* Requisite photo taken with the firemen and we move on.

Later, while Leggy shops ("2nd floor sale ALL shoes, 6 pairs!"), I wait in the plaza by the fountain and watch banner-waving Jesus fans preach to passersby. I talk to a bandana-and-leather-chaps-wearing, tattooed preacher about the devil and why I don't believe in him/her/it. "Then we'd all have an excuse now, wouldn't we?" *Raised eyebrow—at him.*

That's when the Seattle Fire Department medic van pulls up with lights ablaze and two firemen run out to help a cracked-out criminal with a headache. My alert flag goes up. I notice one of the dudes is the hottie fireman from the Seafair Parade! All that banner waving did do something, thank the Lord!

When the rescue head case seems saved, the firemen head back to the van. I excuse myself from Bandana Man and text Leggy: "Hurry up, firemen in the plaza!" then run across the plaza.

"Firemen, hellooo!" They can't hear me over the fountain. I try again. *"Medic! Mediiic!"*

This gets their attention. I explain my need for a photograph of myself with them next to their emergency vehicle, and ask if they'll wait five minutes for Leggy Blonde. (I refer to her as such.) They look at each other.

I coax with: "How many people will really die in the next five minutes?"

They look at each other, eyebrows raised. I check my phone. Nothing. They look at each other.

I relent and ask a tourist to take my photo with them—half-evidence at least. Then they leave. While waiting for Leggy, I admire the photo. Wait a minute. Zoom in: my fly is down *and* I have camel-toe. Lovely. When Leggy arrives, all that's left is the soon-to-be-camel-toe-cropped photo and a brochure-waving Bandana Man.

We go back to my place, nap, follow up with more walking (in requisite heels), then look for a loungy, low-light restaurant-bar-type place. We want a mature crowd but one that's not *too old*. We hit up on several that don't meet muster and end up at El Gaucho, which fits the bill but now we're tired. So we drink champagne we can't afford, eat salads we can, and head home.

There's a lot of girl talk, about the ending of her relationship and whether or not I'll give up my day job(!). (More on that in the next chapter.) We use up our daily allotment of words and then some. Somehow, even with controlled shopping, we still manage to spend too much money. We could have sat at home and had a conversation about the directions of our lives, vulnerabilities, and fears, but then that wouldn't have had the potential for drama, fun, adventure, and prose. And sometimes, when your BFF is going through a separation, what's needed is some not-too-serious distraction.

Conclusion? Seattle is not the fashion capitol of the world, but we're going to walk tall and proud in our four-inch heels anyway. There's no such thing as Prince Charming[1], but we're going to have fun pretending there is until Mr. Not Perfect But Just Right shows up. Running away from stress at home doesn't make it go away, but we're going to run away anyway because the activity recharges the batteries. *Shopping therapy works even if you return everything!* And finally, human connection is vital and friendships are especially important, so cultivate, nourish, and cherish them.

P.S. I Googled the hottie fireman. Not only did he make the Seattle Fireman Calendar cover *twice*, he's also a card-carrying Christian!

P.P.S. I sent a photo of said fireman to California: "Present for you. He's Christian!"

God helps those who help their friends.

∗

What have I learned? Shoes make for superb therapy even when they kill your feet. Dressing up *feels good.*

Homework: Create any-day, every-day occasions to wear my fashionista inspirations! For me.

∗∗∗

[1] According to the book *Prince Harming Syndrome* by Karen Salmansohn, Mr. Right For Me *is* going to be a Prince Charming. Yay! (Dear Lord, please read the aforementioned book. You know my delivery address. Thank you in advance, amen.)

A PAUPER OR A PRINCESS: WILL WRITE FOR SHOES

So, if I do decide to quit my day job and become a literary artist, then I'd better return those Jimmy Choos to Nordstrom A-sap. In other words, writing doesn't pay. (Yet?)

Last year, I said I was done with real estate at twenty years. Twenty years comes at the end of this month. Eek! I had hoped to have transitioned into a *paid* writing career by then, so that I could leave on a high note. As it turns out, my day job is costing me $$ every month. My working expenses are so high—remember I pay for all marketing costs and an assistant—and sales are so slow with the turn of the market that I'm falling behind. Is this a message from the Big Guy? Maybe "God is dropping a piano," as MLM likes to say. Could it also be that my no way, never competitive, always totally cooperative, land pimp, real estate agent associates are catching on to my "secret agent" life (*read*: never being around) and spreading the word, causing my clients' loyalties to falter? Bad real estate agents! Though I'd hoped not, I've already had word from the team that it is so. Fucking realtors. *Sigh*, well, I guess they've got to eat, too. *Still, fucking hungry vulture realtors!*

How can I transition fully? I could sell my house, pay off the investment rental back home, and live like a pauper, but then where *would* I live? HM!

A girl can dream. I text him out of the blue.

"Can I crash at your place for a year?"

"Who is this?"

"Haha, very funny. It's over 5000sqft and you're never there, you wouldn't even notice me!"

"No, really, who is this? I lost my BB [Blackberry] and all my contacts."

I tell him it's me.

"No."

Okay, fine.

I could bunk at my sister's, but it's already pretty cozy there with my mom, brother, sister-in-law, brother-in-law, nephew, and the two kids my sister fosters. (She's been a government-sponsored foster parent of the most unruly teens for over twenty years—and I think *my* job is stressful. Though, honestly, some days it's *practically the same thing*, I assure you!) Mind you, she does have a big yard. I could live in a tent! Or a teepee! (Way cooler! And colder. Hmm, rethinking...)

I could get a roommate! But then I'd still have my house.

An idea flashes through my mind. I could travel.

Yes! I could travel! Housesit the world over. Become a gypsy! Thank you, ridiculous real estate expenses, because I now have enough air miles to travel the world (in coach, but still).

I'm in Starbucks for tea ($2.25), not my usual latte ($4.00+)—no better time than the present to start watching the budget—thinking about my girl time with Leggy. I realize that I have been talking myself out of making more Seattle friends not because I'm a scaredy-chicken, which is only a little bit true still, but maybe because I've already got some amazing gal pals that are kind of hard to measure up to. If only I could transport them down to Seattle. But then again, if I'm going to be a gypsy traveler, that wouldn't really work out either. My self-reflection is interrupted by a call from my mom.

"Hi Dolly, I think you should rent your house . . . and take a sabbatical . . ."

"Hi Mom, are you okay?"

"Oh yes, but I thought I should tell you."

"Um, okay, thanks. I was thinking of gypsy travelling . . ."

"Or join a Christian dating site. I have to go but I wanted to tell you. Okay, love you, bye!"

(I love my mom.)

I'm still confused and everyone is "should-ing" on me. All the theys (friends, family, strangers) say I should keep plugging away at real estate (insert: harakiri[1] mime), sell everything and live like a nomad (I'm halfway there in Seattle), write a real estate series (maybe, but anything real estate isn't really revving my motor right now—refer back to harakiri), and the "shoulds" continue. I say never "should" on anyone, including yourself. So I'm going to pray my heart out and ask for a sign or three or four or a flashing billboard with my name on it, but not my real name because that would be embarrassing, so make it my alias name, and thanks!

Okay, I'll start praying right after I go to the bathroom and look myself in the mirror and say, "God made you and you're perfect. God doesn't make junk," as per my MLM's instructions. (She really means it! God *is* good!) Then I'll read Matthew 11, starting at verse 28, in which God tells me He has an egg for me or something (a "yolk," specifically, which is the best part of the egg, after all). MLM says if you let go and let God, but then turn around and take your problems back, you're not really letting go at all and He'll be all like *okay, dumbass, see what else you can do to fuck this up* and let you take them back again, since apparently you still think you can handle them better than He can, *cough, what a control freak.* (Um, us not God.) I say thank God for my MLM, who comes so full of wisdom in such a tiny package. Her accent may be strong but her message is HD-clear.

*

What have I learned? Letting go isn't the same as giving up. Detachment = destressment!

Homework: Lay off the caffeine, get my ass outside, and write, love, pray, and play, damn it!

***

[1] *Harakiri* (noun): ritual suicide by disembowelment with a sword, formerly practiced in Japan by samurai as an honorable alternative to disgrace or execution. Source: Google, of course.

NICE GUYS FINISH LAST: DATING 101

Still in Seattle near my studio, I'm sitting on the sun-warmed bench outside my brick apartment building, book in hand. I'm trying to live in the now, to be Zen. I've tried the Zen-in-general thing, to relieve my twenty-years-constantly-business-thinking-busy mind, but it's such a challenge to focus on *not focusing* on anything! It goes against my "be productive" grain, but chapter after chapter of breathing techniques and breathing awareness is actually making me *more anxious* because *I can't get to thoughtlessness,* damn it.

It isn't working. Perhaps outdoors in Madison Park—where people watching is so rife—isn't the best place to focus on *quiet.* Cute dogs, fashion faux pas, pretty shoes. Manicures, massages, Asian aestheticians, tipping in cash. Maybe I'll become an Asian aesthetician to get my green card. Hmm... My mind rolls through the thoughts and every few minutes I remember what I'm doing, and remind myself to focus on my *damn breathing.* But it's a lot of non-Zen work and I'm wondering if it's having the opposite effect that it should, i.e., it's making me un-Zen, because I'm only on page six for fuck's sake. Then JP appears on his bicycle. My hero for the day!

I'd never been happier to see him. (Yes, I catch the irony.) I slam the book shut, not marking the page, overjoyed by the distraction. He gets off his bike, tennis rackets poking out of his backpack, and for a moment seems genuinely keen to see me. He gives a bright smile and an enthusiastic "Hi!" Then there's a slight shift in his countenance as he remembers our last encounter. The subtle swing reminds me, too.

I smile through it, and try to think of something positive to erase the memory of the negative. "Hey, I was thinking about you the other day."

JP, encouraged despite himself, smiles and responds, "Really?"

"Yes! Remember last year when we talked about all my dating dealbreakers and how I'd only date a guy with a black Range Rover? Or maybe a Maserati...Well, I have to tell you! I met a guy who drives a VW Golf and I totally fell for him!" I don't mention that I haven't actually met The Italian yet, driver of said econo-car. No objections, please.

JP frowns and mutters, "Great."

I continue anyway. I'll make a friend out of this guy whether he likes it or not. "I know, right?! And there were so many other things on my list he totally failed on, but I still really like him. Isn't that awesome possum?"

His shoulders creep up by his ears and I'm worried they'll cramp and he won't be able to play tennis, but after a bit more conversation, he loosens up, his furrow disappears, and he takes a deep breath. What a trip.

He admits, "I like you because you're refreshing and interesting, okay, and pretty—"

I interrupt, "And shallow and pigheaded. And thank you."

He continues, "You're somewhere in between, but at least you're honest and authentic. And pretty." He chuckles.

My eyes light up, "Really? You think I'm authentic?"

He thinks then responds. "Yes."

I tell him, "Well, you know... When you're with a pretty girl it makes the other pretty girls wonder, 'What's he got going on to be with her?' and all that psychological crap. But it's true."

He's smart. "I already thought of that." (Mischievous grin.)

I mock-gasp. "JP! I'm shocked."

He laughs, appearing relaxed.

A lovely female specimen walks by with long, flowing, lustrous, shampoo-commercial hair, wearing a semi-sheer maxi dress that is the right amount of sexy and feminine. Even my head turns.

"OMG, she's gorgeous!"

He agrees.

We both smile and share a friendly, cheeky grin.

Before I can test my wing-woman superpowers, I decide to take a final whirl in the dating world. In other words, The Matchmaker.

Cut to next scene: I'm decked out in my Bellevue best, a nine-dollar dress I got at Value Village and my well-worn Manolo Blahnik black, patent leather Mary Janes. Since my income could only truly afford *either* designer shoes *or* designer clothes but not both, I went for shoes (and coats), since they last longer and, if well-chosen, can stay in style, like, *forever*, which makes me only half-superficial in the wardrobe department—at least that's how I'm justifying it. But since my secret Seattle escapades have eaten up my clothing budget, Value Village it is, which I totally congratulate myself on because it's not only less shallow but also more environmental! (By the way, the first time I wore the Value Village sheath, I'd gotten retched body odor, which hardly ever happens to me—not a hippy type, remember? But it wasn't me, it wasn't my grime, I found out tonight. It was the dress! This particular artificial fabric doesn't bode well for the nose. *Solution*: Polyester pit pads! I use panty liners in the armpits the next time. Oh yeah!)

For no particular reason, I decide to finally attend an event hosted by The Matchmaker. She found me through a mutual Facebook friend a long time ago. I wonder if maybe her shelves have gone bare. Either way, I'm giving Seattle my last best as Yes! Girl tonight.

The Matchmaker has been inviting me to her Bellevue Put On Your Pout Facebook events for the last year or so. After a perusal of her Facebook page and multiple photo albums—The Matchmaker in various red carpet outfits at what look like various red carpet events—I'd figured I'm not the kind of girl she wants on her roster. Though I like my designer brand shoes, I'm *probably* a little too redneck for her cupid's bow. I mean, it's not like I don't know better than to contain my swearing, but I do like to throw out a few (I'm told) inappropriate sexual innuendos. For instance, I might make innuendo into in-your-end-*oh*! Or, like, if a cute busboy dropped a fork, *(cough)* like at a high-priced steakhouse, I'd be all, "while you're down there..." sort of thing. Uh, not that that happened! (sideways glance)

But this event isn't a "dating" event, per se. No, it's an "educational" event. She calls it "The Soft Hammer." Well, you know how I am about signs. I'd just used the very same expression with CWAD about getting our clients to drop their list prices (for their own good). When I get the invite, I believe the word *synchronicity* must mean something and I'm all, like, "God, you rascal. I got the memo *wink*." Still, I'm wondering if I'll live to regret my belief in the magic of the Almighty.

On the way to the event, I get a random call from The Italian, but I'm trying to read the map on my phone and keep myself from getting caught talking on the phone while reading the map on it, and the results of this can't be good. I've already gotten lost three times and have had to make illegal U-turns where I get honked at and fingered (not in a good way). All of this stunts the conversation and I tell him, "Look, I'm going to have to call you back, I'm on my way to a writing thing," which isn't *exactly* a lie because ultimately I am going to write about what I'm doing tonight, so it really was more of an *exaggeration* than a fib. I'm not as clever as Carrie Bradshaw, who always knew to say "research."

I drive by the hotel thrice, even though I can clearly see the name. I'm assuming (hoping) there's another Cher-a-ton nearby that has marble pillars and an iron gate and white-gloved valets and isn't this Super 8 looking motel that needs a paint job and new parking lot pavement A-sap. I park and on my way in I'm already planning my escape route, which is basically: turn a heel and run! (I've never met these people and would never see them again, anyway. And then all I'd have to do is post a note on Facebook that only she can see that says *Anna died, but had great shoes,* and then I can quietly unfriend her. Easy, breezy!)

Before seeing the unseemly façade, I imagine the event to be standing room only, in a dimly-lit lounge, à la *Pretty Woman*. I picture beautiful people sipping expensive aperitifs and laughing in slow motion, whilst a pianist runs through renditions of old classics. *Cut to next scene*: I inquire at the plain, fluorescently-lit reception desk, fiddling with a dusty, fake, desk plant and looking around for at least one little detail that makes the U-turns worth it. The brown carpet needs a good vacuum and I'm pretty sure I've seen some of the framed wall prints on art.com for $19.99. Everything is hospital-bright, which showcases the thorough drabness. Well, at least it's consistent. The man at the desk is missing at least one tooth and the rest are a greyish-yellow. But he does smile.

I ask for the lounge.

Toothless points behind me. Not off in the dark, not sexy, not soothing, no soft music playing, no intimate conversation in the corner. There it is, *behind the fake fig tree, under glaring lights, right over there.*

Toothless asks, "Is that what you're looking for?"

Um, no. Right over there is an adjacent after-thought area that's been partitioned off with planters of synthetic shrubbery and what looks like a fold-out table with matching chairs surrounding it. At least it's covered in a table cloth. I see a handful of average-looking, average-dressed, and I imagine possibly greasy-haired folk huddled around the table.

I whisper back as though the bright lights might amplify my voice. "Is The Matchmaker here?"

Toothless nods. "Over there."

I look "over there" behind the fake tree to the group of greasies who are in what looks like a board (*read*: bored) meeting. At least The Matchmaker[1] is well polished: her hair is perfectly coiffed, makeup carefully applied including candy-apple red lipstick that matches her nails and scarf. The rest of the forty and fifty-something crowd appears to be clad in their best Value Village finds, only *they look like Value Village finds,* unlike mine that gets red-carpet accolades.

The other tables are vacant. The Matchmaker's acquaintances don't come across quite so chic in this clinical lighting, but maybe no one could. I look down. Yes, I do better in dim lighting, too. I'm sure there are some "nice guys" in the group, but I'm jaded and a little tense and my pit pads are soaked. I decide to hightail it. Thank the Lord for the (fake) fig tree that makes things disappear—it saved Adam and Eve from shameful nakedness and me from two and a half hours of "dating education."

I drive straight home. Okay, not straight home. I get lost again, and *then* drive straight home, replace pit pads, grab my laptop, and deliver my fine, if too fancily-clad, body to Starbucks. This troweled-on makeup will not go to waste. This molten lava cake and glass of Malbec *will* go to waist (and thighs).

I Skype with The Italian while checking out the other patrons from the corner of my eye. Last month when I'd turned to comfort food, he'd said, "It's easier to lose weight than to gain money." In other words, eating is better than retail for a quick fix. (He didn't know I'd been using shopping therapy at Value Village *and* extra calories. But at least double V is a thrift store.) Now, he's looking at me through the computer and saying, "Just how much bigger *are* you going to be when I see you?"

"Very funny. I'll still be delicious, don't you worry." And lick my fork.

He's joking and even though I've always said that there's some truth in every joke, I don't care because I just might be starting to like me the way I am—or at least not detest my fat ass some days, which isn't fat at all, sadly. (No, it's mostly in my belly and thighs, *thanks God.* ← Sarcasm to God: is that a sin?)

Tonight, once I'm done with The Italian, I write. Ahh, freedom, creativity, inspiration, heart's desire—joy.

A few nights later, I'm Skyping with The Italian at home when, at 11:00pm, there's a knock on my door—??—which I don't open (safety first) but instead I call out (while still on Skype), "Who is it?"

"Is that Elaine?" (The visitor actually uses my alias name.)

"Um, yes, who are you?"

"Your neighbor down the hall, Wine Guy." (The visitor actually uses his nickname.)

"Hit the road!" The Italian yells protectively, though his voice does sound like it's coming out of the box it's in (*read:* my laptop not my vagina).

I tell Wine Guy kindly, "I'm busy," and ask him to knock at a more reasonable hour.

The Italian wants to come over and pummel the guy, but he's far, far away.

The next day (at a reasonable hour) Wine Guy knocks again. I think, eh, what the heck, so I go for coffee and then lunch with him—I'd forgotten I'd told him way back whenever that I'd buy him some pizza in exchange for the couple bottles of very nice wine he'd given me. Whether or not he's interested in me, I tell him straight up that I have a boyfriend (fib), I don't date younger guys (anymore), and I don't want kids (still). I invite California and try to set him up with her—he's Christian—but she's now got a Christian fellow (apparently they're coming out of the woodwork) so it's a bust. Well, I tried. Wine Guy and I talk about travels. He's a nice guy. His apartment is a bit bachelor, but more on that in one page.

The Italian says he might get married one day if it's in a small Canadian town with good fishing (and lax marital laws). He also mentions Canada's stellar medical system. I promise my heart to no man. (*Raised eyebrow at life. Smug look.*)

*

What have I learned? At some point, bad boys don't finish first. They keep playing the same game with the same hand of cards, only changing out the players. Nice guys may be too sticky sweet, which, gentlemen, reads as fake and/or spineless, but a good man, though hard to find, is good to keep. (Not to be confused with *a hard man being good to find*—that's back in the bad boy category.) However, no greasy-haired good guy will finish first, either. Lather up, chaps.

Homework: Figure out how to mature faster. Oh, wait, I think I just grew a little bit. Yay me!

✳✳✳

[1]The Matchmaker is *actually* a naturally beautiful woman. I was *probably* wearing more make-up than she was. It *is* rude to try to permanent-marker out pearly whites on a real, live person. Don't try this at home. (Unless you're in running shoes, lest you break a heel whilst high tailing it over lumpy pavement at a Bellevue chain hotel. *Not that this happened.* In case you think I'm this insane: it didn't. Sheesh.)

THE STARVING ARTIST: FREE ROOM AND BOARD

After sucking back No-see-ums (tiny mosquitoes) in the shade at Seward Park, Seattle, dodging suicide squirrels and wiping snot on my sleeve in the chill morning air, I realize my solo cycling sessions are not advancing my social skills. I'm still hiding in shyness sometimes. Elaine, where are you? Yes! Girl? You (all) materialized so I could experience being someone other than the reticent redhead I've been for too long, i.e., the constant subject of merciless teasing, so where are you when I need you? I want to be you—the bold, confident, fun, friendly, fiery, adventurous side(/s?) *of me!* Damn you, fickle multiple personalities!

Okay, that's it. Today I'm getting out of my comfort zone, or at least out of my apartment. Yes, let's start with that.

Cut to next scene: *Location*: Apartment down the hall.

To bring you up to speed as quickly as a writer can: Since I gifted my team all my real estate listings so I could use the extra time to write, I haven't claimed a crumb, so à la thrifty-me it is. (*Read*: I'm broke.) I'm sure the new business model just needs time to mature (*sideways, hopeful expression*), so I'm giving it until the end of summer before intervening. (*Read*: getting my lazy, puff-pancake ass back to work.)

In the meantime, I'm cutting costs and the Seattle studio is one of them.

I'm not giving up Seattle—couldn't bring myself to do it—so instead, when my lease expires, I will be moving in with...Wine Guy. His family owns a homestead and winery a few hours away and he's hardly ever at this home, so I get gratis place to stay until the end of August when we will renegotiate. This means I have about three months to bake cookies and lasagna and win his heart and home via taste buds. What else goes with wine that stores well in the freezer?

Speaking of consumables, while previewing Wine Guy's apartment, here's a list of items that I found:

- Three containers of Philadelphia cream cheese (thankfully in the fridge)
- 4 jars of pickles
- A futon
- Advil, Tylenol, Visine, *Vaseline*
- Old desk
- Old turntable (works!)
- Old recliner
- Old TV (doesn't work)
- Hammock chair
- Leo Tolstoy's *War and Peace*
- Stale Cheerios (I ate them)
- About 17 cases of wine in various stages of consumption
- 3' Christmas tree (decorated) and twinkle lights wrapped around exposed pipe (It's April.)
- Chin-up bar hanging on exposed pipe with twinkle lights
- One black sock

I'm going to like living here.

I've already gone from Gucci to Gap to Goodwill, so now I'll be going from a 500sqft studio with alcove to a 50sqft closet with curtain of mauve (as in my fabric door, since it doesn't have a real one). However! Bonus: All my furniture will fit, and his place can clearly use a lady's touch! (I've offered my furniture in exchange for room and board, which is actually closet and self-bought snacks. Plus, the stale Cheerios I ate.)

In all fairness to me, I did get out of my apartment (and his) by wandering down to Starbucks, where I read on a bench for all of half an hour before meeting California for a catch-up. Naturally, we talk about where we're at with men. She's got a dandy. He's a handsome, nice, thoughtful, *Christian*, emotionally mature, independent, easygoing, has his own hobbies, listens...the-list-goes-on guy. I get the sense that she's totally questioning it! (Then again, I *could be* projecting.)

I tell her about my "friend" The Italian. Hard to get, puts me low on his priority list (okay, last on his priority list, really, though maybe I can't expect much until I actually meet him?), emotionally unavailable, talks about himself, um...is really, really, handsome? All right, a slight exaggeration: I've bitched him out enough that he actually does listen and is getting in touch with his feelers. And he does make me laugh a lot. The low-on-totem-pole bit is true, though.

California and I talk about why we like to chase "bad boys," and it reminds me, once again, of the book, *The Manual: How Men Think, Date, and Mate* (by Steve Santagati). I keep telling him I wish he would write a book for nice guys on how to finish *first*. Here's the whole premise: Be a good guy but let us chase you a bit, for crying out loud, but don't play so hard to get that we give up. (Guess it would be a pretty short book. So, hello! Fill the rest of the pages with half-naked women, because we don't want them to fully objectify us, now do we? Or there could be a reward system, like if they get a certain score on the test, they get to go to page 12 with Pamela on it, but if they fail, then they have to go to page 13, where they'll get Hilary. Then again, that would turn all men into cheaters—book test cheaters but still. It's a slippery slope, my friend.)

There's a fine line in this dating business, between what has potential and what doesn't. California may have Mr. Too Perfect and Available, but I've got a dilemma.

My ex, HBUAB (aka The Fibber), treated me well (aside from all the lying, of course). I did feel like a priority, though. He did make an effort. (By the way, he is doing well: out of rehab, in a relationship, and getting his life in order. *Did I mention he was in rehab?* Can't remember. Prescription painkillers, go figure. Anyway, he told his *new girlfriend* everything about everything: Don't you love it when you leave a man so he can go on to be that amazing person *for someone else?* All I can hope for is that some poor broad is doing the same for me!)

So now I'm "In the Meantime." Not waiting, not looking, just trying to finish this damn screenplay so I can move on. (*Note*: I *will* finish this damn screenplay so I can move on. That's one year on one project. More or less, not including the blog and this book, which has been fun and easy and, hell, that's how I decided I could blog a book together. That's what Jen Lancaster did and now she's got seven bestsellers! I recently, for the first time, read one of her books, *Such a Pretty Fat*. She's hilarious, but maybe I think that because she writes like me. Hello! Or do I write like her? She did publish first. Okay, I'll give it to her. And, of course, anything Jenny McCarthy, or Jen Lawson (The Bloggess) . . . *Holy Shit! Maybe I need to change my pen name to Jenny Anything—seriously.*)

Where was I? Oh yeah, with regard to the screenplay, *sigh*, I *will* get it done. But here's the other thing: *I still don't watch movies.* I'd thought maybe I'd get into the whole film/movie thing since, after all, I was going to have to get on the red carpet in my red-bottomed shoes and know who's who and finally meet The Gerry and all. *Sideways glance.* But, I guess I'm just not that into it, or that kind of girl, a Hollywood-esque girl. The only "TV shows/films" I've watched in the last few years have been TEDTalks and save-the-planet documentaries on Netflix. And that's the ugly truth! I hate to be a (screenplay) quitter (*read:* failure), but maybe this will be the one big thing I tried and didn't succeed at. *And maybe that's even a good thing!*

Save the bees!

*

What have I learned? Aside from the fact that I can't seem to get off this mental merry-go-round?

————————————EPIPHANY!————————————

If I don't have a passion for something (*read:* scriptwriting), why am I trying to force myself into making a damn career out of it?? *(Wasn't I just Realty Lady three seconds ago doing the same thing!? As in doing shit I don't want to? But in the real estate case, at least I was actually making pay. Slap to forehead! Oy.)*

Homework: Do something in the world tomorrow. Church, Cheese Fest, Fremont Market, Museum. Something. Anything! (Um, notice I didn't even mention SIFF, Seattle International Film Festival, though technically I just did, which is only the biggest independent film festival in the country. The only shows on my agenda are the Opening Night Gala— already went and didn't even go to the after party where producers/ actors/directors mix/mingle/movie "network"—and the Shortsfest Night, to view the flick of that student from my writing class, Reel Lady, who already wrote and produced a film that *got accepted*! See now, there's someone who has a passion for the whole f'in works of it!)

***

SURVIVORS VS. THRIVERS: EMPOWERED
WOMEN WANT TO KNOW, NE, GLOW!

I'm drafting out furniture arrangements for Wine Guy's place when I get a text from Little Editor. "Just a few ladies I know. No need to bring anything. Will you come? Saturday, dinner?"

What is this new emotion? It sort of feels like anxiety but with giddy flutterings. I'm not sure how to take myself.

I type out a response: "What kind of dinner? Where? Who's going to be there?" But then I rethink and retype: "Yes! What should I wear?" and hit send before I can change my mind.

I tell myself that courage isn't courage without fear, or whatever this tummy tickling feeling is. Nonetheless, a wee bit of that old timidity lingers, too. In this case: fear of rejection, fear of them seeing the real me or, worse, *the fake me*, which is, yes, fear of not being good enough, which is, yes, more fear of rejection. Damn psychology circles.

Before I can work myself into a fear frenzy, I tell myself out loud, "I'm fucking great! And they can like it or lump it."

I hop off the air mattress, take a shower, get dressed, and head up to Vivaci to write, proud of stepping out of my comfort zone even though I haven't actually done anything yet. I wonder if I'm actually feeling enthusiastic excitement. Hmm.

By the time Saturday arrives, I'm sure of myself and calm and eager, if a tad early—okay, I'm half an hour early, but it's so much easier to meet people one at a time rather than busting in on a gabbing bunch. I'm wearing jeans and a casual top, nothing too loud or overstated. I'm not so much determined to fit in as I am not wanting to offend with flamboyance, though that could be the same thing.

Little Editor's place is a cozy condo with eclectic flair: wooden table with mismatched, India-inspired cushioned chairs, and a wall of picture windows overlooking a side street. The silvery-green needles of tall conifers reflect metallic light in the last of this evening's spring sun. The setting eases any residual nerves I have, and I am grateful for the glass of wine my friend places in my hand.

While Little Editor busies herself in the kitchen, I ask her about her friends. "So, how did you meet these ladies?"

"We met five years ago at a women's empowerment workshop."

"So, do you feel empowered?"

She scrunches her mouth to one side, thinking. "A little." Then adds, "Definitely more than five years ago."

"Awesome possum."

I might point out now that Little Editor knows my childhood history, and she can relate to some of it—though she's discreet. I'm smiling to myself at how far I have come when she seems to read my thoughts.

"Some of the women have been through childhood abuse." She casts a furtive glance.

"Oh, that's great! I mean, it's shitty for them, but a great bonding subject—or is this not something to talk about?"

She's thoughtful before she answers: "It usually comes up in conversation. We sort of, hmm, check in with each other. I thought you'd be okay with it."

"I'll be sensitive about it. I know not everyone thinks the way I do about it."

"I love the way you think about it. It's inspiring."

"But, hey, I'm still fucked up! I'm just *self-aware* and fucked up."

We both laugh.

Where am I on this "stuff"? I remember a conversation I had with HBUAB/The Fibber while I was in Canada. He called to tell me about a notice that was posted on the doors of the townhouse complex he (/we) lived in. A pedophile had been discovered in the 'hood.

Without thinking my visceral and impassioned response was, "Don't you dare stop saying 'hello' to that man!"

I take a quick breath and continue. "He did his time. These people are sick, but they have nowhere to go for help. I guarantee there are plenty of other pedophiles you chat with every day that you don't know about. This man will suffer enough from the rest of the neighbors. Keep [HBUAB's daughter] safe, but don't be hateful. Promise me. *Promise me.*"

I shook until tears fell, then I wondered what the hell had gotten into me. In that moment, though, I also felt—what I didn't recognize fully at the time—love. Not for the perv, but just in general. For everything. For me. Maybe I somehow felt (not that I was aware what I was feeling) that those shackles had been removed, and I had been released. (Yay me!)

What I learned in Choices, intellectually at least, is that *hurt people hurt people*. During the course and for some time afterward, the anger and rage inside me gradually dissipated. I didn't notice it happening. Time just went by. And, no, I don't have Stockholm syndrome—put the "hurt" fuckers in treatment. (At least!)

I lower my voice and tell Little Editor, "If you're an alcoholic and you go to a meeting, you're praised or, at the very least, accepted, and you get a pat on the back for showing up. These people have no one to go to without being judged or thrown in jail." I wait to gauge her response.

She agrees. And though I'm not sure she's convinced, she seems open to the idea.

I continue. "They're fucked up. I'm not saying they're not. They were probably abused themselves as children and even if not—I know that's not an excuse—but there's so little support for them. I'm just saying, 'Don't hate.' Hate isn't good for anyone, least of all the hater."

She can agree with that much and adds, "Some are not ready..." trailing off, but I understand and nod. Some situations require a tender filter.

The first guest, Allison, arrives. She's a solid-framed, deep-voiced woman with short-cropped brown hair and is likely around my age, wearing a feminine, flowery dress. I've already been told by Little Editor that her (lesbian) partner isn't coming.

Allison gives Little Editor a hug, and we're introduced. She gives me a hug, too, and makes herself at home in the kitchen, pouring herself a glass of wine and taking a swig before catching her breath. She's high energy and boisterous and talks a little louder than necessary. "Is everyone coming?"

And before Little Editor can finish her answer of, "Yes, Katie and Gabby are on their way—" Allison is peeking a look in the oven. "Mmm, bacon-wrapped scallops! Tell me what to do."

At the mention of Gabby, I chuckle to myself, remembering our dinner non-date. Guess she just wasn't that into me.

The doorbell rings and Little Editor asks, "Can you let whoever in? The buzzer is broken. Or here, maybe put this in when it boils?" She hands Allison a box of spaghetti and wipes her hands on her apron, which is draped over a fitted, black skirt.

I experience a moment of panic, knowing I'll be left alone to make small talk, but I take a deep breath and a swallow of wine, and I'm fine again. So far, I haven't said much, but I feel content and not unnerved. Again, I'm surprised at myself. (Could be the wine, mind you.)

Little Editor exits. Allison fusses in the open, adjacent kitchen, looking for and then finding a colander. "So how do you know [Little Editor]?"

"We met in a writing class—wow—over a year ago. You?"

"A women's workshop, mostly abuse victims, but not all. But we prefer to say *survivors*."

I think to myself, "I prefer the term *thrivers*." But instead I say, "You're pretty open about it."

"I'm sure she's told you, or you wouldn't have been invited. Trusted friends here." I can tell her direct approach holds no malicious intent.

"That's a nice feeling, maybe a silver lining. I was abused." I'm testing the waters.

She glances at me but then the front door bursts open before she can reply, and three laughing, out-of-breath women enter. There's no elevator in the old building and Little Editor's place is on the third floor. The ladies pile into the compact living/dining room and peel off their jackets. Little Editor takes the jackets to the bedroom and the two ladies hug Allison and garner wine glasses and come back to the dining table where I'm sitting.

Katie is tall and slim with rounded shoulders that make her modest bosom appear slighter than it is. Her longish, light brown hair is parted in the middle and hangs in her face. I guess Katie to be mid to early thirties. She's wearing a long, non-descript skirt, conservative top, and partially-buttoned cardigan. Her face is youthful but etched in seriousness.

Katie smiles without welcoming eyes, then sticks out her hand for me to shake. "Hi. Katie."

"Anna." I smile. She seems irritated—by my presence *or?*

"Hi, Gabby!" I'm glad to see a familiar face.

My only friend in the room smiles, gives me a "Hello!" and a hug that's warm and genuine.

I notice that other than the mascara Little Editor wears, I'm the only one with a full face of make-up. Are they renouncing their femininity? Then again, maybe I'm over-stating my own girliness. I chastise myself, again, for judging and assuming. No wonder chicks don't dig me; I must give off that vibe: critical, catty chick. (*Note to self:* Then again, maybe I'm *just making observations* and trying to figure shit out!)

After the ladies have caught up on the what-have-yous of regular life while intermittently assisting our hostess in the kitchen, we all sit down for the meal: wrapped scallop appetizers, fresh warm French baguette, a delicious spaghetti puttanesca main course, and fresh cantaloupe for dessert. Simple and delicious.

During the meal, the discussion cuts straight to the chase. Allison starts things off. "We had a tough week. You know, shit comes up out of nowhere sometimes. It's hard on her." She looks at me. "My partner. Not abused, sometimes she has a hard time getting it."

I answer, "I get that."

Then she looks at Katie and Gabby to explain: "Anna was abused."

Little Editor takes a sip of her wine and looks out the window at the billowy tree now shimmering in the street light. I try to save her from any awkwardness she might feel. "Think it started when I was four, but I can only remember specifically from six. Not by blood, not that that matters. Hope this doesn't make you uncomfortable." I direct it at Little Editor.

Katie's shoulders relax a little. "Asshole."

Gabby pipes in: "Ten. Though I can't remember everything. Some days I'm not even sure anything happened."

I share, "Yeah, I didn't remember until I was like fifteen. He's dead, now." I pause. "I'm way past the angry stage. I've worked on it a long time."

Katie: "I'm not."

Allison says to me, "She just remembered." Then to Katie, "What, four years ago?"

I try to smile at Katie, but I can see the rage boiling inside her and know nothing I can say will help her right now. I try anyway. "It does get easier."

"Good." I can tell she doesn't believe me.

Gabby asks, "Does it?" As if she genuinely wants to know.

I decide not to share the Pedophile-Posted-Notice story, but say, "Yeah, I was angry for a long time, furious even. 'Don't stand in my path or you'd feel the fury' kind of furious. I took a course, and it helped a lot. Over time, I let it go. Well, as much as we *can* let it go. I'm not tethered to it, at least, and I don't think about it often. Hardly ever, actually."

Katie says, "I think about it every day, every minute."

I want to give her a hug but know it would be the worst thing I could do.

"You're lucky to have such amazing girlfriends," I say. Maybe it'll feel like a hug.

Gabby says, "Cheers to that."

We clink glasses, then Allison asks Little Editor, "How's the divorce coming along?"

Little Editor answers, "He's being difficult as usual, dragging it out with the lawyers." (Even though she's been seeing Can Can Man for a while and has been separated from her ex-husband since before that, she's not officially divorced yet.)

Gabby asks, "And Can Can Man?"

Little Editor says, "That's going better. We had a good talk. He opened up. We're going to try monogamy."

I say, "Cheers to that."

We all clink glasses.

After that, the conversation lightens, and I learn that Katie is over forty and has a boyfriend. I'm surprised not because she's unattractive—she's quite pretty—but because of where she's at with her "recovery." Though now that I think back on my own. I did go through my "angry stage" when I was *with* Good Man. It was another unfair assumption on my part. Sometimes, *I'm* such an asshole. At least in my thoughts. No one's perfect, right? *Right?*

I go home feeling satiated and satisfied, if a little drained. I review the evening in my mind and determine that I want women friends *and* I also need *upliftment*, if there is such a word and if there isn't, add it to my list! (I make up words. My editor dislikes that. But she is very pretty, and I am vain, so she has to like that!) And I get uplifted when I can uplift (or at least entertain) others. I'm not sure I accomplished either, but I'm still really glad I went to the dinner party.

*

What have I learned? Having deeply personal, painful experiences in common can be a bond-builder but, if it brings me down, it can be more empowering for me to pass. I've come a long way, baby!

Homework: Take more chances with the ladies. What have I got to lose but my ego? And dropping that is a good thing. So go ahead and expose my*self*—it's freeing and empowering!—but not by dropping my clothes in a pseudo-lesbian-happy-gay-naked-at-the-County-Fair kind of way.

***

SETTLING FOR MORE: COZY AND COMFORTABLE

Life remains unpredictable.

Marthalicious lost her brother—we'll call him Larry—two weeks ago. Fucking cancer. 'Licious had recently moved to [Big City], Canada, close to where her parents live, but had flown back to our little town in time to say goodbye, while I was still in Seattle. It was unexpected news at the time. Larry was supposed to have been getting better and going home.

Flashback to two weeks ago: I'm trying to organize my move from my tiny studio suite to Wine Guy's pad down the hall, which I have to do in five days so I'm moved in by the end of the month. One evening, I'm meditating (read: laying on the futon in the closet at Wine Guy's) when I get a text from Marthalicious . . .

"Can I call?"

"Of course!"

She calls and tells me Larry has taken a turn for the worse, and the doctors aren't hopeful. Though 'Licious's voice quivers, she's holding herself together with frail hope.

All I can muster is, "Oh no. I thought he was getting better?" I don't want to be pessimistic but I don't want to give false promise. It's a delicate situation.

She tells me her parents' friends have booked them all a flight for the next day (the soonest one available). There's not much I can offer without leaning into some form of expectation: He'll get better. Or he won't. I pray my presence is helpful. I ask questions about what the doctors have said and stick with the clinical. I'm also trying to hold myself together, and though tears are falling, I try to act strong for my friend.

That night, through more tears, I pray, "Dear Lord, I know it's a lot to ask, but *please* let Larry live. And if, for whatever reason, it's not your will, give them strength to get through this. In Jesus' name, amen."

The next day, I get a few texts from her on her whereabouts: on our way to airport, at airport, on way to hospital, at hospital, ttys, please pray he'll be okay. (FYI: "ttys" is "talk to you soon." For those who aren't text gurus. Further, "FYI" is "for your information.")

I don't hear from her until the next morning. My phone rings and I immediately know it can't be good news. Marthalicious, crying, says, "Oh, Anna. He's gone."

I break down, too. "Oh my dearest friend, I'm so sorry."

Through sobs, she says, "I know. I can't believe it."

Wiping my nose on my sleeve, I say, "I don't know what to say. I'm *so* sad for you. I wish I could be there to give you a hug."

Feeling frustrated and wanting to get home to my friend, I cry for the nearly two days it takes me to find help moving my sofa. I cry a lot, more than might be reasonable for empathy: in the line-up at Starbucks and while buying Fran's Chocolate at Bert's and virtually everywhere I go.

I'd so far only half moved to Wine Guy's place because to move that damned white sofa would mean removing legs and apartment door *again*. Finally, California and her boyfriend move it for me while I motor myself home to Canada. (Maybe nice guys *are* the new bad boys?) I am extra emotional. I want to be there for my BFF, yet I can't get there fast enough, all the while I'm remembering the feelings of loss I experienced when my dad died and I'm imagining 'Licious similarly alone and listless.

When I finally arrive, I'm overwhelmed by the hordes of people who have come from far and wide with love, support, food, and the necessary distraction. The love I witness converts my tears to a heartfelt abyss of appreciation. Forgive my dramatics, I might be "on the rag." (That's slang for "riding the cotton pony," which is, yes, more redneck slang.) My friend is deeply saddened by her loss, but takes the devastating event in stride as best she can.

An Engagement Party had been scheduled for friends (whom 'Licious didn't know) of her brother and sister-in-law, which was unexpectedly planned for what turns out to be the night of the memorial. All agree 'Licious's brother would have wanted it to carry on as planned, so it's decided the party will be a celebration of lives, for those beginning a journey together and for he whose journey is complete.

Cut to next scene: 'Licious meets single guy at party who just happens to be moving to [her big city](!) where she just moved! ('Licious has been single for ten years.) *Shut. The. Front. Door!*[1] Both are in town for different reasons, neither knowing the same people. They hit it off. New beginnings ensue. Okay, I am going to say (/write) it: The Lord works in mysterious ways!

Anyway, she comes to my house to say farewell—she's heading home to [Big City]—and shows me a photo of the new prospect from the engagement party. He's handsome in a great, big, cuddly, teddy-bear kind of way. I like the looks of him. (I think of my dad and get all leaky again, and now I know it must be my moon time, *I mean who is this sappy, sentimental girl?*)

We talk about the pluses of a cuddly type over ripped abs of steel: There's the whole "feel great naked" bonus with him because he's not a fitness trainer/model/Mr. Six-Pack. Then there's the assumption that he probably doesn't count calories (how femme) and appreciates food as much as we do! And, finally, he's likely not expecting to unwrap a Jessica pick-any-celebrity-last-name. Hell no, he'd throw that rag doll back until she ate a donut *or fourteen.*

Hmm. Interesting. So...if I date a guy who loves food as much as I do and thinks I look great naked, or at least has bad eyesight, without my ever losing the proverbial "last five to ten" depending on time of month, and I feel safe and cozy bones, um...*What's the holdup?* This thought experiment opens up a whole new catalog of possibilities (not that I'm looking).

'Licious says, "I still want to get in better shape, though, but for me."

I concur, "Me too! No pressure!"

I celebrate with a cupcake. (I don't even like cupcakes, but they're *soo pretty. Animated blinking.*)

When I get back to Seattle, I meet with Tom about my screenplay (revision 5 of draft 5349ish). He likes it. *He likes it!* But. *BUT! Grr* . . . "A few little revisions here and there..." (*Raised eyebrow, menacing pout followed by a very audible exhale and a heavy-duty slump followed by head to table thump.*) *Really?* I'm starting to get the feeling that this is the never-fucking-never plan. Tom's sense of urgency is significantly less pressing than mine. Given he's nearly twice my age, it's all relative, but still, *Tom's sense of urgency is significantly less pressing than mine, people!* The fact that it's my screenplay, not his, and I'm asking something of him, not the other way around, doesn't occur to me until much later. (In fact, until my editor points it out. I figure I'm getting a two for one deal with my editor: grammaticism *and* life coaching on how to be less self-centered, or at least more aware of my selfishness. Thanks! [I think.])

Life is unpredictable, time is of the essence, there's no time like the present, go big or go home, and finally, I've been working on this damn thing for a year, which my editor assures me "is not a long time for a writing project, you know that, right?," but feels like *foreverrr* and I'm going to go postal if something doesn't happen soon, damn it!

I enlist . . . (*cue suspenseful music*) . . . Little Editor. I send her the latest draft of the script. She reads it. She likes it. We agree to meet at the coffee shop to discuss. *(When does one know when to throw in the towel??)* We meet at Vivaci to discuss business. We decide we're going for it. We don't know what "it" is yet, but together we're unstoppable! *And! Scene: looking around the coffee shop avoiding eye contact.*

Little Editor is still seeing Can Can Man, back in the context of an open relationship. Again. Neither of them dates other people, *not really.* Or rather, they keep coming back to each other. (Maybe they're monogamous by default then?) I've changed my thinking about relationships. What's that old saying? "If it comes back to you...?" (Not the "hunt it down" one.) There might be something to it. When you love someone, when he or she is the right one, when you're ready, maybe you don't risk it. Your exploration leads you home. I'm still of the mindset that there are dealbreaking boundaries though, but maybe true love allows, accepts, frees. Maybe the old saying is true. *Maybe someone slipped Ecstasy in my cupcake.* Fuckerson! (By the way, I'm pretty sure I made up this particular f-word. Um, ©!) (My editor reminds me I can't copyright a word. [*Confused countenance.*] I say, why the fuckerson© not?)

Anyway, I hope it works out for Marthalicious and her new cozy cupcake.

Hug for her and her family.

⁕

What have I learned? Love comes in all kinds of packages, so if we think of it like a surprise present, we can unwrap it with childlike abandon and open heartedness when it's finally delivered. (God? Are you listening? *"Finally delivered."*)

Homework:

1. Remove Top 100 Must-Have, Non-Negotiable, Mr. Right-For-Me,

color-coded, laminated, spreadsheet from corkboard. (And purse) (/*es*).
2. Make amends. Just in case.

***

[1] Review: "Shut the front door" means "Shut the fuck up," a slang term of disbelief. No copyright.

IT'S NOT ALL ABOUT ME

Since Marthalicious lost her brother, I've paused to think and re-evaluate life as a death of someone near makes us do. Life isn't all about me. Thank God.

Leggy Blonde got divorced. She ended a relationship that needed ending. And that's all I'm gonna say about that. She and the ex parted on good terms, though, and she seems overall pretty okay with it at the moment. There may be some lingering grief to process before her July 1st goal date of dating again (less than three months from now), but she's a gal after my old heart.

CWAD BMFF loves his single life and while he *is* dating, he's not settling, he's improving his finances, investing in his future, hanging out with friends, and enjoying his many hobbies.

He tells me one day, "I love my life! Summers I get to ride my motor bike or mountain bike. I take Porkchop [dog] to the beach. And winters I get the night pass at the mountain [ski resort]—runs are quiet and no lines. Plus, I tear up the ice playing hockey."

He continues to be a great sounding board and BMFF to me.

Marthalicious is probably making muffins or some other tasty delight right now, crafting some creative art project while shuttling her little man (son) to soccer practice, or cuddling with her big man (boyfriend) on a comfy couch while feeding him homemade chocolate turtles. Save me

225

some! *Mmm . . . 'Licious's turtles . . .*

Little Editor continues the now exclusive (!) dating arrangement with Can Can Man, is content for now, has finished a book she had been working on writing (!), and is awaiting good news. I didn't even know she'd sent it out to publishers! (I want a signed copy.)

California is still dating the Christian, who may be younger than she is (you go girl!) but the same age at heart. He square dances and cleans her car. (Score!)

Realty Lady/Elaine à la *Anna*? In other words, me. I'm still in love with Seattle, even though my lease on my apartment is up and I'm back in Canada now. The last time I was in Seattle, I drove myself to "my" apartment building from a new location without a map. I continue to read the Bible. I'm halfway through the New Testament. I love God but would prefer it if He hired writers who wrote more engaging prose. Maybe I'll do the world a spiritual favor and rewrite the holy bible in AJ prose. Just sayin' . . .

Next week, I'll go back to the U.S. of A. I'm taking myself to the ballet. Solo. A last hurrah, if you will. Not to meet anyone, not to feel the fear and do it anyway, not to advance independence or self-empowerment. Nope, I'm going because I want to see the dancing (and gay men in tights with great asses) and say good-bye to another relationship: Seattle and me. Yay me!

Maybe I'll wear the Jimmy Choos I never did return.

*

What have I learned? People make life interesting. Our connection with others makes life worthwhile. Our connection with ourselves makes the in the meantime parts not so bad, too.

Homework: Take more interest in others. Thank my family and friends for being there for me. (*Thank you! Love you!*)

***

CLOSURE: LET GO AND LET GOD

Canada. Today is a pristine, sunny, spring day. The mountaintops glisten with fresh snow. I'm ready to go snowshoeing. Yet...yet... I put it off. I procrastinate. It seems when I have no obvious commitments, no sense of urgency, it's easy for me to get lazy. Here's how it goes in my mind: I could take that suit jacket in for alterations. (The jacket has moved from my closet to the hall closet to my car and back again. It's in its second cycle of relocation.) I could order the water filter for my fridge that keeps reminding me it needs replacing. I could get that loosened carpet in my bedroom fixed. (I did manage to change the light bulbs in the garage, all by myself, both of them. That felt good.)

I haven't made a lot of forward motion in the "become a writer for real" game plan. I'm not selling my house to run away with the circus or live like a gypsy. (Yet.) I did, however, close the door entirely on personally dealing with clients. Many of them I will miss. The constant pressure I will not miss. The team is more than capable, better at it than I am now. My heart's not in it anymore. I don't want to be the proverbial hamster on that fast moving wheel. New chapter for me: I do the part of real estate I still love *for as long as I love it* and that I can do on *my* schedule—writing, websites, marketing, and management—which I continue to have a high sense of urgency for (it's my nature). The local paper published my real estate article, my first, without a single edit. Over 750 words, thank you very much. (I'm definitely feeling self-congratulatory on this one!)

I realize now that when I said I was "done" at twenty years, it didn't have to mean I'd be completely exiting the real estate business. Because...I don't have to quit my day job to write! Huge bonus. And yes, this may seem obvious to you, but you're not inside my mentally unstable, very cluttered mind. (Plus, I wouldn't have had all that fun as Elaine Kauffman or Yes! Girl if I *hadn't* thought I was quitting, and in Seattle to boot!) This way, I can write for the love of the word, not for necessity. If anything comes of it, great. If not, that's okay, too. Or maybe a better idea will land in my lap! I feel a sense of disconnect, or maybe release or relief, or maybe closure. Whatever. I feel, dare I write . . . ~~fearless?~~ Ne, *courageous!*

On a relationship note, I've often heard that to attract the kind of person with whom one wants to be, one needs to become that kind of person him or herself, i.e., if I want someone who is dynamic and fun, then I better be dynamic and fun, too! Or secure and trustworthy, or whatever it is I seek in another. (This probably means I need to come to terms with being with someone who is slightly insane.) I'd like to add to that I don't have to follow through with whomever is attracted to me, or whomever I'm attracted to, if I'm not in the place in my journey to attract the one I want, i.e., I've got some learning and growing to do to get there because *I'm not that person yet.* (That came out a bit convoluted, but I think you know what I mean.)

In a nutshell, I'm not ready to attract the partner with whom I ultimately want to stay, so I'm gonna chill out until I am! The fact that I'm bored with my own blog and can't be bothered to engage in blog-inspiring drama or dating activities, maybe, *just maybe*, means I'm ready to move on to the next chapter in my life. The drama is overdone and I faded away instead of burning out. (Is that a song or a saying?)

Regardless of my predisposition on the whole topic, I text HM—he comes in out of my life—in an effort to reinitiate a *friendship*. After all, he did at one point say he'd always be my friend. Having been in a "girls and boys can't be friends" frame of mind with ex-HBUAB, it could be said that I did abandon HM, but that was back when I didn't think girls and boys could be friends. So here I am, trying to be friends with a boy. (I'll take my lumps that I've been a bad friend.) I find out that HM was pissed because he thought I was using him for a place to stay in the big city. Partly true, but that was also because it was the only way I could see him, since he never comes to town anymore. *Sideways glance.* Or if he does, he doesn't tell me! *Omg, this part is so true!* (But I guess I could have told him that. Live and learn.) Wait a minute. He sucked as a friend, too! Either way, the past is past and I'm moving forward.

HM inquires via text, "How's the NYC boyfriend?"

"He's not my boyfriend. Yet! Still talking. He needs work."

HM goes on another long rant about how I always do this: find a guy, date him even though I know he's not right for me, try to change him, break up with him, get back together with him, break up with him again, get back together with him, repeat a few more times, give up, break up with him, then blog about it. *Um, WTF, I haven't even "dated" this one?* (Yet, damn it!)

HM is on a roll of a rant: "Either accept the flaws or move on, but don't try to make them perfect (aka change them)!"

"Them? Huh?" *Blink blink!*

And why am I still friends with such a jerk-face? Indeed, I have a hard time fully leaving people. But, also, *he's right.* Here I am again. Same shit, different guy. Even I'm bored with me.

What will happen with The Italian? I don't know. I'm letting go and letting God. I'm practicing living in the now, *starting* now.

I say to HM, "Fine. What will I write about now?"

He answers, "Other people."

Self-reflective, I ask, "Am I shallow?"

He surprises me with, "You're an abyss."

Surprised, I ask, "Are you being sarcastic?"

He replies, "No."

Hmm, I guess it just doesn't show in this "writing voice".

It's time to test my writing skills.

It's time to practice and hone.

It's time to move on.

It's time to trust.

Elaine has left the building...with her box of personal affects.

*

What have I learned?

1. No one is perfect, or everyone is. It's okay to go solo until I find the right-flaws-for-me mate is delivered. If ever. I'm all right either way.

2. I can quit my day job. Or not. I'm all right either way.

Homework: Go snowshoeing!

***

PARTING WORDS: WORK IN PROGRESS

I've been home in Canada for a month. I've made changes. When it's all said and done, there's a moment of pause, and a new book to begin. *Necessary Endings*, by Dr. Henry Cloud. Dr. Cloud's book rightly brings to awareness the necessary endings throughout life—relationships, careers, ideas, projects, and maturity or age-related stages, etc. It's how we handle them that determine our effectiveness, success, and happiness. Certainly, that one sentence simplifies the gist of the book, and is the essence for my take on, and need of, its message.

And now, I see and feel it's time for another ending—the ending of this chapter of my life, and hence this book. (I'll miss you, too.) Before I bid you adieu, there are a few final notes I'll make, a "how far I have come" pause, if you will.

1. I love my age. (End of fear of losing looks? *Hell, no.*)
   a. I've never felt more comfortable in my own alligator skin, but that's not to say I won't "polish the stone" with a touch up here and there.
   b. Yep, I did the Fraxel six days ago (refer back to a), you know, in an effort to keep polishing the stone. Plus, my aha came *after* I Fraxeled, so there. (Shush.) It's relatively quick—one hour numbing cream and a twenty-minute procedure that feels like a thousand needles piercing your skin all at once.

Level six on pain scale. I've been holed up for almost a week.
    i.   Day one: red.
    ii. Day two: red, swollen.
    iii. Day three: less red, less swollen.
    iv. Day four and five: pink, flaky, itchy, patchy, zitty (from ointment), not swollen.
    v.   Day six: light pink, remnant flaking, which disallows for make-up.
    vi. Day seven (today): fully-flaked, pink patches that can be covered by makeup, rough to the touch, will take a month to fully exfoliate, resulting in tighter, smoother skin and less freckles.
c. I finally like my (missing) freckles. But now I can't get them back for three months or I risk scarring.
d. I've bought a cancer-causing tanning package (yes, at a salon) for when I can safely reclaim my trademark spots, of which I will give credit to The Italian for allowing this "unique is desirable" self-esteem building mindset to take root, though it didn't actually sprout until after I'd done the Fraxel. (He says everyone in NYC is an over-processed version of the same pasty, smooth face *and* the most popular models have some unique feature). I like that I'm not. Pasty, that is. Or, rather, won't be once I get my spots back. (Hopefully, without the addition of skin cancer.)
e. I go to the doctor's office on day four for my checkup. The doctor is in my childhood hometown. (Fraxel is not available in my adulthood hometown.) The doctor is a hand and joint specialist (small town multi-purpose doctor), but for some reason I'm not nervous. I sit in the waiting room for the good part of an hour, whilst entertaining the other (mostly little old lady) patients who grasp at their knobby knuckles and knees. The cute doctor asks if I'd prefer to wait in a private room since my face still looks like a truck towed me here. I laugh and say, "No way." If I'm going to do this cosmetic stuff, I might as well be open about it. What kind of a girl do you think I am? (Irony intended.) Let's be clear here: I'm comfortable with aging...gracefully. In my metaphorical book, this includes a little "here and there," as long as the "here and there" is not obvious and I don't try to get all fraudulent by making out like it all comes naturally. If I'm going to embrace this vanity insanity (thank you, Leggy Blonde, for coining that

catch phrase), I'm going to be truthful about it at least. But inasmuch as I'm okay telling people at home what I'm up to when appropriate (which I do in an effort to be honest, not to say that I run around randomly sharing with strangers—well, not *often*—well, unless you count this book), I've been hiding out for a week, meaning I don't want to be seen. We all have our limits. (*Raised—no longer Botoxed—eyebrow at self.*) This is not to say everyone has to expose themselves in public! No way. Disclose whatever you want to, or not! No judgments here. (For real.)

    f.   This Fraxel fix will last three to five years. I'm good with that. And yes, there is a hypocrisy in saying I'm comfy in my skin even though I'm still "enhancing" it from time to time, so perhaps it's more that I'm comfortable sharing my tales of my vain adventures. (*Shrug, whatever.*)

    g.   I don't weigh 115 and I'm okay with that. Honest. (Ish.)

    h.   Since I've decided I don't want kids (my goodness, I'm tired and selfish—and now poor), there's no pressure to find a man, shack up, get married, and ovulate. Hello, all the time in the world! Hello, freedom! Hello, life!

    i.   I only get better with time, "I" as in my personality, which counteracts "negative" physical side effects of aging—ha! This means some men must also. The longer it takes for God to drop *a* Gerry in my lap, the more ready *he'll be for me.*

    j.   Referring back to the feel-good-in-my-own-lasered-skin thing, let's be real: what I'm talking about is being cool with the rogue chin hair, random wrinkles, fuzzy fanny, and sprouting grays—but that's not to say I'm going to let myself go to pot, so to speak.

2.   I gave over all my client-related, Anna J, Realtor, responsibilities to my team: no showing homes, no listing homes, no dealing with offers or clients for me. I'm now focusing exclusively on marketing and writing-related activities and only watch the real estate from a comfortable distance, interjecting when necessary – it's never necessary, but I need to feel needed. (End of twenty years as Realty Lady.)

    a.   As a result, I feel disconnected from my fellow real estate agents and even "my" team. I'm the only real estate agent I know who follows this type of business model, unless you count owner/brokers. I don't know who to go to for support in this grieving process—a natural part of necessary endings—

that would understand and relate. For now, I am simply allowing myself the feeling of grief for the loss of my former-identified self. I believe this must be how people feel when they retire or close a business. For help with my grief, I go to the second hand bookstore for suggestions (reduce, reuse...Anna J, Realtor, reality: I have to watch my pennies). I ask the clerk if he has any books on changing careers, and he leads me to the business rah-rah section. (Hmm.) I ask if he has any books on retirement, and he asks if the books are for my parents. (Hmm.) I ask if he has any books on *"I don't know who I am if I'm not Realty Lady."* I end up with *The Half-Empty Heart*. Though the title goes against my Pollyanna grain, the book explains a diagnosis I can identify with: dysthymia—either low-grade depression (not me) or chronic discontent (me! me! me!). Not to be confused with chronic unhappiness (not me).

b. I feel an underlying anticipation, an excitement, about the freedom I now have to pursue my passion of writing. But writing can come with urgency and deadlines. I have been so driven, so goal-oriented, so needing to *be productive and successful* all my life, that I feel lost without due dates looming over my head. For now, I'll take it one day at a time, no pressure. (*No pressure!*) (That was for me.)

c. I can be me. I am no longer Realty Lady. Although it was always my choice: I always chose business advancement over personal authenticity and freedom. That's not to say Realty Lady wasn't also me, but she was only a small part of me, the only part I permitted the public to see. (As I've said before.) Trust me, clients wouldn't hire me if they saw me at the coffee shop in costumes from my tickle trunk (I'd give Mr. Rogers a run for his money, I assure you). Not that I'll be doing that now, anyway, but I could if I wanted, and it wouldn't matter. (Well, it might, but let's pretend.)

d. I can work from here. I can work from there. Wherever *there* is. The funny thing is that ever since I've come to terms with being the real me(s) right here at home, this place isn't so bad anymore. Well, that's not entirely true: the winter is still long, gray, and wet, and yes, it is a sleepy little town on Vancouver Island with limited cultural activities. However! Rainy days are ripe for writing (as I learned back in Seattle) and I now have my own pink snowshoes! In the summer, there's no better place to be for outdoor recreation, and in the winter, I can leave whenever I want and go wherever I want because living here in this little town is so affordable! *Yeah, baby, yeah!*

3. I've thrown in the towel on *potential* relationships. (End of fancying fixer-uppers.)

   a. HM is coming to town. After a few "float the balloon (let's see where it goes), can I sleep in your bed" jokes (pretty standard fare with HM), he understands that if he's to be in my life at all, friendship is the only option. Be respectful, I tell him, and that goes for me too. We'll see.

   b. Ex-HBUAB contacted me the other day. I was expecting it. I just knew. I hadn't heard from him since last fall when I asked him not to contact me anymore. He tells me more about his drug detox experience in a clinic far far away. Apparently he was addicted to Oxycodone while we were together, which does explain a few things. (Does this mean I'm prepared for The Gerry, who was also *reportedly* addicted to painkillers? Right, fixer-upper. Minor relapse.) I didn't feel angst or knots in my tummy when I heard from him. His words were thoughtful and sounded genuine. He apologized and asked me to apologize for him to my family and friends for lying to me and hurting me. I replied kindly and, though I'm curious about his journey, I have no desire to rekindle the old flame. Aside from his being on a better path, he has a long way to go. Even drug addiction doesn't fully distort, or excuse, character. I wish him well.

   c. The Italian and I are still cyber-communicating. I will love myself first and foremost and act accordingly, which also includes learning, growing, and bettering me. I am far from perfect, and that's *perfectly okay.*

   d. I'm ready to let go and let Dude. (Déjà vu?) For real this time. No dating sites, no matchmakers, no events focused on "will *the one* be there," no "I must look my best wherever I go, just *in case,*" no speed dating, no burlesque dancing, no overly friendly but innocent overtures in Madison Park Starbucks, no lists and spreadsheets and quality control checks, and no desperate "time is running out, where is he already?" attitude. Living now. Accepting. Allowing. I hope all this lasts, people!

P.S. HM is now a true friend—he opened up. And slept in the spare room.

P.P.S. I haven't heard from him since. *Pfft.*

*

What have I learned? Thought-riddled ramblings don't necessarily mean I'm fully committed to (total) change, but I have made some significant (to me) changes and I'm doing my best, *and that's good enough.* And sometimes, just sometimes, good enough just is.

Homework: Think first, act second~~, put up sticky note~~.

***

POST-SCRIPT

Still back in Canada in my cozy abode, I'm Skyping with The Italian, who's been MIA for a few weeks. I'm sharing my melancholy woes of winding-downs and endings and he is gentle and supportive.

"You'll be all right, Anna. You're a brave little bird. You have a lot of talent and you're smart. It'll all work out."

"Thank you, I needed to hear that."

"I want to thank you for supporting me through my recent negative mini-crisis." (I'd finally given up—let go—and decided to listen instead of preach. Sometimes being a real friend is lending a shoulder to someone who needs to vent.)

"Really?" I swallow and my lip quivers.

"Yes, Monkey. Don't cry."

I think for a moment, and then take a deep breath. "I want to meet you. I'm going to come to New York."

He laughs. "Well, you'd better hurry up. I'm moving to L.A. in a month."

What the—? I've been so consumed with my own shit I haven't even asked what's been going on in *his* life. *Additional WTF:* He's been freely giving me the stage rather than hogging it for himself, this, the guy I judged as being all me me me. *Aww.* But back to Big City Flight. Apparently, he's also tired of cold winters and his job is portable so he's heading to La La Land, as in *Hollywood.*

Blink blink. Blink!

Immediately after we finish our conversation, I call MLM. "Mom, when's the last time you saw your brother in L.A.?"

"Oh, let me think . . . Twenty jears."

"Mom . . . We're going to L.A.!"

In case you didn't figure it out, Sexy Italian and Steve Santagati are one in the same. Here's a photo of us together with him holding his (Pea)cock.[1]

**

[1] Actually, it's a pheasant, but that doesn't sound quite so naughty, now does it.

MLM

The events of this memoir happened before My Little Mom was diagnosed with cancer in early 2016. She was a fiesty, little spitfire almost up to her last days when she passed away at home with her three children holding her hands. It was an honor and privilege for us to care for her so intimately and an experience that broke my heart yet filled it with indescribably unconditional love. Love you, Momma!

REFERENCES (AKA ADMIRED AUTHORS)

Byrne, R. *The Secret*. New York: Simon & Schuster, 2007.

Chapman, G. *The Five Love Languages*. Chicago: Northfield Publishing, 2009.

Cloud, H. *Necessary Endings*. New York: HarperBusiness, 2011.

Doidge, N. The *Brain That Changes Itself*. New York: Penguin Books, 2007.

Downs, A. *The Half-Empty Heart*. London, England: St. Martin's Griffin, 2004.

Ford, A. *Kiss Me, I'm Single*. Berkeley, CA: Conari Press, 2007.

Gilbert, E. *Eat, Love, Pray*. New York: Penguin Books, 2007.

Harvey, S. Act Like a Lady, Think Like a Man. New York: Amistad, 2011.

Hay, L. *You Can Heal Your Life*. Carlsbad, CA: Hay House, 2009.

Jeffers, S. Feel the Fear and Do It Anyway®. New York: Ballantine Books, 2006.

Lancaster, J. *Bitter is the New Black*. New York: NAL Trade, 2006.

---. *Such a Pretty Fat*. New York: NAL Trade, 2008.

Payson, E. The Wizard of Oz and Other Narcissists. Royal Oak, MI: Julian Day Publications, 2002.

Robbins, A. *Unlimited Power*. New York: Free Press, 1997.

Salmansohn, K. *How to Be Happy, Dammit*. Berkeley, CA: Celestial Arts, 2001.

---. *Prince Harming Syndrome.* New York: QNY, 2009.

Santagati, S. *The Manual.* New York: Harmony, 2008.

---. *Code of Honor.* Coral Gables, FL: Bad Boys Finish First, LLC, 2012.

Tolle, E. *The Power of Now.* Novado, CA: New World Library, 2010.

---. *A New Earth.* New York: Plume, 2006.

Vanzant, I. In The Meantime: Finding Yourself and the Love You Want. New York: Touchstone, 1999.

ABOUT THE AUTHOR

You know too much already! But, to summarize, I'm a half-Mexican, half-Danish, all-Canadian redhead writer(!) who used to be a real estate agent in Comox, BC, Canada. Born in Comox, BC, a pretty small town, I was shuttled back to the logging camp where my parents worked as a first aid attendant and logging truck driver. Secluded, tiny, and isolated with no road access, the tiny town didn't allow for a lot of socializing (less than a dozen kids, total, lived there) but it did allow for a solid rooting of redneck-esque.

Though I've always felt something of a free spirit, I rooted myself by venturing into real estate at the age of twenty. I was a natural at it, but after twenty years in the business, it was time for a change. Now, after escaping to Seattle for a couple of years to live the writer's life (think thrift stores and starving artist lodgings), my free spirit gets to travel, and now I write for a living, and by "living," I mean I live to write and I write to live. And yes, as of this writing, I am over forty. But! I made it!

Like Anna's style? Find more of Anna's writing at www.naughtypottyblog.com and www.wingmam.com 'cause I'm a dating, love, and relationship coach now, y'all! Yay me!

Shut the front door.

Made in the USA
Monee, IL
26 February 2022

91887008R00152